Enterprise Architecture Fundamentals

Enterprise Architecture Fundamentals

Using the PAGODA BLUEPRINT

Rémy Fannader

IZZARD INK PUBLISHING

PO Box 522251

Salt Lake City, Utah 84152

www.izzardink.com

LIBRARY OF CONGRESS CONTROL NUMBER:

Cover Design by Andrea Ho
Cover Images:
Original Illustrations by Herve Leroux (Albert)

First Edition

Contact the author at info@izzardink.com

Hardback ISBN: 978-1-64228-049-4

Paperback ISBN: 978-1-64228-061-6

eBook ISBN: 978-1-64228-048-7

Contents

An organization's ability to learn and translate that learning into action is the ultimate competitive advantage.

— Jack Welch, Former CEO, General Electric

Preface

Enterprise architectures mix physical & symbolic artifacts,
with a built-in ability to change

Premises & Pillars

Architecture can be understood both as an activity (what architects do) and an outcome (what architects build). On that account, there is a frustrating imbalance between enterprise architecture (EA) as a set of practices and as a discipline. This book is an attempt to bridge the gap by establishing the discipline on principled foundations.

To that end, the book stems from three premises:

- Enterprise and systems architectures must be set apart.

- EA must be understood as a mix of symbolic representations, organization, and computer systems.

- The primary objective of EA is to ensure consistent and continuous adaptations to changes in environments.

The book is built on four pillars:

- A modeling paradigm based on the Stanford Symbolic System Program (SSP), which defines symbolic systems as containers that manage the representations (or surrogates) of relevant actual or symbolic objects and phenomena

- The Pagoda blueprint, an extension of the Zachman framework, which is used to chart EA's mix of symbolic, organizational, and systems components

- Three established approaches (Agile, Use cases, Model-based systems engineering), which are commonly understood but not uniformly applied; their integration provides a proof of concept of the proposed paradigm and a smooth learning curve

- Ontologies and Knowledge graphs, for an all-inclusive representation of data, information, and knowledge, and the integration of Artificial intelligence and Machine-learning technologies

Organization

The book is divided into five parts: enterprises and systems, EA objectives and frameworks, EA and knowledge, EA engineering, and enterprises as viable organisms.

Part I outlines the basics of EA modeling:

- *Chapter 1* establishes the foundations in terms of maps (or blueprints) and territories (environments, systems, processes).

- *Chapter 2* introduces the basics of modeling languages (syntax and semantics) and symbolic representation (objects and behaviors, anchors and aspects, surrogates).

- *Chapter 3* applies the modeling paradigm to EA models (descriptive, prescriptive, technical) and engineering (workshops and decision-making).

Part II sets forth the ends and means of EA as a discipline:

- *Chapter 4* makes the case for a distinction between business and systems perspectives; the former focused on value chains, and the latter, on architecture capabilities.

- *Chapter 5* expounds the benefits of frameworks for mapping architectures and managing changes, and sets guidelines for selecting the right one.

- *Chapter 6* is a detailed presentation of the Pagoda blueprint, revisiting the Zachman framework.

Part III deals with the all-inclusive representation of data (environments), information (systems), and knowledge (enterprise):

- *Chapter 7* expounds on the modeling principles introduced in chapter 3, and specifically on the use of anchors to attach the prescriptive models of systems to the descriptive models of business environments and objectives.

- *Chapter 8* considers the pros and cons of patterns, profiles, and meta-models, and the benefits of ontologies.

- *Chapter 9* examines how ontologies and Knowledge graphs can be used to turn the representations of environments, organization, and systems into actionable maps that weave data, information, and knowledge with enterprise organization and systems architectures.

- *Chapter 10* considers the benefits for decision-making of the integration of the systems and representations discussed in chapter 9.

Part IV deals with engineering and the transformation of enterprise architectures:

- *Chapter 11* takes a bird's-eye view of requirements and puts their taxonomy in an EA perspective.

- *Chapter 12* sets guidelines for the refactoring of requirements along EA concerns, with a focus on digital transformation.

- *Chapter 13* considers the management of EA engineering projects, with a focus on Use cases as modeling interfaces between business and enterprise objectives, on the one hand, and user-driven and architecture-based developments, on the other hand.

- *Chapter 14* puts Model-based systems engineering (MBSE) at the hub of enterprise architecture transformations. At the systems level, an augmented backlog mechanism ensures the dynamic integration of business-driven (Agile) and architecture-based (MBSE) developments. At the enterprise level, the morphing of augmented backlogs into Knowledge graphs ensures the conceptual integration of engineering with business strategies and enterprise modernization.

Part V puts enterprise sustainability in the broader perspective of cybernetics, Artificial intelligence, and Machine learning:

- *Chapter 15* considers architectures' agility in terms of versatility and plasticity. For enterprises competing in digital environments, it means that sustainability depends on their ability to make the most of the flux of information; in other words, to limit entropy. That understanding is used to revisit Capacity maturity model integration (CMMI).

- *Chapter 16* takes a strategic view on the impact of Artificial intelligence and Machine-learning technologies at the systems and enterprise levels. The focus is put on organizational behavior, innovation, and their impact on intangible assets.

- *Chapter 17* concludes with the issue of enterprises' resilience to systemic changes and EA significance with regard to externalities.

Audience

The book is organized to reflect the interests of three typical audiences:

- Parts I and II are written for anyone with an interest in EA: business analysts, systems architects, software engineers, managers, and students.

- Part III is more specific and requires a good understanding of modeling issues.

- Part IV is also more specific, with a focus on engineering issues. It should be of special interest to MBSE practitioners.

- Part V explores broader organizational and cognitive issues, and is aimed at a wider readership of EA enthusiasts.

Highlights

This book is characterized by:

- A focus on the specificity of enterprise architecture and its relationship with systems

- A shift in the modeling paradigm to encompass environments, business objectives, organization, and systems

- A formal, open, and concise kernel of concepts and definitions

- A thorough reinstatement of established concepts and methodologies (e.g., Agile, Use cases, Model-based systems engineering, Capacity Maturity Model Integration), supported by Knowledge graphs and Deep-learning technologies.

To enliven highbrow arguments, core concepts are illustrated by original cartoons.

PART I

Enterprises
& Systems

CHAPTER 1

Maps & Territories

Enterprise architecture must provide actionable symbolic representations (maps)
of physical environments, systems, and processes (territories)

An Opening Note on Information Systems

Enterprises as collective ventures have been a pillar of human societies for millennia. Across agriculture, trade, manufacturing, and finance, they have been characterized by their collective organization — the way people collaborate in carrying out their activities — and sustainability — their ability to progress or simply survive in adverse environments while keeping their collective identities.

Keeping Tabs

The need to write down representations of people, social or economic status, objects, and activities appeared when small wandering groups of hunters and gatherers, living day-to-day, were replaced by agricultural communities trying to make the most of locations and seasons. As these polities grew larger and more differentiated, their sustainability depended on their ability to keep tabs over time on people, assets, ownership, and usage.

From a functional point of view, today's information systems have much in common with the governance of the centralized empires of ancient Egypt and Mesopotamia. All of these systems record who people are, what they own, and what they do, among other things.

Implementation technologies have changed, of course, moving from clay tablets to silicon ones. But more importantly, what has changed is the need to document how information systems are being built and transformed. In industrial societies, representing the changes is not enough: information systems must keep track of changes in how representations are designed.

Keeping Track of Tabs

In order to maintain the continuity and consistency of complex systems in changing environments, not to mention the turnover of people in the know, organizations have to keep track of changes in representations; i.e., what is deemed relevant (territories) and how it is represented (maps).

At their simplest (flat, nondescript territories), representations must ensure the continuity of individual records (e.g., who paid what to whom). As territories and organizations become more complex, maps must ensure continuity and consistency in the face of the changing human, geographic, and economic landscape. And the way maps are designed (or territories projected in two-dimensional representations) has to be documented in order to maintain and update them. Real challenges appear when changes affect not only the territories but also the design of the maps themselves. For example, the Roman Republic had to keep track of changes in the definition of citizenship with the expansion of Roman polity, so as to take into account sheer numbers, the idiosyncrasies of the polities that were taken over, and the variety of related settlements, if any.

That dynamic dimension of social structures means that enterprise architecture (EA) as a discipline should be defined both in terms of outcomes (maps) and activity (the mapping of territories).

Regarding outcomes, enterprise architecture mixes symbolic representations of business environments (e.g., regulations, demographics) and enterprise objectives, on the one hand, and actual organizations, processes, and assets, on the other hand. Regarding corresponding activities, enterprise architecture is a continuous and dynamic endeavor because change is part and parcel of the life cycle of enterprises:

- At the enterprise level, architecture keeps organizations and systems in line with changing environments.

- At the system level, architecture synchronizes changes in organizations and processes with the corresponding digital counterparts (or surrogates in technical parlance) managed by supporting systems.

As a practice, enterprise architecture employs blueprints for maps and territories, and processes for the management of changes across and between maps and territories.

EA Blueprints

What Is Represented

Compared to brick-and-mortar architectures, which are tangible and perennial, enterprise architectures are works in progress to be carried out all along the life cycle of enterprises. Therefore, maps are needed to monitor external changes in business and technical environments and to ensure the traceability and consistency of their representation (or surrogates) in enterprises' organizations and systems.

Whatever the doctrine, these primary objectives should determine the basic structure of blueprints:

• At the enterprise (or organizational) level, blueprints describe business environments, concepts, objectives, organization and processes.

• At the technical (or operational) level, blueprints describe physical and digital
environments, systems interfaces, and platforms.

A third level between enterprise and technical ones describes systems and ensures the transparency and consistency of maps and territories between business and
physical environments (figure 1-1).

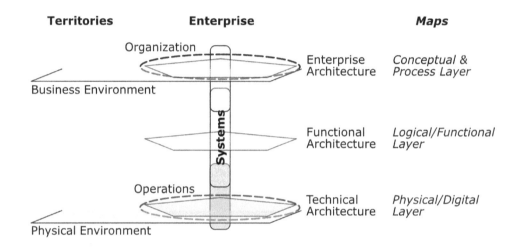

Figure 1-1. Enterprise Architecture Overview

For all intents and purposes, that ternary view of architectures (enterprise, functional, technical) holds true independently of the labels used (e.g., layers, levels, tiers),
or the perspective applied (e.g., business, data, applications, technologies). This tripartite understanding also aligns with the traditional hierarchy of models: conceptual
and process, logical and functional, and physical or digital. More practically, the layered approach provides a robust framework for problem-solving:

• At the enterprise level, problems are defined by environments and objectives,
and solved by organization and processes.

- At the (system) functional level, problems are defined by business processes and solved by functional architectures.

- At the (system) technical level, problems are defined by functional and operational requirements and solved by technical architecture, application design, and platform configurations.

That separation of concerns is critical because ensuring the consistency of changes across the corresponding layers with regard to environments (business or physical), nature (maps or territories), and time frame (external for environments, internal for enterprise) is at the core of enterprise architecture.

Current Shortcomings

While that layered representation often supports EA practices, at least implicitly, its significance is widely ignored. Practical and conceptual reasons for this misunderstanding point in the same direction: enterprise architectures are usually understood as an extension of systems architectures, with the same scope, objectives, and concepts. The ensuing myopia has two key consequences for enterprise architecture as a discipline:

- A double confusion, first, between environments and enterprise, and second, between maps and represented territories: environments, organization, and operations

- A blind eye to change as part and parcel of EA, and consequently to the importance of actionable maps

Attempts to find the foundations of enterprise architecture thus generally end with shallow representations or flights to abstraction:

- Shallow representations: colored arrays of boxes and arrows with generic labels are used to represent EA components and activities without being specific about architectures' constitutive elements and their relationships.

- Flights to abstraction: generic descriptions are scaled up the abstraction ladder until they become detached from actual contexts and concerns, thus becoming irrelevant truisms.

These shortcomings can only be overcome with a modeling paradigm that weaves together enterprise architecture blueprints and processes.

EA Processes

What Is Processed

If, as propounded by Stafford Beer (cf. bibliography), enterprises are viable systems, their sustainability depends on their continuous and timely adaptation to their environment. This adaptation cannot be achieved without dynamic feedback between changes in territories and their representations in maps. EA processes should therefore ensure:

- Continuous and consistent attachments between identified elements in territories (e.g., product sales) and their projection in maps (e.g., share of market segments).

- Transparency and traceability in both directions: changes in territories are reflected in maps (e.g., new distribution channels), and changes in the way territories are mapped (e.g., new market segments).

The ill-famed Waterfall development model epitomizes the consequences of detached systems engineering on the continuity of representations. The Waterfall paradigm takes a file-and-forget view of requirements, assuming that comprehensive and accurate requirements upfront can secure a continuous alignment of enterprise architectures with their business target, and so make further modeling redundant. As demonstrated by a costly track record, that assumption comes with two major flaws:

- Sizable engineering projects set across business domains and architecture assets take time, and the longer they take, the higher the likelihood that initial requirements will become redundant or obsolete.

- Since architectural projects usually involve a number of stakeholders with different agendas, collaboration is often an intrinsic part of their management; by preventing valuable adjustments, hasty decisions etched in stone may turn into projects' epitaphs.

The plights of Waterfall have prompted corrective approaches based on Agile principles. But, if Agile development models — and iterative ones, more generally — are best for business-driven applications with well-defined scopes and stakeholders, they are much less effective for architecture-oriented projects with overlapping scopes and distributed stakeholders. To that end, engineering processes must be directly geared to maps, and work units explicitly attached to architecture components.

Current Shortcomings

To be of any use, enterprise architecture must be actionable, which means that static (EA blueprints) and dynamic (EA processes) descriptions must be conceptually integrated.

That requirement is often either overlooked, because processes are defined in terms of one-size-fits-all activities (e.g., requirements, functional analysis, design), or misunderstood, because engineering processes mirror architecture layers.

The idea of a parallel between systems architectures and engineering processes is arguably a critical flaw for EA, for principled as well as practical reasons.

With regard to principle, if architectures are meant to support processes through shared assets and mechanisms, one may assume that they are set along orthogonal dimensions; otherwise architectures would be turned into silos dedicated to subsets of specific processes.

With regard to practice, enterprise architects are supposed to balance the specificity and volatility of business opportunities with the consistency and perennity of shared assets and mechanisms. Overlooking the inherent opposition between business opportunities and asset sustainability would erase a key aspect from the job description of enterprise architects.

Workshops

If the orthogonal dimensions of enterprise architectures and engineering processes are to be combined, and work units geared to architecture artifacts, engineering purposes must be crisscrossed with enterprise, systems, and platforms layers. Borrowing from customized manufacturing processes, systems engineering should be carried out through four basic workshops (figure 1-2):

- Enterprise: organization and business processes, interfaces with supporting systems, locations and communication channels

- Domains: conceptual, logical, and physical models

- Applications: business logic, business functions, development and tests

- Systems: operational processes, services, configurations, and deployment

The actual sequence of projects would be determined by the changes in territories (enterprise and systems workshops) and maps (domains and applications workshops).

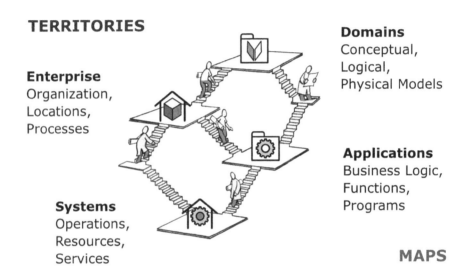

Figure 1-2. Enterprise Architecture Workshops

This dual description of engineering in terms of maps and territories provides the rationale for Model-based systems engineering (cf. chapter 14).

CHAPTER 2

Enterprise Architecture Modeling Primer

Surrogates are digital substitutes meant to reflect the state of objects or phenomena identified in the environment

Models come first in an architect's toolbox, whether the target is a concrete edifice or an abstract polity. Applied to enterprise architecture (EA), models have to consider different kinds of elements: physical (hardware), logical (software), human (organization), and conceptual (business). By that account, the standard modeling paradigm (epitomized by languages like UML or SysML) is floundering at the top and bottom of the modeling spectrum: with respect to architectural concepts at the top, it overlooks environments and organizational concerns; concerning architectural implementations at the the bottom, it is overloaded with software concerns.

What is needed is a shift to refocus the modeling paradigm on the specificity of enterprise architecture as compared to systems architecture.

Syntax & Semantics in Modeling

From a formal point of view, languages are made of syntactic, lexical, semantic, and pragmatic components. For natural languages, developed over time from shared deeds and beliefs, these layers overlap and mingle. But not so for modeling languages, which are symbolic tools designed with purpose. Thus, a clear-cut distinction should be maintained between modeling syntax and semantics, if only because the former can be defined independently of purpose, whereas the latter is contingent on context and concerns.

The semantics of descriptive models should be applied to business domains, in order to identify business categories of objects and phenomena. Given the fleeting nature of consumers' behaviors and competitive pressure, such semantics are, by nature, specific (to make a difference) and open-ended (to make the best of new opportunities).

The semantics of systems, by contrast, are meant to deal with bounded and well-defined technical domains; they are thus best for prescriptive models, whose purpose is to specify how systems' components should be designed.

That double perspective on language (syntax and semantics) and on the purpose of modeling (descriptive and prescriptive) can be used to simultaneously distinguish and connect systems and enterprise architectures. Systems architectures (prescriptive models) are focused on the design and implementation of systems' components,

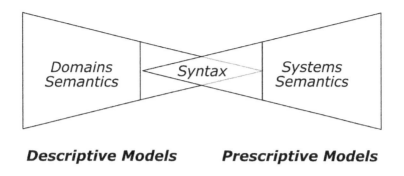

Figure 2-1. Syntax as a Bridge between Descriptive and Prescriptive models

whereas EA is primarily concerned with the interoperability of representations of business environments and objectives (descriptive models), and of organization and supporting systems (prescriptive models).

A small number of syntactic constructs provides the glue between descriptive and prescriptive semantics.

Syntax

In contrast to their mingling in natural languages, syntax and semantics are supposed to be kept well apart in modeling languages. Taking advantage of syntax neutrality, the main pillar supporting the bridge between business descriptive and systems prescriptive models should be a core group of well-accepted syntactic constructs that could be shared by both kinds of models without interfering with their respective semantics:

- Anchors (#) mark elements that are continuously and consistently identified in EA, both in maps and territories.

- Identifying associations tie the identity of the tail (source) to the identity of the head (destination).

- Containers (or collections, *) denote entities that manage sets of identified elements independently of the nature of the elements (e.g., lists of items or staff in organizations).

• Partitions (or powertypes, [2]) denote entities that represent subsets of identified elements (e.g., hybrid cars as a subset of cars).

• Specialization connectors are used between sets and subsets; structural specialization is apt for sets and subsets of individuals, whereas functional specialization is for sets and subsets of behaviors.

• Structural connectors (or diamonds) are used for composition (parts identified through their owners) and aggregation (parts identified independently).

• Functional connectors are used for peer-to-peer associations between entities that are identified independently.

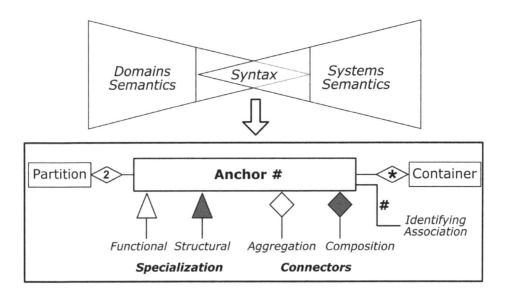

Figure 2-2. *Basic Connectors*

Ensuring syntactic (or shallow) interoperability between descriptive (e.g., analysis) and prescriptive (e.g., design) models is the easy part, providing that the constructs are formally defined. For example, composition, aggregation, and collection can sometimes be used without a semantic label (e.g., the association *is a part of* placed between *Meal* and *Order* doesn't need further explanation); otherwise, the meaning of associations must be set by context (e.g., the association *beneficiary* placed between *Account and Person* has to be explicitly defined).

The real challenge is to ensure a semantic (or deep) interoperability between domain-specific and systems models. Taking into account a broad consensus about the semantics of systems architecture, enterprise architects should focus on those semantics used to describe what stands between systems and environments; namely, the symbolic representation of domains, processes, and organizations.

Semantics

Tasked with mapping enterprises' territories, the architect's learning curve starts with a menacing swerve that may lead rookies astray with little chance of getting back on track. Hazards come from a series of potential mix-ups. At the outset, because territories have to be documented one way or another, preliminary outlines and depictions can easily be confused with maps. Hence, initial descriptions of objects and phenomena in environments (figure 2-3, left) should be set apart from their systems' representations (figure 2-3, right).

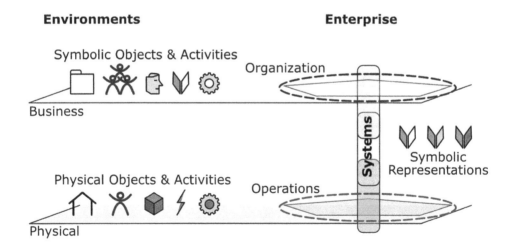

Figure 2-3. A 3D Perspective: Physical, business, Representations

Compounding the difficulty, modelers have to differentiate between items that are physical (e.g., Bob's car) and those that are symbolic (e.g., the model of Bob's car as marketed by vendors), while working on morphing territories' elements into mapping categories. Physical items are set in territories (figure 2-3, bottom left), whereas symbolic ones are seemingly placed somewhere in no-man's-land (figure 2-3, top left).

Confusion can be avoided by distinguishing between symbolic objects and symbolic representations. Symbolic objects are intangible entities defined by social understanding, whether institutional or customary (e.g., contract, music). By contrast, symbolic representations are digital (or clay, or quantum) depictions (e.g., car maintenance record, music sheet) that mirror the state of external entities, which can be tangible (e.g., actual cars) or intangible (e.g., car registration, song). These symbolic substitutes (or surrogates) constitute the raison d'être of information systems; they serve as the symbolic counterparts of external objects or phenomena, which are meant to be managed through supporting systems:

- Physical: containers, persons, active objects (i.e., possible source of events), passive objects, noncountable (NC) objects, events, processes

- Symbolic: containers (e.g., a team), collective agents (e.g., organizational units), objects, roles, activities, partitions (or powertypes[2])

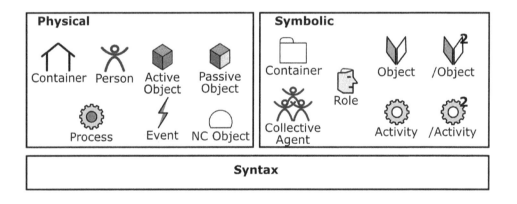

Figure 2-4. Modeling 101

Those actual and symbolic categories are then combined using a compact set of unambiguous syntactic constructs shared by modeling languages.

The corresponding surrogates will then distinguish between passive (all blue), active (half orange), and real-time (half red) representations.

Applied to a diner case study, modeling would first consider business objects and activities independently of supporting systems:

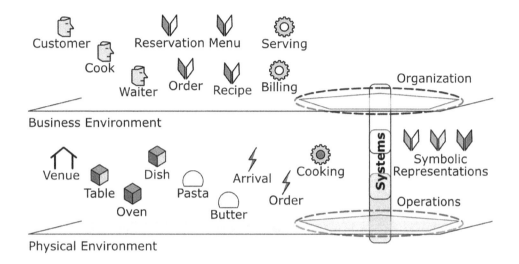

Figure 2-5. 3D Perspective for a Diner

This triptych (business environment, physical environment, and surrogates) marks the difference between enterprise- and systems-architecture modeling: the former has to deal with the whole picture; the latter, only with surrogates.

Systems' Representations

Models define categories. Compared to the categories used to represent systems architecture, the ones pertaining to business environments and enterprise organization are set by business objectives and are meant to change with environments, time, and opportunities. For enterprise architects, the difficulty is to carry on implementing changes while ensuring the continuity of representations. As long as there is no explicit modeling of environments, as is the case for systems architecture, the continuity of representations is circumscribed to existing business operations and relationships. This limited perspective ignores other aspects or circumstances until a broader approach is called for by business needs — as happened when banks, taking notice that their customers were buying insurance products from other sources, had to reorganize their databases around customers instead of accounts.

What Should Be Represented

As defined by Stanford University's Symbolic Systems Program, symbolic systems are:

"…agents that use meaningful symbols to represent the world around them so as to communicate and generally act in the world."

This seemingly plain definition implies:

- A unified understanding of people, organizations, and systems as agents with the ability to process symbolic representations

- A threefold modeling paradigm: for environments, both symbolic and physical objects and phenomena, and for systems, symbolic representations of environments

- A conceptual distinction between enterprise and systems representations: the former, open-ended and pragmatic; the latter, finite and normalized

The significance of this modeling paradigm is best understood when compared to the one upheld for systems by the Object Management Group (OMG):

"A UML model consists of three major categories of model elements [classifiers, events, and behaviors], each of which may be used to make statements about different kinds of individual things within the system being modeled."

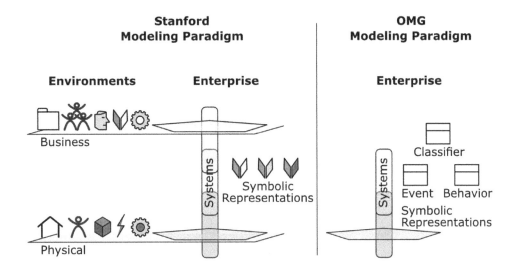

Figure 2-6. *3D (Stanford) vs. 2D (OMG) Modeling Paradigms*

The difference is akin to one between 3D and 2D representation. Whereas the Stanford paradigm encompasses environments (including agents) and their symbolic representation by systems and organizations, the OMG paradigm deals only with symbolic representations, unconcerned by what they are meant to represent. It ensues that trying to apply the OMG paradigm to enterprises and environments is doubly misleading:

- It props up a "file and forget" approach and the belief that environments will remain as they were when they were modeled — a dubious assumption for enterprises immersed in digital environments.

- Since Object-oriented (OO) modeling is the established standard for systems and software design, the implicit inference would be that objects and behaviors in business environments should also be seen through OO glasses — something akin to a reversal of Plato's allegory of the if the people outside were the embodiment of their shadow on the wall.

Constraining representations into classifiers, events, or behaviors may have limited impact at the application level. But that's not the case at the system and enterprise levels, where that one-sided approach introduces clear modeling fault lines; in particular:

- Classifiers epitomize the flight-to-abstraction syndrome: defined as an "abstract metaclass," they can be applied to any kind of object, event, behavior, interface, aspect, etc. That's not a problem for systems architectures given their closed context and finite number of well-identified concepts. By contrast, the range of business meanings is open-ended as well as shifting, offering an unlimited number of skylights open to abstraction that are detached from any actual semantics.

- Most importantly, enterprise architecture has to make a conceptual distinction between agents (environment), roles (organization) and actors (systems). That's not possible with the OMG paradigm.

- Likewise, a conceptual distinction is necessary between business and systems events: the former correspond to changes in environments; the latter, to changes in the state of representations. It's easy to understand the consequences of a confusion between a business state of affairs (e.g., bills due) and recordings in systems (e.g., bills paid).

These points can be illustrated with the diner case study (figure 2-7):

- While a seated *Customer* (role) is not necessarily modeled as *Individual* (agent), he must be in the cases of takeaway or delivery, if some upfront guarantee of payment is requested.

- *Order* can be modeled as an event, a business (passive) object, an active object, or a behavior attached to a business object. These options come with architectural implications that are better understood when the descriptive physical and business dimensions are modeled separately.

- More generally, activities, whether physical (e.g., *Cooking*) or symbolic (e.g., *Serving*), can be represented by active objects, behaviors, or directly implemented by applications. These options can be made explicit with the three-pronged Stanford modeling paradigm, but not with the alternative unidimensional OMG approach.

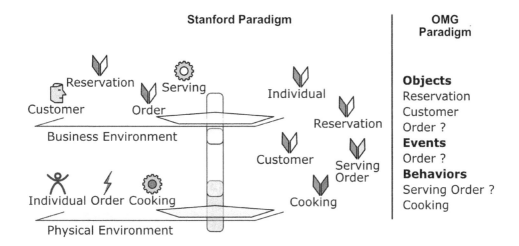

Figure 2-7. Upgrading the Modeling Perspective

Needless to say, experienced modelers will deal with these issues whatever the paradigm. But that's not the point. Since EA models are meant to be used across organizational units (with different objectives) and over protracted time frames (i.e., without direct communication between primary modelers and subsequent users), the semantics of modeling languages should not be confined to systems but should also embrace enterprise organization and business environments (with different meanings). Compounding these challenges, the fleeting nature of business domains means that shared modeling semantics have to be regularly updated.

Anchors

Like cartographers hooking geographic maps to physical locations, enterprise architects should keep to a simple mantra: maps must be anchored to territories through a set of locations continuously and consistently identified independently of concerns or perspectives.

Like travelers using maps as they go or for planning, the anchoring of EA maps to territories serves two basic purposes:

- Supporting a fine-grained management of organizational structures and systems capabilities

• Maintaining business sustainability with a comprehensive, reliable, and consistent representation of environments

Using maps while traveling relies on synchronous but transient associations with physical (e.g., river, mountain, town) and/or symbolic (e.g., road sign) objects in the environment.

For enterprises, it means that processes, once anchored to territories, are carried out on the assumption that maps remain aligned with territories until the processes' completion. For systems, synchronization also implies that the processes' execution secures exclusive access to targeted territories and no external event should interfere.

By contrast, using maps for planning relies on asynchronous but persistent associations with physical or symbolic objects in the environment.

For enterprises, it means that objects of business interest (or entities managed by systems) can be continuously and consistently mapped independently of the operations performed by business processes.

Taking both the travelling and planning usages into account, three kinds of coupling should be considered (figure 2-8):

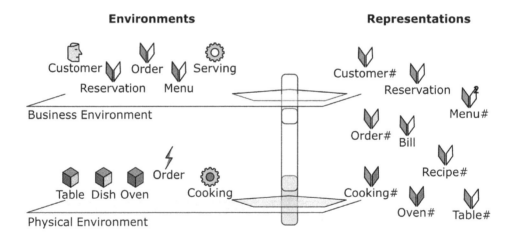

Figure 2-8. Anchors

- Persistent representation of individual entities; e.g., *Table*, *Customer*, *Menu*

- Transient (or nonpersistent) and asynchronous representation of activities (icon with half-orange icon) at the system level; e.g., *Serving*

- Transient and synchronous representation of activities (icon with half-red icon) at the system level; e.g., *Cooking*

On that account, two categories of anchors (#) are needed: one for persistent representations (business entities), and the other for transient ones (processes). The modeler's choice of anchors should reflect business objectives as well as physical constraints; for example:

- Business: *Reservation* (no anchor) can only be taken for identified *Customer#* (business anchor)

- Physical: systems must know the status of *Oven#* objects and *Cooking#* processes (synchronous process anchors)

- Mixed business and physical considerations: *Order#* (asynchronous process anchor) can be served with a time lag, depending on the nature and complexity of the dishes (and customer patience)

Anchors are the building blocks of enterprise architecture as they serve a dual purpose:

- They bind individuals in environments to their symbolic counterparts in systems.

- They bind structural descriptions identified at the enterprise level to functional ones defined at the domain, and consequently system, level.

At the system level, anchors also reconcile aspects with Object-oriented modeling paradigms, a key benefit for architectural design and engineering.

Aspects

Enterprise architecture must cope with conflicting objectives: on the one hand, symbolic representations must be continuously and consistently anchored to environments. On the other hand, enterprise architects must allow for the semantics of representations to differ across business and organizational contexts, and to change over time.

Reconciling those two objectives can be achieved by setting apart structural and functional descriptions from one another, applying common syntactic connectors uniformly to all business and systems descriptions, and using domain-specific semantics for business descriptions. Anchors and syntax would thus secure the consistency and continuity of identities and structures, whereas aspects would be used to describe features and behaviors separately. The syntactic connectors introduced above could then be used to bring together anchors and aspects (figure 2-9):

- Composition (♦): for elements that can only be identified through their owner (a)

- Identifying connectors (#): from elements identified by their owner (b)

- Aggregation (◇): for elements that can be identified on their own (c)

- Association (—>): between identified individuals (d)

- Structural inheritance (▲): between sets and subsets of instances (e)

- Functional inheritance (△): between sets and subsets of features (f)

- Stereotypes (<<business role>>): for semantic extensions meant to qualify classifiers (g); as such, stereotypes can be seen as a special case of abstract subtyping (f)

The question is, could these syntactic constructs be applied uniformly to business and systems models and thus serve as a bridge between the corresponding semantics? The short answer is yes, for constructs targeting instances (composition, aggregation, association), and no, for constructs targeting categories (inheritance and stereotypes).

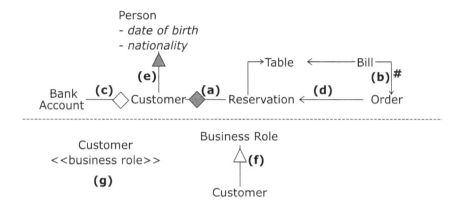

Figure 2-9. A Sample of Basic Syntactic Constructs

Composition, aggregation, and association connectors are defined in terms of identification, and can be applied to business entities independently of the semantic context, business or systems. As a corollary, models can combine heterogeneous representations, for example (figure 2-10):

• ***Bank Account, Customer*** and ***Table*** represent business objects

• ***Reservation, Order***, and ***Bill*** represent systems surrogates

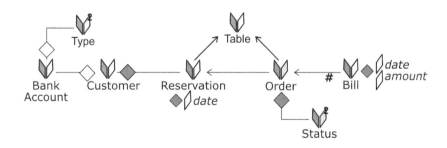

Figure 2-10. Syntax with Semantics

It must be noted that these connectors (to be refined in chapter 7) are not meant to fully describe the features and associations of objects, but rather only the constraints pertaining to enterprise architecture.

Nonetheless, the sharing of syntactic constructs in descriptive and prescriptive models can only be justified for associative connectors; i.e., ones defined with regard to instances. That is not so for inheritance and stereotypes, which apply to modeling categories (or classes), and therefore depend on the modeling languages used for their representation in descriptive and prescriptive models.

Abstractions

If the structure of anchors in systems models mirror their business counterpart, could generalization and specialization also be applied uniformly in descriptive and prescriptive models (figure 2-11) ?

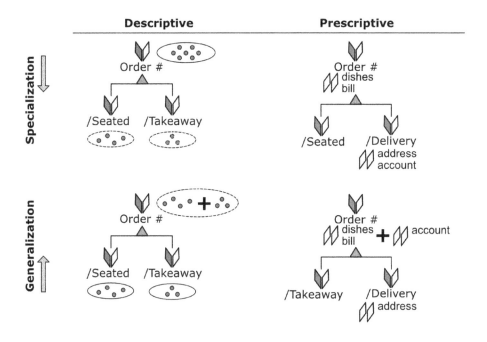

Figure 2-11. Abstraction Semantics

Descriptive models (figure 2-11, left) apply categories to identified objects or activities, tangible or otherwise. Specialization is achieved by setting apart subsets of individuals with specific features (e.g., specifying */Seated* and */Takeaway* from **Order**). Generalization merges groups of individuals with shared features (e.g., regrouping */Delivery* with */Seated* and */Takeaway* under **Order**).

Prescriptive models (figure 2-11, right) take the opposite perspective: they don't classify individual objects or activities but define how artifacts should be created. Specialization is achieved by adding specific features to designs (e.g., **address** and **account** are added to **Order** to characterize **Delivery**), and generalization is accomplished by factoring out a subset of shared features (e.g., **account** would characterize a generalization of */Delivery* and */Takeaway* under **Order**).

This definite difference in abstraction semantics clearly rules out mixing specialization or generalization across descriptive and prescriptive models. And it must be added that the divide has nothing to do with the modeling languages but is rooted in the theoretical foundations of modeling: descriptive models are extensional, which means that they deal with (or denote, in semiotic parlance) actual populations; prescriptive ones are intensional, which means that they deal with specifications.

Often used to represent ill-defined abstractions, stereotypes (<<stereotype>>) can be seen as the jack-of-all-trades of systems modeling. On that account, they can denote inheritance in systems models or serve as planks spanning the semantic gap between systems and business representations; for example (figure 2-12):

- Inheritance of complex data structures (from a technical model): **Recipe** is implemented by **<<graph>>** from a library of abstract data types (a)

- Inheritance of features (from a prescriptive model): the stereotype **<<order>>**, packaged with the development context, will be used to design **Delivery Order** independently of the programming language (b)

- Semantic reference (from a descriptive model): **Oven** is characterized as a **<<cooking device>>**, whose meaning is to be found in a **Kitchen** business profile (c)

These examples epitomize the issue of abstraction: stereotypes are semantic extensions that come with no strings attached. As such, they open the door to overlaps or conflicts with the native semantics of the modeling languages.

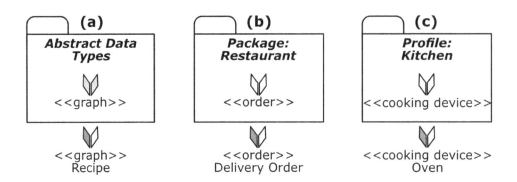

Figure 2-12. Stereotypes

That's not a problem when stereotypes point to technical models, because no more modeling is called for (a). Likewise, it shouldn't be a problem when stereotypes are used as semantic references independently of syntax or semantics (e.g., thesaurus) (c).

By contrast, pitfalls appear when stereotypes involve inheritance, as is the case for **Delivery Order** inheriting from **<<order>>** (b). The risk is a mixing of abstraction semantics: one defined by the modeling language (figure 2-11) and one defined by stereotypes (figure 2-12).

These issues are fully developed in part III.

CHAPTER 3.

Enterprise Architecture Modeling Paradigm

Descriptive models represent environments; prescriptive ones represent surrogates

Architecture begins with blueprints. For enterprise architecture (EA), blueprints (or models) can be descriptive (e.g., requirements' analysis) or prescriptive (e.g., software design). Although that distinction may remain implicit at the system level, it takes on a new significance at the enterprise level, wherein the divide is explicit between the business environment and objectives, on the one hand, and the part played by supporting systems, on the other hand.

Given that double perspective, enterprise architecture has two primary objectives:

- Integration: EA blueprints must bring under a common roof all representations pertaining to business, organization, and systems.

- Transformation: in contrast to brick-and-mortar architectures, enterprise ones are meant to be constantly adapted to changing environments.

That can only be achieved with actionable maps gearing representations to organization and architectures.

Enterprise Architecture Modeling

Taxonomy of Models

Like any symbolic representation, blueprints (or models) can be characterized by a combination of targets and purposes:

- Descriptive models record all relevant aspects of the business environment and the ways to deal with them; they can be compared to the map projections (e.g., Mercator) used to flatten the earth's surface into geographic representations.

- Prescriptive models focus on managed elements (e.g., organization, processes, artifacts, systems), and how their representations in systems can be defined, designed, or built.

- Predictive models add a virtual dimension to descriptive and prescriptive models for simulations, expectations, or objectives.

From a formal point of view, these distinctions can be expressed in terms of modal logic (figure 3-1):

	Descriptive Models (extensional)	Prescriptive (intensional)
Actual	Business Domains, Organization, Processes	Functional & Technical Architectures
Virtual	Business Intelligence	Business Models

Figure 3-1. A Formal Taxonomy of Models

Descriptive representations are meant to provide serviceable models of targeted environments. Such models are said to be extensional, because their objective is to classify observations of objects and phenomena (or extensions) into categories. Actual descriptive (or analysis) models are used to organize the relevant features of domains; virtual models, like data analytics ones, are used to extrapolate from observations of actual environments to putative contexts and concerns.

Prescriptive representations go the other way, because their purpose is to define presumptive artifacts or activities. They are said to be intensional, because they denote sets of features meant to characterize individuals, instead of sets of individuals denoted by extensional categories. Actual prescriptive (or design) models deal with artifacts built at the system level; whereas virtual ones, with intended objectives or behaviors, deal with artifacts built at the enterprise level.

The distinction between descriptive and prescriptive representations can be illustrated using US Navy classes: the (descriptive) ten nuclear-powered aircraft carriers are built on the (prescriptive) *Nimitz*-class aircraft carrier model.

Such a formal understanding of models sets the foundation of enterprise architecture as a discipline, establishing a principled understanding of architectures and representations (figure 3-2):

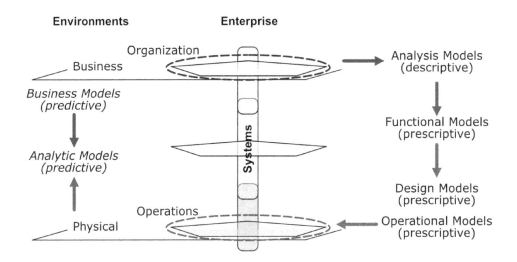

Figure 3-2. Enterprise Architecture & Models

- Prescriptive models define classes of artifacts at the functional (systems), technical (platforms), or operational (resources configuration) levels.

- Descriptive (or analysis) models define categories of objects, events and activities in environments, as well as enterprise organization and processes.

- Predictive models are hypothetical descriptive ones: instead of actual environments and organizations, they deal with possible (analytic models) or planned (business models) ones.

It must be noted that, as illustrated by the *Nimitz* example, models can overlap: objects built from prescriptive models can subsequently be represented by descriptive ones. For instance, deployment models combine actual locations with hardware and software components; locations and hardware also appear in descriptive models.

The differentiation of predictive, descriptive, and prescriptive models, and their threading with architecture layers pave the way for the integration of organizations, systems, and knowledge — a critical issue for enterprises immersed in changing digital environments.

Capabilities of Architectures

As already mentioned, the primary objective of enterprise architects is to plan and manage perennial assets while keeping ahead of the competition in changing business environments. All too often, that objective is defined in terms of business capabilities, sweeping the very challenge of enterprise architecture under a delusional carpet. The fact of the matter is that business revenues and asset capabilities are set along orthogonal lines, if only because of the contrary momenta and life cycles of shifting markets and steady architectures. More importantly, the dynamic adjustments between the drive of business opportunities and the constraints of systems capabilities are at the root of businesses' competitive advantage. Managing these adjustments at the enterprise and system levels can thus be seen as the raison d'être of enterprise architects.

At the enterprise level, the objective is to align organizational capabilities with business objectives, as materialized by business processes. To that end, organizational capabilities can be described in terms of maps (roles, representation of business objects, business logic) and territories (physical objects and locations, events, and processes execution). Enterprise capabilities would thus be defined by:

- Agents and roles: communicating, collaborating, and making decisions

- Business objects: acquiring, processing, and managing data, information, and knowledge

- Activities: defining business logic and managing business transactions

- Events and processes: monitoring environments, synchronizing activities, and supporting decision-making

- Physical objects and locations: servicing distributed assets, resources, and operations

At the system level, functional capabilities are best defined with regard to time and collaboration between processes. Systems architecture capabilities would thus be defined by:

- Boundaries: support of transient and local or individual (nonshared) functionalities

- Persistency: continuity and integrity of the shared representation of business objects (or surrogates) independently of their use by processes

- Controls: synchronization and consistency of transient and shared functionalities

- Services: consistent and timeless execution of shared functionalities independently of the operational context

- Systems: support of wrapped functionalities (boundaries, persistency, controls, and services) independently of their implementation (physical, virtual, or in the Cloud)

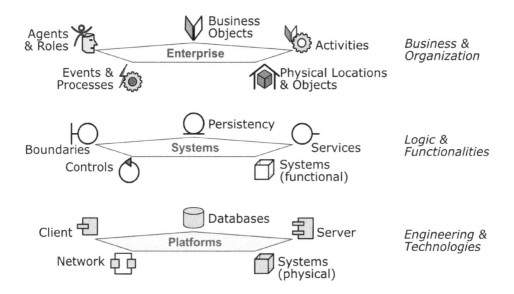

Figure 3-3. Enterprise Architecture Capabilities

As it happens, that taxonomy neatly aligns with the generic and well-established Model (for persistency), View (for boundaries), Controller (for controls) (MVC) pattern.

At the platform level, technical capabilities can be defined directly as the implementation of functional ones using standard design patterns. Although the definitions vary with technologies, technical capabilities can be summarized in terms of:

- Client: implementation of transient and local or individual (nonshared) functionalities

- Database: implementation of persistent storage independently of the use of data by processes

- Network (or middleware): communication within and between systems

- Server: implementation of transient and shared functionalities

- Systems: implementation of wrapped functionalities (boundaries, persistency, controls, and services)

Defining systems architecture capabilities in terms of functional patterns ensures the transparency and traceability of three kinds of adjustments:

- Between business processes, supported by organization, and applications, supported by operations (enterprise to platform levels)

- Between organization and systems (enterprise and system levels)

- Between architecture and engineering (system and platform levels)

That modeling framework is the key to enterprise architecture transformation.

Models for Change

Scope of Models

Change is the raison d'être of enterprise architecture. Accordingly, grand layouts and planning are of little use because architectures are not built in a single shot but originate and develop on a continuous basis along different dimensions, whether pulled by design or pushed by necessity.

Planned or emerging, changes must be managed — and that cannot be achieved without models. Monikers may vary (e.g., layers, levels, tiers) but enterprise architects should focus on three kinds of models congruent with architecture layers, borrowing from Model-driven architecture (MDA) modeling levels:

• Computation independent models (CIMs) describe organization and business processes independently of the role played by supporting systems.

• Platform independent models (PIMs) describe the functions supported by systems independently of their implementation.

• Platform specific models (PSMs) describe applications and systems components, depending on implementation platforms.

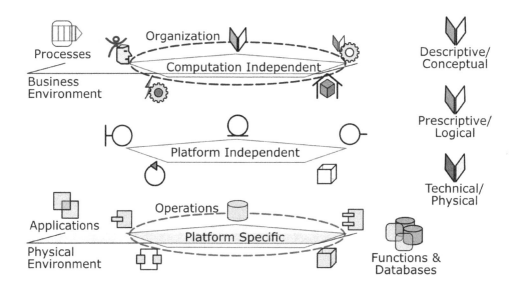

Figure 3-4. Model-driven Architecture (MDA)

Not surprisingly, these modeling levels coincide with the modeling framework presented above, as well as with the organization of models into conceptual-, logical- and physical-database categories:

- Conceptual models describe business objects that are managed persistently and consistently, independently of business processes and representations (subset of descriptive models).

- Logical models describe the symbolic representation of conceptual models (subset of prescriptive models).

- Physical models describe the implementation of logical models as digital objects (subset of technical models).

As far as enterprise architecture is concerned, the focus should be on changes in environments, organization, and systems architecture, as represented by Computation independent (or descriptive) and Platform independent (or prescriptive) models.

Descriptive Views of Changes

Modeling views, as depicted through diagrams, are commonly grouped into four categories; typically the four basic UML diagrams:

- Symbolic objects: domains, features and associations (class diagram)

- Symbolic activities: roles, business logic, and data and control flows (activity diagram)

- Actual activities (processes' execution): events, states, and transitions (state diagram)

- Physical objects (people, devices, systems), locations, and channels (object diagram)

Use-case diagrams provide the glue between diagrams (cf. chapter 13).

Given their neutrality, the syntactic constructs defined in chapter 2 can be applied uniformly to modeling views to ensure their seamless integration (figure 3-5).

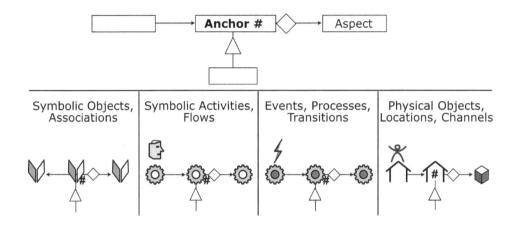

Figure 3-5. One Syntax, Four Modeling Views

That unified syntax is instrumental to hinge descriptive (business environment and processes) and prescriptive (systems functional architecture) models.

Engineering Views of Change

Enterprise architecture mixes descriptive and prescriptive blueprints (what is to be built and why) with engineering (how systems are to be designed and built). This combination requires actionable relationships between architecture blueprints and engineering processes.

There is, for the most part, an implicit consensus about systems architecture views (barring lexical discrepancies), typified by Philippe Kruchten's "4+1": View Model of Software Architecture (cf. bibliography):

- Logical view: design of software artifacts

- Process view: execution of activities

- Implementation (or development) view: organization of software artifacts in development environments

- Physical (or deployment) view: mapping of software components across physical environments (platforms)

Use-case diagrams (cf. chapter 13), a brain child of Ivar Jacobson, provides a fifth view that describes the interactions between systems and business processes.

At first, Krutchen's model appears to be congruent with cursory views of enterprise architecture (e.g., logical view for data, process view for applications, physical view for technology). But labels may be misleading when applied indiscriminately to software architecture (views) and systems architecture (layers): contrary to views, which are solely defined by concerns (independently of targeted structures), layers reflect definitive assumptions about architectures. That confusion between views and layers, illustrated by the miscellany of tabular and pyramidal representations returned by search engines, critically hampers the modeling of changes, and consequently, a key aspect of EA.

As it happens, the confusion can be worked out if Kruchten's views are associated with four engineering workshops, each one crisscrossed with each architecture layer from its specific angle:

- Enterprise workshop: dealing with organization, business processes, supporting-systems interfaces, locations, and communication channels

- Domains workshop: dealing with the symbolic representation of business objects at the conceptual, logical, and physical levels

- Applications workshop: dealing with business logic, systems functions, and programs development

- Systems workshop: dealing with operations and processes, services, configurations, and deployments

That organization brings two critical benefits:

- Workshop attributions are completely neutral and can support any kind of engineering process (cf. chapter 13).

- Engineering processes and work units can be directly defined with regard to development flows and targeted artifacts instead of pre-defined activities, a necessary condition for Model-based systems engineering (cf. chapter 14).

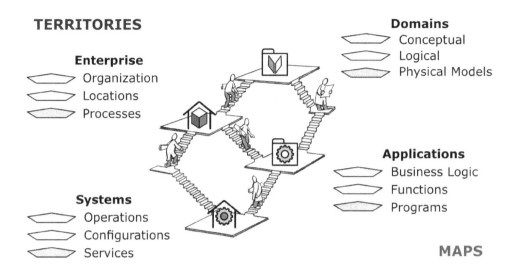

Figure 3-6. EA Engineering Workshops

Enterprise architects can thus manage changes according to their footprint (e.g., organization, business, resources), granularity (e.g., applications, functions, processes), and responsibilities (e.g., business units, domains, systems).

Decision-making

Managing changes across business units, assets, and time frames can be seen as the alpha and omega of enterprise architecture. In large, diversified, and complex organizations, managing change calls for distinctive decision-making apparatuses that combine contexts (business, regulations, technologies), concerns (revenues, assets) and horizons (operational, tactical, strategic).

Compounding the difficulties, the immersion of enterprises in digital environments and the merging of business and engineering processes are erasing many of the familiar guidelines for enterprise decision-making.

To make up for the overturning of customary benchmarks, enterprise architects have to reinvent ways to depict the rationale and footprint of changes.

Depicting the rationale of changes uses descriptive, predictive, and prescriptive models to document the pivot (or root cause); typically a change in policy or a change in environment. Causes or justifications can then be traced backward, and consequences, actions, or anticipations projected forward.

Depicting the footprint of changes with regard to their causes, pivot, and consequences, is best done in terms of maps and territories, beginning with a distinction between the changes confined to either territories or maps, and changes affecting both.

Confined changes are meant to occur below the floor of enterprise architecture; i.e., without affecting the mapping of territories or the coupling between enterprise architecture and environments (figure 3-7):

- Territories: local changes at the level of enterprise (e.g., organization) or systems (e.g., operations) do not require updates of architecture blueprints.

- Maps: local changes in models of domains or activities do not affect the anchoring of enterprise and systems architectures to their environment (e.g., new features or business rules).

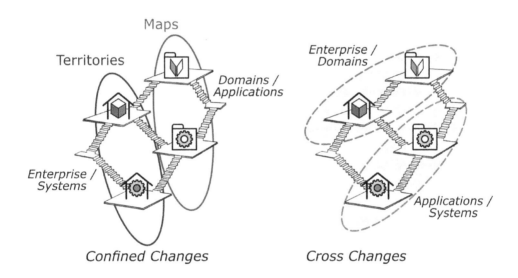

Figure 3-7. A Taxonomy of Changes

Conversely, changes above the floor of enterprise architecture, whether originating in territories or maps, affect the coupling of enterprise architecture and business or technical environments:

- Territories: changes in operations (e.g., new capacities) induced by changes in activities (e.g., new distribution channels)

• Maps: changes in business domains induced by changes in enterprise environments (e.g., new regulations) or business objectives (e.g., new products or services)

With the benefit of a comprehensive and actionable mapping of territories, enterprise architects are in a better position to refine the rationale and footprints of changes, and plan them accordingly. Fine-tuning the granularity of changes is of particular importance for planning, given the ubiquity of software in business products and services and the ensuing blurring of business and technology time frames.

Such fine-grained mapping of territories could then be used to support the Observation-Orientation-Decision-Action (OODA) decision-making loop (cf. chapter 10):

1. Observation: understanding the nature, origin, and time frame of data in business environments (or territories)

2. Orientation: assessing the reliability and shelf-life of pertinent information (or maps) with regard to objectives, risks, and current positions and operations

3. Decision: weighing options with full knowledge of enterprises' stakes and capabilities

4. Action: carrying out decisions according to the operational context and time frames

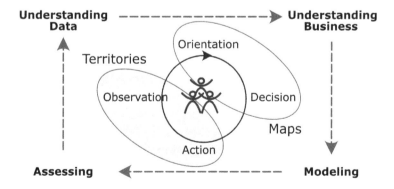

Figure 3-8. EA Decision-making Process

The decision-making loop must be backed by a comprehensive, accurate and up-to-date processing of data, information, and knowledge:

- Understanding data: gives form and meaning to observations from environments

- Understanding business: charts data observations with regard to business objectives and policies

- Modeling: integrates data and business understanding with information-systems models (descriptive, predictive, or operational)

- Assessing: evaluates and improves accuracy and effectiveness in support of objectives and decision-making, and fine-tunes or redefines data-analytics models accordingly

That seamless integration of architecture blueprints, engineering processes, and knowledge management constitutes the nexus of enterprise architecture as a discipline.

Enterprise Architecture Objectives & Frameworks

The first part of the book introduced the fundamentals of enterprise architecture (EA):

- Scope: environments and organization, on the one hand, and symbolic representations as systems surrogates, on the other hand

- Purpose: making the best of enterprise capabilities, and managing continuous adaptations to competitive business environments

- Means: using models (or maps) to ensure the consistency of changes in systems and environments (or territories)

This second part takes a closer look at the role of architectures in harnessing purposes and means.

Enterprise architectures are meant to be driven by purposes. First among them is the perennial harnessing of business and systems perspectives on enterprise capabilities, which can only be done through a seamless integration of architecture blueprints and engineering processes (cf. chapter 3, and part IV).

If enterprises are to change with competitive environments, their architectures cannot be developed separately in vitro before being deployed in vivo in environments. Changes should instead be understood as an intrinsic part of enterprises' transformations, shaped by a combination of patterns, both emerging (from operations) and designed (by organization). Going ahead with the transformation of architectures without affecting business performances can only be achieved with frameworks that ensure the transparency and consistency of representations, models or otherwise.

CHAPTER 4.

Business & Systems Perspectives

Value chains are meant to cross the delivery of products and/or services to customers with the supporting activities

Silos cannot serve as pillars of enterprise architecture, if only because the raison d'être of architectures is to share assets and resources. Nevertheless, because silos are bound to develop when specific answers are required in response to external menaces or opportunities, enterprise architects have to keep reconciling the initiatives of business analysts and systems architects.

Business Processes & Systems Capabilities

Business capabilities can be compared to the medieval philosopher's stone, once deemed to turn base metals into gold. In truth, successful managers and seasoned architects know better; the former are well aware of the singularity of business achievements, and the latter are usually appreciative of the universality of computer systems.

Yet, even when they agree that their perspectives must converge, opinions differ about the end point: summarily, should IT systems be upgraded to integrate business functions, or should business functions be expanded and IT services cast as utilities?

However, these controversies are self-defeating: like diggers tunneling from opposite directions, they will succeed as one or fail on their own. Enterprise architects should arrange the meeting of minds.

Problem & Solution Spaces

Broadly speaking, business analysts are meant to formulate problems and systems architects, to frame solutions; in between, enterprise architects act as matchmakers with a long-term view on their respective expectations and commitments. It ensues that, in contrast to business analysts and systems architects dealing with self-contained problems and solutions, enterprise architects have to decide how problems are to be expressed and where solutions are to be found. As usual, that can be best achieved through a separation of concerns (figure 4-1):

- At the enterprise level, problems are defined by the business environment and objectives (or business models), and solved by organization and processes.

- At the system level, problems are defined by business and functional requirements, and solved by supporting systems' functionalities.

- At the platform level, problems are defined by operational objectives (e.g., locations, processes, size), and solved by applications and operations.

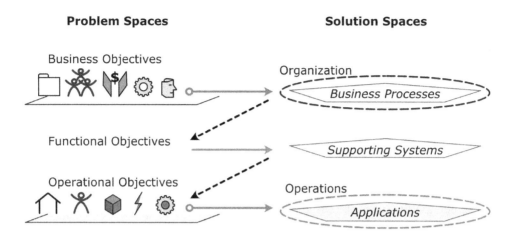

Figure 4-1. *Separation of Concerns*

In addition to feedbacks between problems and solutions, the layered approach introduces a dynamic dimension to enterprise architecture decision-making (figure 4-2):

A systems perspective, going from the bottom up: focused on the way processes support business objectives and are implemented by functions and applications

A business perspective, going from the top down: focused on the way systems support processes and are congruent with the organization

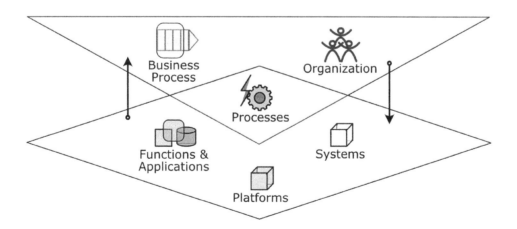

Figure 4-2. *Dynamic Alignment of Business Processes & Systems Capabilities*

That double perspective puts processes at a juncture where issues could be resolved with the assistance of enterprise architects.

Processes & Business Logic

At the enterprise level, the semantics of business domains and systems architectures are too far apart for a consensus on a comprehensive and actionable model, if only because of the former's inherent variability compared to the latter's expected stability (cf. chapter 3). But as far as processes are concerned, there is no need for an all-inclusive agreement, and practical collaboration can be achieved based on a common understanding of problems and solutions. Accordingly, processes is where business analysts and systems architects could work out the alignment of processes and capabilities.

In principle, Business processes models (BPM) describe the concurrent execution of activities by using business semantics to flesh out formal structures (e.g., Pi-Calculus, Petri nets, State machines).

In practice, Business processes models mix the definitions of business logic and dialogues between users and systems, and languages like Business process model and notation (BPMN) (cf. chapter 13) make no difference between them. The ensuing modeling assortment of organizational, operational, and business-specific concerns undermines the architectural relevance of models. That confusion is of particular importance for business logic, which should be managed independently of systems architecture because:

- Business rules are prone to changes in response to market circumstances, in contrast to organizations and architectures, which are supposedly stable.

- Business rules are meant to be shared between applications (e.g., credit-rating functions) and should therefore be defined independently of the context of their execution (e.g., online or in branch).

As it happens, leading Enterprise Resource Planning (ERP) providers have long understood the benefits of setting apart integrated business functions and business-specific logic, and have designed their platforms accordingly. With the digital transformation and the generalization of industry-specific Cloud and mobile software, that distinction between business-specific logic and integrated enterprise services has become a key component of enterprise architectures (cf. chapter 12).

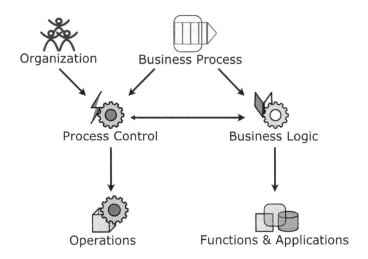

Figure 4-3. *Setting Apart Logic & Control*

Assuming a common understanding of the business entities involved (cf. anchors in chapter 2), the next step of a project inception would be to associate business processes with architecture capabilities (figure 4-3).

Value Chains & Capabilities

Business processes can be assessed with regard to value (as defined by business units), feasibility (as defined by systems capabilities), and returns on investment (as assessed at the enterprise level). Besides balancing business value and feasibility, assessing the returns of processes at the enterprise level must take into account asset depreciation, the shelf-life of applications, and opportunity costs. Enterprise architects can help by tracing contributions across systems architecture.

The concept of value chain, introduced by Michael Porter (cf. bibliography) in 1985, has long served as a reference to assess business processes. Summarily, value chains are meant to chart the activities associated with the delivery of products or services to customers, with the purpose of mapping business values to the resources and assets involved (figure 4-4).

The influence of Porter's concept comes from the key distinction between primary and supporting activities, which puts the focus on enterprises' two orthogonal dimensions: one set by fleeting business opportunities; the other, by perennial supporting systems.

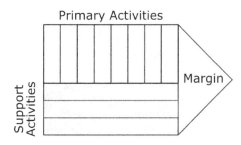

Figure 4-4. Porter's Value Chain

But the digital transformation and the ensuing pervasiveness of software components in business processes have blurred the boundaries between primary and supporting activities. Thus, a redefinition of the relationships between business processes and supporting systems is required (figure 4-5), one that understands supporting activities in terms of organizational capabilities, binding business objectives and processes to EA capabilities, as defined in chapter 3:

• Agents and roles with shared access to supporting systems

• Business objects shared between business processes

• Business logic and functions shared between business processes

• Locations and objects accessed by processes, and the communication channels connecting them

• Events and control mechanisms contributing to processes' execution

A fine-grained analysis should then plot each activity to enterprise architecture capabilities (figure 4-6):

• Roles (Who)

• Inward and outward flows of data, information or knowledge (What)

- Functions (How)

- Ties to physical locations and objects (Where)

- Execution modalities (When)

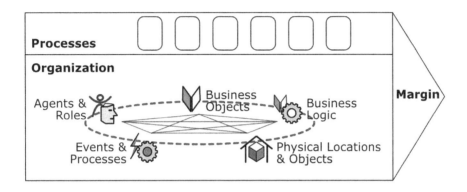

Figure 4-5. Crossing Processes & Organization

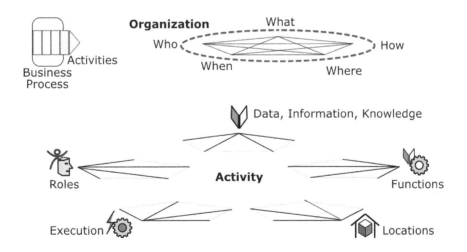

Figure 4-6. Crossing Activities & Capabilities

Assuming the traceability of EA capabilities (cf. chapter 3), the contribution of five generic layers' capabilities to business processes could be then assessed selectively (figure 4-7):

- At the enterprise level: people and organization, as described with Computation independent models (CIMs)

- At the system level: functional architecture, as described with Platform independent models (PIMs)

- At the platform level: technical architecture, as described with Platform specific models (PSMs) and operational configurations

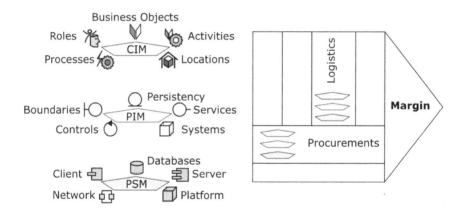

Figure 4-7. *Charting Primary & Supporting Activities to Architecture Capabilities*

As already mentioned (cf. chapter 3), systems' functional capabilities are congruent with the well-established Model-View-Controller (MVC) pattern for systems' architecture:

- Boundaries (or Views): for interactions with users

- Persistency (or Models): for the continuous and consistent upkeep of business entities

- Controls (or Controllers): for the orchestration of enterprise processes' execution

- Services: for shared business functions

- Systems: for Cloud-based solutions

That alignment of functional capabilities with an agreed upon systems architecture paradigm ensures the consistency of the whole of enterprise architecture, from organization to platforms.

Value Chains & Value Streams

Given the alignment of systems functional capabilities with the MVC system architecture pattern, the mapping of value chains between CIMs and PIMs can be delegated to systems architects. Enterprise architects, for their part, can focus on the traceability of value chains between business processes and enterprise architecture capabilities.

In order to deal with that dual perspective (business processes on the one hand, software design on the other), Agile approaches often introduce a distinction between the operational (or business) and development (or engineering) aspects of value streams. Assuming shared ownership and continuous delivery (cf. chapter 13), both streams can be managed at application level.

Yet, value streams also rely on the implicit assumption that the semantics of business processes can be unambiguously mapped to CIMs. Such a direct mapping of business value to enterprise capabilities would imply that domains would not be shared between processes (to avoid semantic overlaps); as a corollary, no business value would be found in synergies between value chains (which would otherwise induce semantic overlaps).

Whereas these assumptions can be justified for business-oriented requirements, business analysts and systems architects need more than collaboration at the process level to secure the consistency of their approaches at the enterprise level.

Business Domains & Enterprise Architecture

Finding a common ground between business and systems people is arguably a priority for enterprise architects. Although consummate practitioners can routinely collaborate at the process level, discrepancies soon appear when domains have to be crossed, as illustrated by the motley of schemes meant to provide a generic information reference model, including: Data Reference Models, Master Data Management, National Information Exchange Model, and Semantic Web. That variety of options can be explained by the confusion between concepts, information, and data.

A Matter of Words

Enterprise architects have to deal with two kinds of semantic discrepancies (figure 4-8):

- Between the conceptual representation of business objectives and the logical and functional representations of systems capabilities (a): these discrepancies are supposed to subside with the integration of CIMs and PIMs into enterprise architecture

- Between business-specific concepts and domains (b): these are bound to persist and even be renewed by the winds and waves of competitive environments

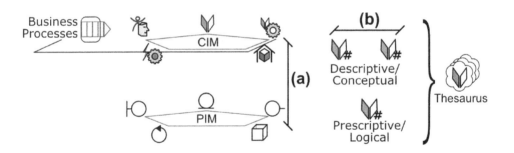

Figure 4-8. Double Entendre

Lexicons or glossaries can manage flat (i.e., lacking abstraction levels), final (unchanging meanings), and nonoverlapping definitions; but they cannot cope with mixed and unsteady semantics (between domains) set at different levels of abstraction (conceptual and logical for business domains, logical and functional for systems architecture). Thesauruses should ensure that conceptual and logical mappings don't work at cross-purposes; i.e., the stability and reliability of the latter should not be affected by the shifts and fuzziness of the former.

Beginning with conceptual/logical mapping, a thesaurus weaves together the diverse, open-ended, and changing semantics of business domains with the homogeneous (single perspective), definite (no ambiguities), and steady (not prone to changes) semantics of systems architecture. That can be achieved with the two-tiered semantics introduced in chapter 2: one tier of generic concepts serving as pivots between business domains and architecture capabilities, and the second tier used for the specific aspects of business domains.

Then, thesauruses will bring the semantics of pivots and aspects under a common conceptual roof in order to manage the semantic overlaps between business domains; for instance (figure 4-9):

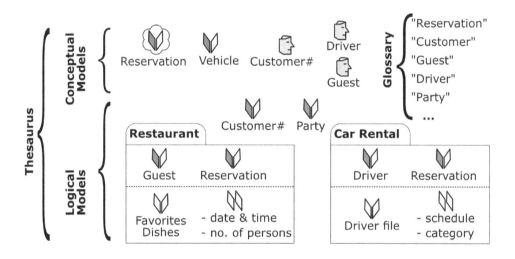

Figure 4-9. Glossaries, Models, Thesauruses

Business domains **Restaurant** and **Car Rental** share the semantics of the **Customer** anchor, which may or may not coincide with domain-specific **Guest** and **Driver**. But there is no common semantics for **Reservation**, which applies to seats in **Restaurant** and cars in **Car Rental**.

As a consequence, the enterprise thesaurus will represent **Customer** as a business entity shared across domains, but **Reservation** will only appear as a concept to be logically modeled as a business entity at the domain level.

Thesauruses can thus serve as a glue between different levels of descriptions:

- Glossaries are for terms used independently of representations in models.

- Conceptual (or descriptive) models deal with the representation of business objects and activities independently of their representation by systems; e.g., *Reservation* (concept), *Vehicle* (business object), *Customer* (role).

- Logical (or prescriptive) models deal with the representation of business objects by systems; e.g., *Customer* (enterprise level), *Reservation* (domain level).

It must be noted that, contrary to models, thesauruses have no organizational or engineering significance. Accordingly, entries may be introduced at will or remain implicit; e.g., *Party*, representing the accounting footprint of agents in transactions (customers, staff, suppliers, etc.), may appear as a business surrogate without a corresponding entry at the domain level.

These different levels of understanding may appear unwarranted at the system level; but at the enterprise level, they are required to manage meanings across domains and their change over time. That can be achieved with information models (conceptual, logical, physical). One step further, ontologies will be required if knowledge (i.e., the ways information can be used) has to be taken into account (cf. chapter 9).

Facts, Categories, Concepts

As far as systems architecture is concerned, modeling languages provide principled and effective schemes that bridge the divide between business analysts' requirements and software architects' designs. But enterprises' endeavors and behaviors cannot be fully fitted into systems-oriented modeling categories, and pressing on in that direction would hamstring the ability of enterprises to anticipate changes in business environments. The immersion of enterprises in digital environments reinforces the inhibiting impact of looking at business environments through systems-modeling glasses:

- Facts, once captured through discrete observations and ready to be interpreted, have turned into raw, massive, and continuous data floods swamping predefined categories.

- Concepts, once built on explicit models and logic, are now emerging like new species from the primordial soup of digital environments.

Typically, business analysts take the lead extending symbolic representations on both fronts: toting learning machines for facts and waving knowledge graphs for concepts. Positioned in the no-man's land between fast-flowing facts and shifting concepts, systems architects have to deal with a two-pronged encroachment on their information models:

- Regarding facts, systems architects have to build a Chinese wall between observed data and managed information in order to comply with privacy regulations.

- Regarding concepts, they have to continuously integrate emerging concepts with the categories managed by information systems.

That brings a new light on the so-called conceptual, logical, and physical "data" models, which are key components of enterprise architecture:

- Physical data models are meant to be directly lined up with operations and digital environments.

- Logical models represent the categories managed by information systems and must be congruent with their functional counterpart in systems architecture.

- Conceptual models represent the enterprise's explicit knowledge of business domains and objectives; such models should also be amenable to the implicit knowledge embodied in people and organization or elicited from environments through Deep learning.

Logical models (pertaining to information) serve as a modeling hub between business facts (observed through data) and concepts (used as knowledge axes or pillars), securing the adjustments of representations and environments; typically (figure 4-10):

- Knowledge is used to analyze data sets that could identify and inform prospective business categories (a).

- Knowledge uses business categories (information) to build new marketing data sets (b).

- Data sets are crossed with business categories (as managed through information models) in order to assess and improve marketing knowledge (c).

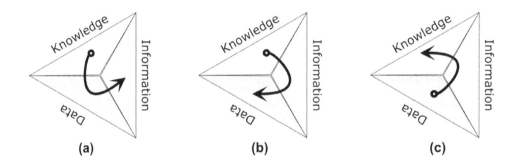

(a)   **(b)**   **(c)**

Figure 4-10. The Knowledge Loop

With everything turning digital, these distinctions could be easily overlooked were it not for the extensive adoption of Knowledge graphs and Deep-learning technologies. Digital strategies cannot be built without a clear understanding of digital contents; that's a prerequisite.

Then, in order to compensate for digitally levelled playgrounds, enterprises need a discriminating and transparent governance apparatus.

Merging Business & Systems Perspectives

Ingrained habits die hard, and mental ones are the last to be disrupted. The sway of pyramids to represent enterprise architectures is one such habit, and the significance of such representations is more than metaphoric.

But for our purpose here, it is enough to say that pyramids are actual as well as metaphoric architectural dead ends: like homes carved in stone for the departed, they are immutable and closed for business. Thus, as a representation of enterprise architectures, pyramids induce two major misconceptions:

- The juxtaposition of an information layer on top of or beneath other ones (e.g., application, technology, business) obfuscates the ubiquity and role of information as a neurotransmitter across enterprise architecture layers.

• A flat and indiscriminate representation of data, information, and knowledge flies in the face of the digital transformation, which is characterized by the emergence of data factories as an industry of its own, the advent of data privacy as a strategic issue, and the spreading of Knowledge-graph technologies with their layered architecture.

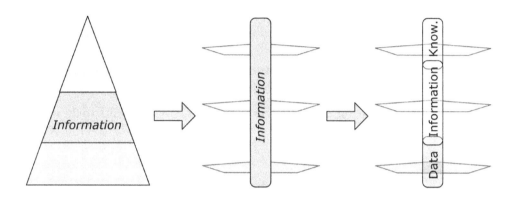

Figure 4-11. EA: From Vault to Pillar

By contrast, defining information along an orthogonal axis set across enterprises' architecture layers establishes information as a mainstay that unifies business and systems perspectives:

• Data, from direct observations or as a product of data factories, can be neatly separated from information managed by systems — a necessary condition for compliance with privacy regulations.

• Information, for the subset of data that fits within the categories pertaining to business objectives (e.g., customers, accounts), can be continuously and consistently managed as systems surrogates.

• Knowledge, for individual or collective skills and expertise, can be explicitly represented in conceptual models, Knowledge graphs or ontologies.

That separation of concerns and its alignment with enterprise architecture layers (organization, systems, platforms) brings clear and direct benefits for the governance of enterprises bound up in digital environments. As represented by the Pagoda Blueprint (cf. chapter 6), the integration of systems and knowledge architectures also ensures the convergence of business and systems perspectives:

• Business/symbolic level: anchoring models of business environments and objectives to enterprise architecture

• Logical/functional level: aligning information systems and business categories

• Physical/digital level: merging observations from environments (data mining) with operational data (process mining)

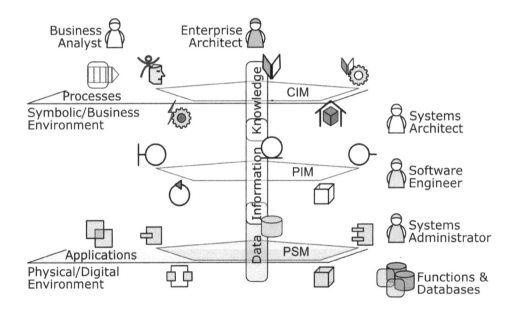

Figure 4-12. Enterprise Architecture's Pillar of Wisdom

Responsibilities should therefore be primarily defined with regard to these basic perspectives before taking into account the specifics of enterprise organization. Job titles will often differ between organizations, but the remits should be clear: business analysts, enterprise architects, systems architects, software engineers, and systems administrators.

In parallel to organizational responsibilities on EA transformations, the integration of architecture layers and representations will provide a built-in traceability of changes across business and engineering processes.

Collaboration Schemes

The omnipresence of software in products and services, and the continuous gearing of engineering processes to business time frames, are compelling managers, analysts, architects, and engineers to cooperate on a steady basis. Yet, as much as being induced by the specificities of industries, enterprises' organization is the result of their history and corporate culture; and idiosyncrasies may even give enterprises a competitive edge.

On that account, responsibilities should not be set according to a one-size-fits-all template but rather on a case-by-case basis, depending on the scope and purpose of business or technical requirements (cf. chapter 13):

- Scope: business analysis (enterprise) or software engineering (systems)

- Purpose: business value associated with processes and applications, or assets materialized by organization and systems architecture

These distinctions should determine collaborations depending on ownership (stakeholders) and skills (analysts, architects, engineers).

Four collaboration templates (figure 4-13) emerge when requirements are refactored along the enterprise architecture perspective (cf. part III):

With regard to business-driven applications:

• When business requirements can be circumscribed to single domains, business analysts and software engineers can collaborate directly through iterative developments, typically Agile projects (a).

• When business requirements are set across domains, collaboration between development teams and architects should be supported by models (b).

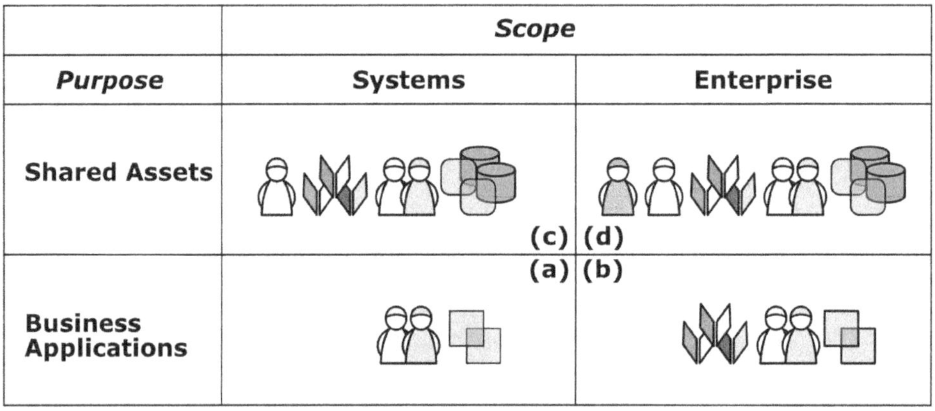

Purpose	Scope	
	Systems	Enterprise
Shared Assets	(c)	(d)
	(a)	(b)
Business Applications		

Figure 4-13. Squared Collaboration

With regard to shared assets, like business functions or services:

• Assuming requirements can set apart functional and organizational issues (cf. chapter 13), business analysts should use models to collaborate with systems architects and engineers building the models for systems' functions, services, or databases (c).

• Organizational issues introduce a collective dimension to decision-making and commitments, which can only be dealt with at the enterprise level. As a corollary, enterprise architects should collaborate with business analysts, systems architects, and engineers (d).

Collaboration between business and systems stakeholders and contributors thus appears as a major aspect of enterprise architecture, with collaboration occuring not only between individuals but also between collective entities. Moreover, the changing nature of enterprise architectures means that collaboration must be an intrinsic capability of such architectures. That issue will be further discussed in terms of supporting frameworks (next chapter), knowledge management (chapter 9), decision-making (chapter 10), and the maturity of organizations (chapter 15).

CHAPTER 5.

Frameworks

Frameworks are meant to manage the consistent descriptions of typical artifacts and associated modus operandi, and to support their enactment

Architecture is all about sharing: dwelling or activities for buildings; organization, assets, and business processes for enterprises. Enterprise architecture (EA) adds two critical dimensions to the archetype: one for changes, and the other for symbolic artifacts.

Like urbanism, EA is as much about change as it is about structures — more so when the ability to change becomes a key success factor. And the perspective of sustainable success reinforces the appeal of comprehensive and consistent blueprints.

But it's the symbolic dimension introduced by information systems that constitutes the specificity of enterprise architectures: a tight and singular combination of organizational, physical, and software components, supported by a uniform digital representation, from models to artifacts. The purpose of frameworks is to manage the whole.

Like the frames of paintings, frameworks are meant to make the best of what is framed. For EA, the most important benefit of using a framework is in the enhanced quality of the maps produced, with particular attention to transparency and transformation:

- Transparency: frameworks help to map business objectives and processes, on the one hand, and organizations and systems blueprints, on the other hand.

- Transformation: frameworks pave the way to actionable maps, providing guide rails for a continuous and consistent adaptation of enterprises' architectures to their business and technical environments.

The focus put on actionable maps should serve to identify core framework requirements, and to discard substandard solutions and pick the best ones, depending on enterprises' business, organization, and systems.

Objectives

Frameworks are meant to support processes and methodologies, not to replace them. On that basis, EA frameworks should focus on a) mapping territories, and b) integrating the trio of business, engineering, and decision-making processes.

Mapping Territories

As there can be no enterprise governance without transparency, frameworks must provide comprehensive, accurate, and up-to-date representations of environments, organization, and systems. Thus, mapping should be:

- Purposeful: the first objective of EA mapping is to distinguish between the representation of environments, organization, and systems; the second is to be actionable (i.e., to support the management of changes across corresponding territories and maps).

- Neutral: lest they inhibit or bias the work of business analysts and systems architects, EA maps must be focused on the concerns of enterprise architecture and ignore the representation of the specifics of business domains or systems architecture.

- Reliable: to be error-free, maps must be built from a small set of established and unambiguous concepts from which all relevant representations of contexts, organization, and systems could be logically derived.

- Open: like geographic ones, framework maps should be modular and open to extension.

Integration of Business & Engineering Processes

As already stressed, enterprise architecture is all about managing changes; hence, it is important to have actionable blueprints that could associate business and engineering processes with the relevant artifacts in supporting architectures. Such integration determines the framework's leveraging impact on business agility and engineering efficiency.

Agility

While the Agile development model often appears as a default option, amalgams of Agile processes are more likely to be cumbersome and loaded with overheads than pliable and versatile; moreover, adding procedures will make things worse. Frameworks, by contrast, can extend the benefits of Agile to enterprise architecture; first, by enhancing projects' visibility through greater transparency and traceability, and second, by harnessing business-driven requirements (carried out with Agile development methods) to architecture functions.

Efficiency

As it's safe to assume that large and complex organizations cannot rely on one-size-fits-all solutions, frameworks should further synergies from the integration of:

- Iterative development models (epitomized by Agile) for business-driven projects (cf. chapter 13)

- Model-based systems engineering (MBSE) for architecture-oriented ones (cf. chapter 14)

Integration of Business, Engineering & Decision-making Processes

The digital transformation raises the capabilities of EA frameworks to a new dimension by paving the way to a seamless integration of actual and symbolic artifacts and architectures (cf. chapter 9).

Taking advantage of the digital convergence between business and systems perspectives (cf. chapter 4), EA frameworks could go further and merge systems and knowledge architectures into a continuous decision-making loop (cf. chapter 10).

The benefits of weaving together decision-making with the processing of data, information, and knowledge can be illustrated using the Observation-Orientation-Decision-Action (OODA) loop. On that basis, frameworks should help to design and build business and engineering processes:

- Observation (data): changes in territories (environments and systems) can be monitored and assessed at the digital (e.g., data- and process mining) and enterprise (e.g., business intelligence) levels.

- Orientation (information): accurate, relevant, and up-to-date maps uphold the assessment of business observations with regard to enterprise commitments and anticipations.

- Decision (knowledge): alternative courses of action can be presented according to the nature of commitments: business, organization, or platforms, and the windows of opportunity.

- Action (data again): decisions can be carried out in a timely and consistent way, and their implementation can be fully monitored.

Such integration of business, organizational, and technical dimensions with knowledge management and decision-making processes can be a decisive factor for enterprises' success when competing in digital environments.

Prerequisites

Embarking on an architectural framework is a long-term endeavor, bearing upon a wide range of activities, and is thus bound to induce profound transformations in organization and systems. As a corollary, the outcome could be doomed from the outset: once on a wrong path, the best, if not the only, option is often to cut the losses as soon as possible and ascertain the correct path. Fortunately, there is no reason to hurry when devising the framework, and every reason to take time for an in-depth evaluation.

The first step should be to establish a short list of frameworks worthy of further assessment. For that preliminary selection, only form (and not substance) should be taken into account, with the focus on scope and clarity of purpose.

Scope & Separation of Concerns

Considering the role of enterprise architects as arbitrators between business and systems perspectives, frameworks have to bring under a common roof the representations of all relevant contexts and concerns in order to support the monitoring and management of objectives, projects, and time frames.

On that account, frameworks should allow enterprise architects to focus on the relationships between environments, organization, and systems, without being side-tracked by the details of applications. Conversely, frameworks should not hamper prompt and business-driven adaptations to environments.

Checklist:

- A compact set of reasoned and actionable representations of environments, objectives, assets, and processes: this set is needed for the swift and consensual definition of projects and responsibilities.

- Clear decision-making criteria to set apart self-contained projects that could be carried out under the radar of enterprise architecture, and those pertaining to organization or systems architecture.

Clarity of Purpose & Consistency of Definitions

EA frameworks should be more of a compass than a handbook, drawing clear lines of action without delving into the specifics of implementation. Lest architects get lost in compilations of ambiguous or overlapping definitions and rules, frameworks must come as compact sets of clear and reasoned abstractions and smooth learning curves, ensuring a selective and incremental adoption by decision-makers, business analysts, systems architects, and software engineers.

Checklist:

- The meaning of a small set (a dozen at most) of primary terms (e.g., event, role, activity, process, business object), regardless of monikers, should be uniquely and unambiguously defined based on core principles, independently of enterprises' organization and processes.

- Circular or overlapping definitions are to be ruled out as evidence of confused understanding; the same can be said of quantitative distinctions (e.g., large vs. small, higher vs. lower) not borne out by specifics regarding the nature of measurements.

A rough indicator of a glossary's efficiency is the ratio of entries to the number of unambiguous terms directly and independently defined (i.e., without referring to other glossary terms).

How to Choose

Frameworks are meant to support the design and governance of enterprises' organization and systems without adding undue methodological constraints. Therefore, given a short list of frameworks checked for key objectives and prerequisites, enterprise architects should decide among them based on frameworks' effectiveness and usability, rather than their idiosyncrasies. Effectiveness should be assessed by practicality and reliability, and usability, by ecumenisms and learning curves.

Practicality & Reliability

Adopting a framework should help with decision-making and reduce uncertainty. On that account, systems engineering roadmaps built from predefined activities (e.g., Requirements, Planning, Analysis, Design, Test) are deceptive because they rely on the implicit assumption that all issues can be fitted into prefabricated solutions; such a commitment is either too vague or too rigid and, in both cases, increases uncertainty. Taking for granted that positive outcomes can never be guaranteed independently of circumstances, frameworks should be ranked according to their ability to support enterprise architects in assessing situations, defining the courses of action, and deciding between them.

That's where the importance of maps and territories appears in full: frameworks need to provide specific and reliable roadmaps with clear signposts and unambiguous criteria that support enterprise architects' decision-making.

Ecumenism & Learning Curve

Prerequisites are necessary conditions that may have to be weighted differently depending on the specifics of individual enterprises; for example:

- Comprehensiveness and modularity are critical for enterprises with diversified lines of business and complex organizations; less so in the case of narrowly defined industries, stable environments, or hierarchical organizations.

- Clarity and consistency are obviously primary criteria in choosing a framework, but so is continuity with enterprises' embedded skills and proven practices. Frameworks should therefore be amenable to methods and tools already in use with established effectiveness.

More generally, given that continuity is a basic tenet of enterprise architecture, frameworks must be assessed with regard to their ecumenism; i.e., their interoperability between organizational, methodological, and technical contexts.

Although discrepancies will have to be dealt with, ecumenism, and consequently a smooth learning curve, can be achieved through a common understanding of established architectural concepts:

1. Architecture layers: platforms, systems, organization

2. Modeling levels: Computation independent, Platform independent, Platform specific

3. Functional capabilities: Model-View-Controller pattern

4. Database modeling schemas: conceptual, logical, physical

First and foremost, an EA framework has to be in line with the well-understood ternary distinction between platforms (technical and operational environments), systems (functional and logical descriptions), and enterprise (organization and business processes).

Second, to ensure continuity between EA and systems engineering, EA's three layers must be aligned with modeling levels. Again, labels may differ, but Model-driven architecture (MDA) provides a principled and ecumenic reference for concepts (cf. chapter 3):

• Computation independent models (CIMs) for organization and business processes

• Platform independent models (PIMs) for systems functionalities and information

• Platform specific models (PSMs) for systems components

It must be stressed that as far as EA is concerned, using adapters to contrive the alignment of layers is not an option. Adapters hinder traceability and transparency, which runs counter to the very purpose of a framework.

Third, with regard to systems functional architecture (PIMs), an EA framework should be fully congruent with the well-established Model-View-Controller (MVC) pattern, arguably the leading functional architecture pattern whatever the guise:

- Model (persistency capability): shared functions with life cycles independent of business processes

- View (boundary capability): stand-alone functions with life cycles limited to interactions

- Controller (control capability): shared functions with life cycles set by business processes

A functional archetype can be added to take into account Services oriented architecture (SOA), with services representing shared functions with no life cycle.

Fourth, an EA framework has to be aligned with the de facto consensus among leading database providers about conceptual, logical, and physical schemas:

- Conceptual: describe business objects and processes independently of their symbolic representation by systems

- Logical: describe the symbolic objects to be managed by supporting systems as surrogates of business objects and activities, independently of their physical implementation

- Physical: describe the actual implementation of symbolic surrogates as binary objects

Endorsing these four basic understandings independently of the labels employed (as a rule, enterprise architects should avoid definition games) would ensure the framework's continuity, interoperability, and smooth learning curve.

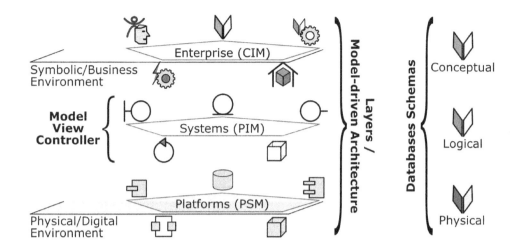

Figure 5-1. *Frameworks should be Aligned with Established Understandings*

The importance of a smooth and piecemeal adoption of a framework's concepts and modus operandi is often overlooked, leading either to delays, overheads, and project failures, or to giving up the mastery of the framework to external consultants (which, to all intents and purposes, undermines the rationale of adopting a framework).

How to Weigh Value Propositions

Pledges about stakeholder expectations, holistic commitments, and Agile achievements often come front and center in framework brochures; but the choice of a framework should be driven by the actual value propositions, not by declarations of intent.

An in-depth assessment of a value proposition is obviously a challenging and time-consuming undertaking. So, instead of conducting a shallow and misleading appraisal, the value proposition of a framework should be measured by its degree of specificity, in particular, with regard to its description of EA and systems engineering processes.

To that end, a simple yet reliable ranking should be established as follows:

• Frameworks with all-inclusive commitments would serve as a null option (thus lending themselves to the bottom of the ranking), because they make no difference between the items of their value proposition.

- The likelihood of commitments should serve to estimate the degree of specificity. Assuming that no framework would purport to ignoring business needs or not being Agile, specific commitments should be understood as being more open to a thorough assessment. This transparency alone should give more credit to the value proposition of a framework.

Short-listed frameworks could then be ranked according to the level of specificity of their commitments.

CHAPTER 6

The Pagoda Blueprint

*The objective of the Pagoda blueprint is to align EA frameworks
with enterprises' physical and business environments*

Overview

An online search for "enterprise architecture" yields five kinds of returns, typifying the diverse understandings of the term:

- Posters with large graphical arrangements of boxes and arrows are labeled with customary activities and views associated with software and systems.

- Architecture-modeling languages, like Archimate, which can be understood as bottom-up approaches, focused on systems.

- Meta-modeling languages, like Object Management Group's UAF (Unified Architecture Framework), which exemplify the flight to abstraction with a mix of syntax and semantics detached from contexts (systems, organization, environments) and concerns (descriptive, predictive, prescriptive).

- Process-oriented frameworks, like TOGAF, which are focused on activities and procedures applied to predefined views and artifacts.

- Systems-oriented frameworks, like Zachman's, which are focused on architecture capabilities, with some latitude given to enterprises regarding engineering processes.

Architecture-modeling languages put the focus on systems architectures, with a limited perspective on enterprises' business environments, objectives, and organization. Their main benefit comes from their straightforward integration of Model-based systems engineering (MBSE) (cf. chapter 14).

Meta-modeling languages are of little use to enterprise architecture, either because of their high level of abstraction - and consequently their detachment from actual architecture matters - or because they make no built-in distinction between software, systems, and enterprise issues (cf. chapter 8).

Process-oriented frameworks can be seen as extensions of the development-process paradigm. They try to detail activities related to enterprise architectures, but because maps and territories are introduced as an afterthought, a mass of overlapping definitions, often fuzzy or circular, ensues. Process-oriented architecture frameworks create a crucial imbalance between detailed procedures and fuzzy artifacts, which consequently leads to a lack of transparency and traceability between processes and architectures — a critical flaw for change management and MBSE. Moreover, the focus on detailed and specific procedures induces discontinuities with existing organization and methods, as well as steep learning curves.

Systems-oriented frameworks focus on architecture (as opposed to processes), and thus come with a comprehensive and consistent conceptual mapping mechanism. Accordingly, these frameworks are more amenable to enterprise architecture, organization, and methods. This perspective is the one developed in this book.

The Zachman Framework

The Zachman architecture framework (cf. bibliography), first introduced in the 80s, comes with a sound conceptual standing; nonetheless, its actual imprint on enterprise architects' practices has been limited. Apart from common prejudices against conceptual approaches, that somewhat disappointing outcome can be primarily explained by Zachman's tabulated presentation and a later functional misrepresentation.

Tabulated Presentation

Clarity and concision are arguably the main strengths of the Zachman architecture framework, exemplified by its tabulated presentation crossing six columns and five lines:

- Columns are set according to the traditional distinction between roles (who), objects (what), activities (how), locations (where), timing (when), and motivation (why).

- Lines are set along enterprise layers (business concepts and organization, systems functions and logic, engineering and technologies), with contexts added above and operations below.

- Cells are aligned with established stereotypes, as defined in chapter 3.

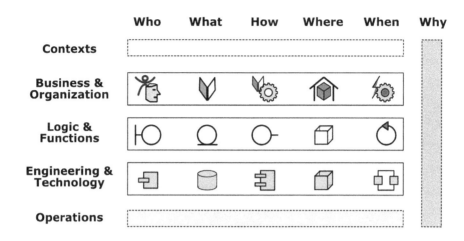

Figure 6-1. Stereotyped Zachman Lines & Columns

Yet, despite the soundness of the concepts, the tabular arrangement comes with some discrepancies, as it mixes architectural artifacts (lines 2–4 and columns 1–5) with contexts, instances (Operations), and purposes (Why).

This should not be problematic for the top and bottom lines, as they make room for new developments with regard to business intelligence (top) and digital environments (bottom).

However, the same cannot be said for the sixth column. Contrary to the other five, which characterize capabilities, the sixth is meant to deal with objectives, which are arguably better understood and managed when defined for capabilities (columns) than for layers (lines).

A straightforward graphical translation that substitutes pentagons for lines can redress the presentation of the core architecture's backbone without affecting its semantics (see figure 6-2) .

This neutral transformation, congruent with broadly accepted views of systems architecture, could have secured a sound extension of the Zachman framework to enterprise architecture by using the contexts and operations lines as bridges to business and digital environments, respectively. But that transformation was preempted by a functional misrepresentation.

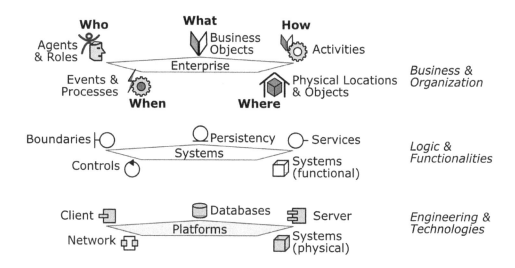

Figure 6-2. Graphical Translation of the Zachman Framework

Functional Misrepresentation

The Wikipedia definition the Zachman framework illustrates the issues raised by its transformation:

"... an enterprise ontology and a fundamental structure for Enterprise Architecture which provides a formal and structured way of viewing and defining an enterprise. The ontology is a two dimensional classification schema that reflects the intersection between two historical classifications."

Such a definition compounds two critical confusions:

- It overlooks systems architecture, which is at the root of the Zachman framework, and puts the focus on the enterprise perspective, a later extension.

- Ontologies are much more than frameworks or classifications, whatever the number of dimensions.

Such a misrepresentation has induced a number of misuses. Instead of providing a sound and pragmatic basis for systems architecture to be extended to enterprise organization and business, the Zachman framework has often been turned on its head and seen as an abstraction detached from actual and direct realizations of systems architecture. More critically, the framework has been presented as an ontology and its lines redefined in terms of perspectives (e.g., business executive and management, architect, engineer).

These changes have broken the framework's conceptual consistency by introducing confusion between views, meant to be set by concerns, and layers, meant to frame the ways architectures are defined and built. That confusion has a limited impact for stable software or systems architecture. But it turns out to be critical for enterprise architecture, where the challenge is to secure continuous mutations without affecting uses, and even more so for frameworks, whose primary objective is to serve as a gear between the views from supported business processes, and the engineering of supporting systems.

To offset the semantic blur newly introduced to the cells (diversely labeled as architecture, system, model, diagram), attempts have been made to redefine columns in terms of phased generic activities: definition, representation, specification, configuration. But, as a consequence of replacing the conceptual soundness of architecture capabilities with indeterminate (with regard to architecture) engineering phases, the framework has been refocused along a process perspective, losing its original clarity of purpose and consistency.

The aim of the Pagoda blueprint is to reinstate the conceptual integrity of the Zachman framework within the broader context provided by the digital transformation and its consequences for enterprise ontologies.

The Pagoda Blueprint

The spreading of digital technologies to every kind of activity requires, as well as facilitates, explicit and homogeneous representations of business and physical environments, respectively. Organization (for the business environment) and operations (for the physical environment) serve as interfaces with enterprise architecture. This explicit representation of business and physical environments neatly coincides with the top and bottom of the Zachman framework's tabulated representation.

The Zachman Framework Revisited

At the top, the symbolic representation of business models, objectives, and processes puts organizations at the juncture between enterprises and their business environments. That's where relevant entities and categories are identified, territories mapped, and systems anchored to environments (cf. chapter 3).

At the bottom, the intermingling of business processes and digital flows puts operations at the nexus between enterprises and their physical environments. That's where systems surrogates can be instantiated, modified, or just compared to facts, reflected by data.

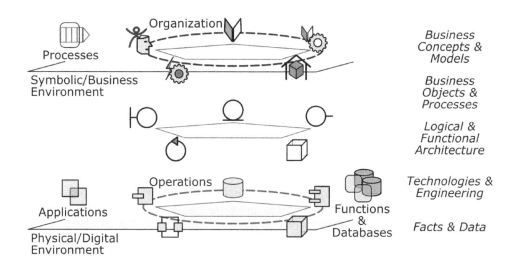

Figure 6-3. The Zachman Framework Revisited

In between, systems logical and functional architecture ensures the smooth integration of maps and territories, and thus the sustainability of the enterprise's activities.

Spanning the Semantic Divides

The various labels, and thus understandings, applied to the cells of Zachman's tabulated representation illustrate the importance of actionable maps; they determine how to define architecture artifacts, how they work together, and consequently, how architectures can be transformed.

That is what the Object Management Group's Unified Modeling Language (UML) is doing for systems and platforms layers: ensuring consistency, continuity, and traceability between artifacts' representation in models and their engineering into systems components. But with its roots in software design, UML is ill-suited to cope with the semantics of business domains - which is arguably a requisite for enterprise frameworks meant to support business and systems semantics, as well as the relevant mappings. The UML's intrinsic shortcoming can be redressed with the Stanford modeling paradigm.

As explained in chapter 3, the guiding principle of the paradigm is to anchor enterprise architecture to its environments through business entities, which are continuously and consistently identified at the enterprise level independently of their use by business domains or processes. That's what the executive (top) level of the Zachman tabulated framework is meant to do, with the resulting anchors (#) providing the architecture's backbone. Domain managers can then define their own categories and associated semantics, and flesh out anchors with relevant aspects.

The distinction between anchors and aspects (cf. chapter 2) plays a key role in ironing out the discrepancies between business and systems semantics. While the semantics of anchors (e.g., ***Customer***) in descriptive (business environment) and prescriptive (systems representations) models should be aligned at the enterprise level, that's not the case for other business entities (e.g., ***Reservation*** or ***Menu***) and aspects (e.g., ***dish*** and ***wine***), which can be interpreted differently by business domains. The alignment of these latter two categories with types or classes in prescriptive models (systems functional architecture) can then be decided by systems architects and software engineers.

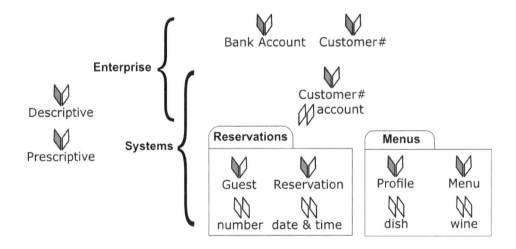

Figure 6-4. *Semantics of Anchors & Aspects*

That twofold mapping, first for anchors, then for aspects, is key to ironing out the semantic discrepancies between conceptual and logical representations (figure 6-5):

- The identity and semantics of anchors are defined at the enterprise level (descriptive models) and remain consistent across prescriptive and technical models.

- The identity and semantics of other business objects are defined by domains in descriptive or prescriptive models.

- Aspects can be defined at the enterprise or domains level, in descriptive or prescriptive models.

- Business logic is defined in descriptive models.

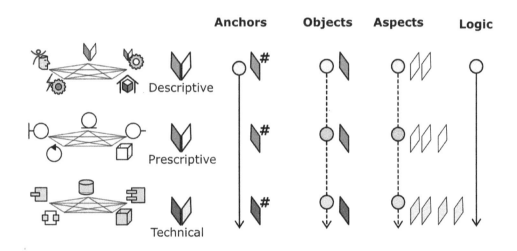

Figure 6-5. Spanning Semantic Gaps

The mapping of systems representations to business anchors induces leveraged benefits across EA layers:

First, it aligns the representations of business environments and objectives, organization and processes, and systems functional architecture.

Then, given the maturity of systems functional architecture patterns, like MVC (cf. chapter 5), and of software design patterns, epitomized by Eric Gamma's Gang of Four (cf. bibliography), it also brings technical representations into the fold of a consistent EA framework, from organization and business analysis to the design and programming of applications.

Swinging with Environments

The digital revolution bears out the dynamic dimension of enterprise architecture and, as a corollary, the necessity for frameworks to integrate blueprints and change management:

- Blueprints: to keep their edge, enterprises have to manage relevant, accurate, and up-to-date symbolic representations of their business environment and architecture capabilities.

- Change management: architectures must come with a built-in ability to learn from environments and operations, and to integrate operational decision-making with long-term strategies.

Pagodas epitomize sustainable architectures designed for unstable environments. Central pillars provide intrinsic strength and resilience to external upsets; layers attached to the pillars are allowed to move with the whole or to be modified independently.

The benefits of the Pagoda blueprint in digital environments come from its ecumenism: in line with the Stanford paradigm, the blueprint can be applied to all kinds of symbolic systems: equipment, computer, or organization.

To begin with, the immersion of systems in digital environments ensures a seamless continuity between the platforms layer and Cloud implementations (figure 6-6).

More generally, the Pagoda blueprint ensures proper communication between all kinds of systems through the alignment of layers with language capabilities: digital, symbolic, and natural.

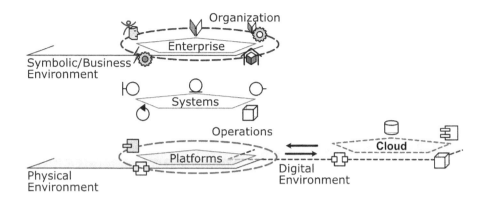

Figure 6-6. Systems in the Cloud

The significance of these points can be demonstrated with the Internet of things (IoT) and Service-oriented architecture (SOA) (figure 6-7):

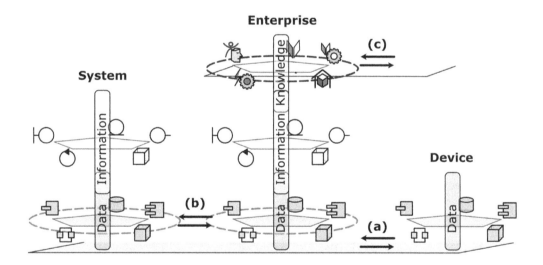

Figure 6-7. Architectures & Communications

- Broadly speaking, the term IoT covers everything connected to the internet; but, as a technology, it is focused on the nonsymbolic connections of devices (whether or not these devices come with symbolic capabilities) in order to use basic and fast communication channels in digital environments (a).

- Systems functional architecture, typified by services (cf. chapter 12), uses symbolic communication channels at the operational level (b).

- EA's top layer adds natural languages and human interfaces to enterprises' communication and collaboration capabilities at the organizational level (c).

Such alignment between communication channels, languages (digital, symbolic, natural), and architecture layers points to a broader integration between EA's layers and its ability to deal with digital data, to process symbolic information, and to use it as knowledge (cf. chapter 9).

Knowledgeable Architectures

Mirroring their alignment with languages and communication capabilities, the Pagoda layers are also aligned with corresponding symbolic capabilities: data for digital environments and operations, information for systems, and knowledge for organization (cf. chapter 4).

That integration of structures with communication and symbolic processing capabilities can greatly enhance the performances and sustainability of enterprise architectures in digital environments:

- At the operational level (platforms), digital osmosis secures reliable and timely observations of shifts in environments.

- At the functional level (systems), the integration of symbolic processing capabilities enables a dual feedback between observations from environments (data) and categories managed by supporting systems (information).

- At the enterprise level, the harnessing of organizations and systems can be decisive in supporting collaboration, and building collective knowledge and decision-making.

From a practical perspective, such a framework must rely on MBSE (cf. chapter 14). But models fall short in dealing with the whole range of business and engineering knowledge, as demonstrated by the ubiquity of Machine-learning technologies. A broader representation framework, one that could reach beyond modeled categories, is needed to encompass the whole of enterprise architecture concerns (figure 6-8).

Thesauruses can provide the conceptual glue between systems models, concepts, and uncategorized data in predictive models, enabling bottom-up processing of data into information and knowledge, and top-down knowledge and systems management.

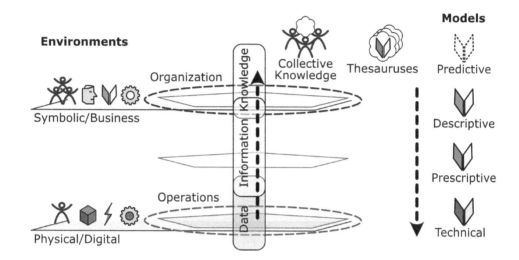

Figure 6-8. Knowledgeable Architecture

But thesauruses are not enough to support knowledge-based enterprise architecture. For that purpose, ontologies are required.

PART III.

Models
& Knowledge

The digital immersion of enterprises in their environments induces a seamless integration of computer systems, symbolic artifacts, and organization into business processes. As change becomes the rule of the game, architectures must be actionable, which requires maps and territories to be tightly coupled (cf. part I). Frameworks should then be introduced to ensure the sustainability of enterprise architecture (EA) through a dynamic alignment of business and systems perspectives (cf. part II).

This part focuses on the extension of maps from systems to enterprise architecture and, more specifically, on the use of ontologies to bring together all symbolic representations pertaining to systems, organization, and business. Chapter 7 expounds on the modeling principles introduced in chapter 3; namely, the use of anchors to attach prescriptive models of systems to descriptive models of business environments and objectives. Chapter 8 considers the limits of profiles and meta-models and the benefits of ontologies. Chapter 9 examines how ontologies can be used to turn the representation of environments, organization, and systems into seamless actionable maps that weave data, information, and knowledge with enterprise organization and systems architectures. Chapter 10 considers the benefits of ontologies for decision-making processes.

CHAPTER 7.

Models & Perspectives

A modeling paradox: opposite transformations (removing vs. adding scythe blades) can both be understood as specialization depending on the perspective: business (descriptive model) or engineering (prescriptive model), respectively

Whichever doctrinal tenets are held, at the end of the day, enterprise architects have to trade the value of business ventures with the returns on shared assets. This balancing act makes communication between analysts, managers, architects, and engineers a primary concern, and models the tools of choice.

As expounded in chapter 3, descriptive and prescriptive models form the main pillars of enterprise architecture, representing business and systems perspectives, respectively. In contrast to the file-and-forget policy adopted in systems modeling, descriptive models are meant to be continuously maintained in order to enable the continuity and consistency of changes in enterprise architectures. This requirement of continuity and consistency constrains EA in two ways: it has to be maintained between descriptive models and environments, and between descriptive and prescriptive models. That can only be achieved if descriptive models are built according to clear and reliable principles regarding:

- Defining the scope of models

- Anchoring the enterprise to environments

- Aligning prescriptive models with anchors

- Defining anchors' abstraction levels

Adhering to these principles would enable patterns and policies to be defined.

Scope

Separation of Concerns

To be of any use, enterprise architecture must ensure trustworthy communication between stakeholders and analysts, on the one hand, and architects and engineers, on the other hand. For large and complex organizations, collaboration critically depends on models that are precisely tailored with regard to purposes, users, and the time frame defining the models' validity.

Regarding purpose (figure 7-1), the critical distinction made by EA is between descriptive models for contexts and concerns, and prescriptive models for systems engineering. Predictive and technical models take the back seat; the former is best for alternative or virtual representations of environments (e.g., for data mining and business intelligence) or systems (e.g., for process mining), and the latter, for design and implementation. Patterns are higher-level models that are used to connect customary models (typically descriptive and prescriptive ones), and more generally, to connect generic models of problems and solutions (cf. chapter 8).

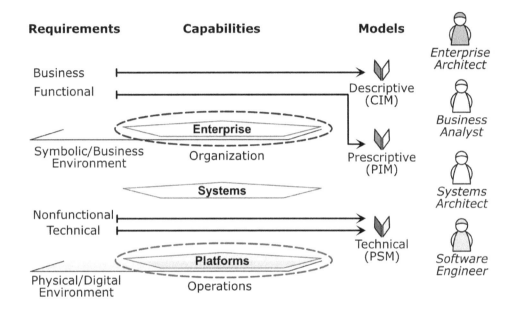

Figure 7-1. *Requirements & Models*

Models stem from requirements (cf. chapter 11) and should be subject to clear rules of ownership (cf. chapter 3):

- Descriptive (or Computation independent) models: business analysts and project owners

- Prescriptive (or Platform independent) models: systems architects, software engineers, and project managers

- Technical (or Platform specific) models: systems configuration managers, software engineers, and project managers

These broadly defined responsibilities should make room for the specificities of enterprises' organization and methodologies.

Divide & Conquer

Reflecting the lack of maturity of enterprise architecture as a discipline, practitioners are often faced with a dilemma: either delving into a miscellany of models and trying to sort out responsibilities, or following organizational directives and assignments.

A more principled approach would be to determine the architectural relevance of models according to their intrinsic properties, including owners, users, status, and shelf-life. To that effect, three categories must be considered:

Engineering models are meant to be detached from environments, due to either their nature (e.g., functional or technical patterns) or their status (e.g., reusable models with explicit shelf-lives). Once their semantics and consistency are validated, these models can be managed and used by different units across organization and over time, depending on targets, purpose, and time frame (cf. chapter 14).

Business intelligence models are meant to describe actual or hypothetical environments and objectives, independently of systems representations. Because they are bound to specific environments and purposes, the validity of these models is fleeting by nature. While the representation of their objectives and outcomes should be shared across EA, their content doesn't have to be.

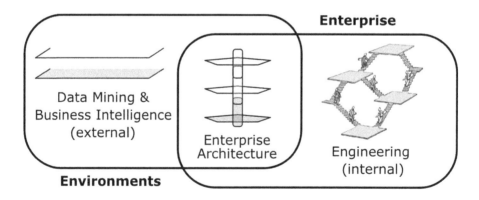

Figure 7-2. EA Attaches Enterprise to Environments

Enterprise architecture models mark the overlap between enterprises and environments in terms of business processes (organization), business functions (systems), and physical implementation (platforms). As such, EA models constitute the core of enterprise architecture as a discipline, operating as gears between enterprises and environments.

Anchoring Enterprise to Environments

Anchors & Aspects

As already stressed (cf. chapter 3), the primary objective of EA is to manage changes, and specifically to coordinate internal, designed changes with external, unplanned ones. The challenge for enterprise architects is therefore to build secure hinges that would attach enterprise and systems architectures to environments without inhibiting changes; that can be achieved with anchors and aspects (figure 7-3):

- Anchors are business objects whose identity and meaning are continuously and consistently aligned in environments and enterprise, independently of domain semantics and modeling languages (a).

- Regular (i.e., non-anchor) business objects (or entities) are defined by domains (b).

- Aspects are features or operations whose meaning can be defined independently of business objects; some are shared across domains (c), whereas others are specific to business domains (d).

- Some aspects are parts of anchor structures (e, solid arrow), whereas others can be attached to anchors or to regular business objects (f), depending on their semantic footprint (enterprise or domain).

- The structure of anchors must be maintained in prescriptive models (g, solid arrow); as for the business objects not used as anchors, choices are made at the domain level (h, dashed arrow).

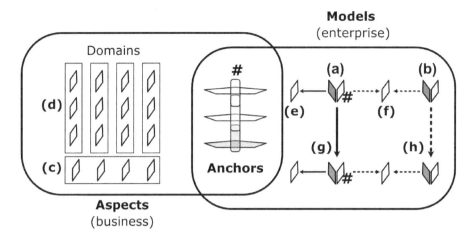

Figure 7-3. Anchors & Aspects

Anchors are built in three-step iterations:

1. Setting apart business entities and aspects; the former for categories of individuals, the latter for elementary or structured features (properties or operations)

2. Setting apart anchors from regular business entities; to be decided by business analysts, and enterprise and systems architects (see below)

3. Fleshing out anchors and regular business entities with structural and functional aspects

Identified at the enterprise level, anchors are meant to serve a double purpose:

• Provide a hub where business analysts and systems architects can collaborate in refining and fleshing out aspects

• Secure the consistency of external (descriptive) and internal (prescriptive) symbolic representations

These objectives can only be achieved through collaboration between business analysts and systems architects, with enterprise architects as facilitators. That collaboration implies a shared understanding of core generic constructs that are common to business and systems modeling languages but detached from the semantics specific to business domains (cf. chapter 2). That can be done through anchors: on the one hand, they secure consolidated semantics; on the other hand, they serve as beacons for business aspects still unmodeled (yet defined in thesauruses) or partially modeled (defined only in thesauruses and descriptive models).

Structuring Anchors

Here the focus is on modeled anchors and aspects (unmodeled ones and thesauruses are considered in chapter 9). Once identified in descriptive models, anchors must be fleshed out with aspects. Since business analysts and systems architects are meant to collaborate, they must agree on the semantics of modeling connectors used as glue between business objects (including anchors) and aspects.

As already noted in chapter 2, there are two kinds of connectors (figure 7-4):

- Composition and aggregation characterize links between instances of objects, or their association with aspects.

- Subtypes apply to modeling categories (or types, or classes) but not to instances.

		Business Object	Aspect
◈	Composition	*Parts identified by owner*	*Mandatory aspect*
◇	Aggregation	*Parts identified independently*	*Optional aspect*
▲	Structural subtype	*Subset of individuals*	*Qualified range*
△	Functional subtype	*Subset of aspects*	*Qualified domain*

Figure 7-4. Basic Connectors in Descriptive Models

It ensues that the semantics of the connectors pertaining to instances can be defined independently of modeling languages; but that's not the case for the ones pertaining to modeling constructs. As a corollary, the former can be matched in descriptive and prescriptive models, but not the latter.

Composition & Aggregation

Composition is used for structural connections between sources and targets. Referenced entities cannot be identified independently, and targeted aspects are mandatory.

Taking the diner case study as an example (figure 7-5):

- Applied to business entities, composition means that the part is identified by the owner; that could be represented by an identifying reference (#) from *Reservation* to *Customer*, or by a composition (black diamond) of *Customer*.

- Applied to aspects (properties or operations), composition means that the aspect is intrinsic and thus mandatory; e.g, *Passport* is a mandatory property for *Non-citizen*, and *Open* and *Close* operations are always supported by *Bank Account*.

Aggregation is used for functional connections between sources and targets. Referenced entities can be identified on their own, and targeted aspects are optional. Returning to the diner case study:

- In contrast to the reference of *Reservation* to *Customer,* the reference of *Customer* to *Bank Account* can only be defined as aggregation (and not composition), because *Bank Account* (contrary to *Reservation*) is identified in the business environment independently of *Customer*. *Owner* appears as a mandatory property of *Bank Account*, but not as a reference to *Customer*, because its semantics is set by the context independently of *Customer.*

- Depending on the category of *Reservation, change()* is an optional operation, and *last visit* is an optional property of *Customer.*

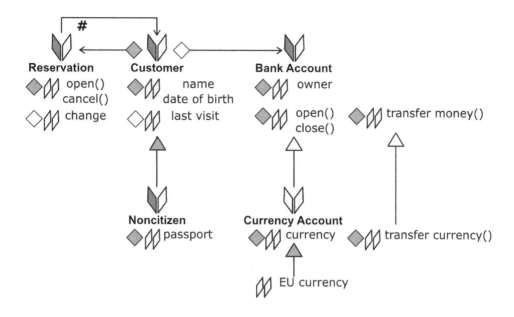

Figure 7-5. Basic Connectors for a Generic Reservation Case Study

Subtypes

Subtypes are not defined between individuals but between the sets of individuals represented by the categories (or classes, or types) considered.

Structural subtypes define subsets of individuals (referenced entities) or values (qualified aspects); for example:

- **Noncitizen** defines the subset of customers who are foreigners.

- **European Union (EU) currency** (as a list) has a qualified range compared to the **currency** list.

Functional subtypes define subsets of aspects independently of the individuals concerned. For categories, functional (or behavioral) specialization implies only the

inheritance of aspects; for aspects, it implies that the specialized one inherits the domains of use of its parent; for example:

- **Currency Account** is not defined as a business entity but as a set of features (or
  interface) that add **currency** features to **Bank Account**; that choice enables multiple and changing currencies to be attached to the same account.

- **Transfer currency()** operates like **transfer of money()** in the context of **Currency
  Account**.

The systematic use of semantically neutral connectors should significantly reduce
domain-specific contents in EA models, thus enabling their uniform and unambiguous understanding, and consequently a better collaboration between analysts, architects, and engineers. However, these connectors are too coarse-grained to support
extended consistency checks; hence the benefits of using standard logic extensions.

Logical Refinements

Descriptive models are the primary repository of business requirements and, consequently, the primary reference for quality checks. To that end, as far as EA is concerned, their content should meet two basic conditions:

- Lean: everything represented has to serve a clear purpose at the enterprise architecture level.

- Unequivocal: there should be no ambiguity regarding the intent or meaning of
  what is represented.

The first condition can be satisfied if the visibility of associations is limited to
the ones involving anchors (e.g., **Customer**) or business entities identified in environments (e.g., **Bank Account**).

The second condition is met if connectors are refined in line with established
logical operations (figure 7-6):

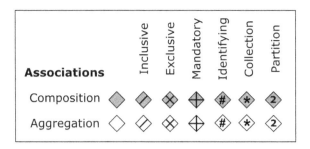

Figure 7-6. Logical Extensions

• Inclusive composition: a bill can be paid in cash, by cheque, or by credit card (payments are identified by bills)

• Inclusive aggregation: the payment of a bill can be shared by personal or corporate customers (customers are managed independently)

• Exclusive composition: a bill must be paid either in cash, by cheque, or by credit card

• Exclusive aggregation: a bill must be paid either by a personal or a corporate customer

• Mandatory composition: telephone numbers are not managed independently

• Mandatory aggregation: bank accounts can be managed independently

• Identifying connectors are both exclusive and mandatory

• Collective composition: payments for a bill

• Collective aggregation: orders paid by a bill

• Composed partition: bank accounts ranked with regard to credit rating

• Aggregate partition: bank accounts grouped with regard to currencies (currencies are managed independently)

Logically refined connectors enable an effective collaboration between business analysts and systems architects, and allow for consistency checks of descriptive models, and their integration with prescriptive models.

These connectors can also help to iron out the semantic discrepancies between modeled business domains and the unmodeled or partially modeled (cf. chapter 4) ones. A clear remit of enterprise architects, these modeling transit areas are managed by thesauruses along modeled domains. Whether these representations are meant to remain outside systems architecture concerns (e.g., business intelligence) or to be progressively integrated into descriptive and prescriptive models, they should all rely on a common set of connectors with consistent meaning.

Picking Anchors

In setting apart anchors from regular business entities, the role of enterprise architects is to make sure that business and systems stakeholders share the same architectural principles without hindering their autonomy; in particular (figure 7-7):

- Anchors are tied to elements identified in the environment, either permanently (e.g., *Party#* to *Person* or *Organization*) or during the execution of a process (e.g., *Booking#* to *Event*).

- Business entities identified and managed in environments independently of enterprises (e.g., *Person, Organization, Bank Account*) should not be directly defined as anchors but represented as roles (e.g., *Party*) in descriptive models, with representations in prescriptive models determined at the domain level (e.g., *Customer, Provider*).

- Business entities managed by domains but not identified in environments (e.g., *Reservation*) should not be defined as anchors.

- Process (or transient) anchors should be introduced when the continuity and consistency of regular (nonanchor) business entities must be maintained until the completion of a business process (e.g., *Booking*).

With anchors and regular business entities identified, the next step is to align prescriptive models with descriptive anchors.

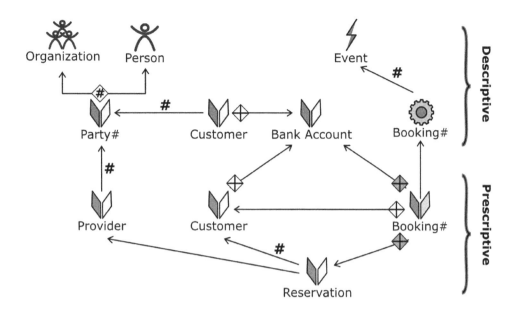

Figure 7-7. Anchoring Descriptive & Prescriptive Models

The use of an ontology (cf. chapter 8) enables a seamless integration of models; for example, the entry for ***Party#*** can be first introduced as a role (descriptive), then updated as an entity (prescriptive), an anchor, and finally, as a class (technical).

Aligning Prescriptive Models with Anchors

From a systems perspective, models are means to engineering ends, and their assessment is thus focused on internal consistency. External consistency is reckoned with as a by-product of requirements, falling under the responsibility of business analysts.

From a business perspective (cf. chapter 4), models are means to organizational ends, with feasibility assessment the responsibility of systems architects.

That leaves a quality no-man's-land in-between, where neither expectations nor commitments are checked; that hiatus can be curtailed with descriptive models that span from the business side, and prescriptive ones that span from the systems side.

Objects & Aspects

The alignment of anchors in descriptive (business) and prescriptive (systems) models should secure the structural continuity of systems representations. But it will do little for the functional consistency of models and, consequently, for the systems' ability to change and adjust in digital environments.

To deal with the issue, enterprise architects can distribute responsibilities for objects and aspects in descriptive and prescriptive models (figure 7-8).

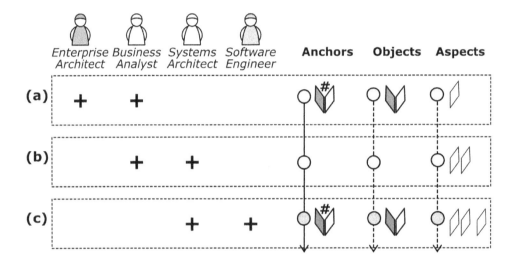

Figure 7-8. Basic Responsibilities

- Enterprise architects and business analysts identify anchors and regular business objects depending on the business environment, objectives, and business entities already managed; apart from identity and intrinsic (or structural) properties, no assumption should be made regarding modeling constructs (a).

- Business analysts and systems architects flesh out anchors and regular business objects with aspects using logical connectors (figure 7-6), whenever possible (b).

- Systems architects and engineers proceed with the translation of descriptive models into prescriptive ones, taking into account the structure of descriptive anchors. The detachment of nonstructural aspects and the distinction between logical connectors and semantic ones give them enough latitude for design (c).

Those three steps, meant to be repeated in loops, sum up the EA modeling process, from the expression of business aspects and logic, unconstrained by modeling language, to actionable models constrained by systems architectures.

The asymmetry between unconstrained business analysis and constrained systems design is epitomized by the Object-oriented (OO) paradigm, a de facto modeling standard for systems architectures and software design.

Simply put, OO modeling considers targeted contexts as sets of objects whose properties and behaviors can only be addressed through interfaces that hide their inner workings. Classes are meant to represent subsets of objects with shared properties and behaviors, as well as the methods encapsulated behind the interfaces.

The basic OO concepts of objects and interfaces appear to be in keeping with the anchors, business objects, and aspects used in descriptive models, suggesting a straightforward translation into prescriptive ones. But that apparent congruence is misleading because it is limited to flat descriptions and falls short when different levels of representations are used. In that case, the alignment of descriptive and prescriptive representations would require that subtypes and inheritance have the same meaning in both types of models.

But there is no reason to assume an OO symmetry between software objects in systems and their business homonyms in environments. As a matter of fact, the sundry, fuzzy, and shifting nature of business domains, on the one hand, and the homogeneity, accuracy, and stability necessary for systems continuance and performances, on the other hand, all point the other way: environments and systems are different beasts better kept apart by business models and organization. Nonetheless, since descriptive models have to be implemented by prescriptive ones, principles should be defined to map business objects into systems ones.

Where to Put Anchors

Managing changes is a primary objective for enterprise architecture, and that can be done by shifting aspects between descriptive and prescriptive models. But changes should not affect the consistency of representations, especially not the consistency of individuals in environments and systems.

Anchors' (or structural) consistency implies that relevant objects in business environments are uniquely represented by surrogates in systems, and that each surrogate represents one, and only one, business object. It ensues that selecting a descriptive category as an anchor means that surrogates in systems (represented by prescriptive categories) will always match their counterpart in environments. That may be trivial for physical objects with intrinsic identities (e.g., people), but is much less so for those that are statutory (e.g., contract) or designed (e.g., concept car).

Figure 7-9. External Instances & Systems Surrogates

When anchors are set at the physical level (figure 7-9, left), external instances (e.g., people) and their systems surrogates stand at the same physical (or digital) level; in other words, all categories involved (no matter their number) can be folded into a flat model supporting a direct mapping between external instances (*a,b,c,d*) and their surrogates (a,b,c,d).

By contrast (figure 7-9, right), when anchors are set in symbolic environments, the mapping of external symbolic instances (*m,n,o,p*) to digital surrogates (m,n,o,p) cannot be taken for granted. One way is to bestow digital identities to symbolic instances (e.g., contracts); more generally, mapping will be achieved through descriptive and prescriptive categories.

Consider *Employee* and *Customer* in the diner case study (figure 7-10). On the left appear individuals in physical (*Person*) and symbolic (*Customer* and *Employee*) environments; on the right are two options for their representations as descriptive (green) or prescriptive (blue) categories.

Symbolic Anchors

If anchors are attached to business categories in descriptive models (e.g., *Customer#* and *Employee#*, figure 7-10a), corresponding prescriptive models will let domains manage individuals independently. An additional prescriptive category (e.g., *Person*) can be introduced at the enterprise level to manage the overlaps between domains. Internal consistency could thus be secured by linking *Customer#* and *Employee#* to *Person*; but since *Person* is not a descriptive business object, the external consistency of identities is not a built-in property of models but depends on verification procedures.

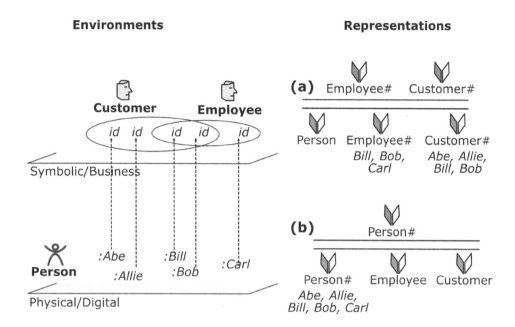

Figure 7-10. Symbolic (a) & Physical (b) Anchors

Physical Anchors

Conversely (figure 7-10b), if **Person#** is used as an anchor in the physical environment, instances for prescriptive categories **Employee** and **Customer** could be consistently identified through the prescriptive anchor **Person#**. While that will secure external consistency, it will also bar business domains from managing **Employee** and **Customer** roles independently of the externally defined **Person#**.

Hybrid Anchors

Anchors could be attached to objects that combine symbolic (e.g., social security number) and physical (e.g., fingerprints) identities. Such hybrid anchors, spanning symbolic and physical environments, could solve the overlapping issue of symbolic anchors and remove the constraints associated with physical ones. But they come with issues of their own.

First, business objects — and anchors, in particular — must be identified uniformly. For the identification mechanism for hybrids, two options are possible: either the symbolic part is given a digital identity (e.g., cryptocurrency) or the physical part is given a symbolic one (e.g., a person's national identity). In practice, given that anchors are supposed to be defined at the enterprise level, hybrid ones will become a mix of symbolic and physical business objects wrapped in symbolic envelopes. The question is how to represent these mixes in models (figure 7-11).

Descriptive hierarchies of subsets must be ruled out because sets and subsets must be identified uniformly; for example, *People* and *Organization* (identified externally) cannot be defined as subsets of an enterprise business object *Party*. Instead, *Party* will be identified through an identifying (#) and exclusive reference to *People* and *Organization*.

Then, should the business object *Party* become an anchor? If it does (figure 7-11a), its prescriptive counterpart *Party#* should make no structural reference to environments. Otherwise (figure 7-11b), there would be no constraint on the design of *Party*, which could bypass descriptive anchor *Party#* and make exclusive references to anchors *People#* and *Organization#*, or use an OO abstract class for *Party*, with *People#* and *Organization#* as subtypes.

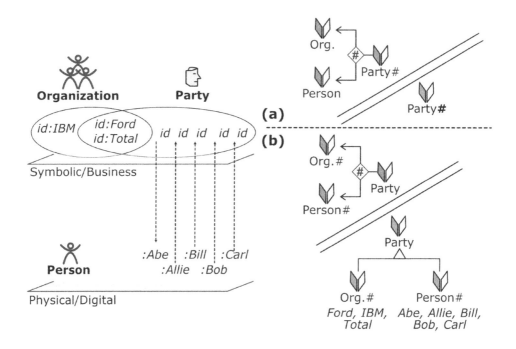

Figure 7-11. *Hybrid Anchors*

Hybrid anchors shed light on basic modeling principles:

1. Descriptive and prescriptive models are not symmetrical: the former target heterogeneous environments and thus can make no modeling assumption about the semantics of representation levels; the latter target artifacts and their only constraint is to be explicit and consistent about their modeling approach, typically OO.

2. All references to business objects in environments should be done through descriptive models.

3. Casting business objects as anchors introduces a constraint on their prescriptive counterpart, which must mimic the descriptive structure.

Those principles serve as guidelines for managing changes.

Anchors' Abstraction Levels

Given that ensuring the consistency of changes is at the top of the EA agenda, changes should be defined and managed through anchors in descriptive and prescriptive models. To that effect, enterprise architects should distinguish between local changes that are carried out through specialization, and architectural changes that are carried out through generalization.

Using the example in the illustration that introduced this chapter:

- From a business perspective, removing scythe blades from war chariots so as to use them in victory parades would appear as a specialization of descriptive models without any impact for engineering.

- Conversely, if officers ask engineers to add scythe blades to chariots in order to weaponize them, it would entail a specialization in prescriptive models.

That example illustrates the asymmetry of descriptive and prescriptive representations: opposite changes (adding and removing scythe blades) can both appear as specialization depending on the perspective: business use (descriptive model) or systems engineering (prescriptive model).

Specialization of Anchors

Changes through specialization are meant to add new functionalities without affecting the semantics of existing ones. They can be initiated at the enterprise level through descriptive models, or at the domain level through descriptive or prescriptive models (figure 7-12).

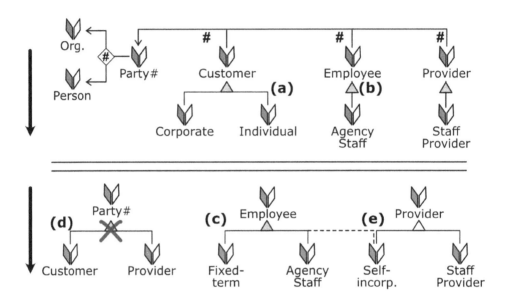

Figure 7-12. Specialization (downward arrow)

As noted earlier, no modeling assumption (e.g., OO) should be made regarding descriptive models. Accordingly, specializations should only be understood in terms of subsets; this implies that identification mechanisms for business objects (anchors or regular) cannot be affected. For example (figure 7-12, top):

• *Customer* can be specialized as *Corporate* and *Individual* (a).

• *Employee* can be specialized as *Agency staff* (b).

- As already noted, ***Party#*** cannot be specialized into ***Org.*** and ***Person*** due to the difference in identification mechanisms.

With regard to prescriptive models, specialization semantics are defined by modeling languages, with the OO paradigm the default option. However, there is a proviso for the specialization of prescriptive anchors, which must reproduce the structure of their descriptive counterpart; for example (figure 7-12, bottom):

- The descriptive specialization of ***Employee*** (a regular object) can be redefined by the prescriptive model in line with OO guidelines and management objectives (c).

- A prescriptive specialization of ***Party#*** (an anchor) by ***Customer*** and ***Provider*** would mean that both subtypes are identified by ***Party#***, but the descriptive model says the opposite (d).

In principle, specializations should be checked and set down explicitly in EA models. In practice, given that modeling is not an exact science, successive transformations of models may introduce overlaps. Consistency checks should thus be carried out regularly through the tracing of identifying associations; for example:

1. The starting point is a prescriptive model with an exclusive specialization of ***Employee*** (c).

2. A prescriptive ***Provider*** is introduced with a nonexclusive specialization for ***Agency staff***.

3. Two extensions are introduced from different domains, at different times, for a ***Self-incorporated*** specialization of ***Provider***, and of ***Employee*** (e).

4. Functional consistency is not supposed to be affected by specialization, and identities can be traced back and reconciled to ***Party#***: one through ***Employee***, and the other through ***Provider***.

Since changes through specialization are not supposed to affect existing functionalities, managing their impact on enterprise architecture can be straightforward, providing their footprint is clearly defined with regard to:

- Visibility: domain or enterprise

- Level: descriptive or prescriptive model

- Target: anchor or regular object

By contrast, difficulties arise with generalizations.

Generalization of Anchors

Compared to specialization, which is mainly driven by the extension of existing business activities (cf. chapter 13), generalization is often motivated by the extension of architecture capabilities — typically to deal with the merging of enterprises, business domains, or information systems. The intents, if not the achievement, of such mergers are usually not limited to increased revenues or reduced costs, but also aim to transform the whole of organizations.

From a modeling perspective, generalization means that sets of objects or activities initially defined separately are redefined in order to factor out a number of shared features and operations. As a corollary, and contrary to specialization, generalization can modify the semantics of existing functionalities — which is, in many cases, an explicit purpose of architectural transformations.

Leaving aside predictive models (which have no direct impact on architectures), generalizations should be explicit with regard to these changes in descriptive and predictive models.

Blank Generalizations

As a zero option mirroring the semantic neutrality of specialization, blank generalizations can be defined as ones that don't change the semantics of existing objects and aspects. From an architectural point of view, a blank generalization means that changes can be reversed, thus making room for smooth transformations and improved architectural plasticity (cf. chapter 15).

The reversibility of changes first requires that identities not be affected by the generalization, enabling operations to be consistently applied to individuals independently of the level of representation (e.g., VIPs should remain customers). That condition can be easily checked in descriptive models because the levels of representation are defined by subsets; not so for prescriptive models, which allow for a wider range of abstractions (e.g., instances of **Self-incorporated** can be identified as **Employee** or **Provider**, figure 7-12).

Assuming that changes can be circumscribed to systems representations, prescriptive generalizations can introduce new objects or rename existing ones. For instance (figure 7-13), a new class **Customer** can be added to manage aspects shared by **Individual Customer** and **Corporate Customer**. Instead of being tied by identifying associations to the externally defined **Person** and **Organization**, **Individual Customer** and **Corporate Customer** will still have the direct reference but their identity (**#**) will be managed through **Account#**, an enterprise anchor. Since the generalization is exclusive (black triangle) and existing aspects are not affected, the change can be handled as an engineering issue and even reversed, if need be, without affecting descriptive models.

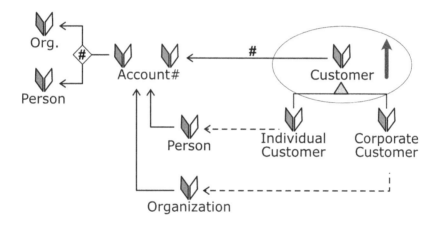

Figure 7-13. *Blank Generalization (upward arrow)*

However, that will not be the case if changes in statuses are taken into account (e.g., individual customers becoming entrepreneurs).

Prescriptive Generalizations

With blank generalizations set apart, the next ones to consider are those that can be circumscribed to systems architecture.

Such transformations are supposed to deal with overlapping (e.g., between *Provider* and *Customer*) and dynamic (e.g., from *Agency staff* to *Fixed-term employee*) prescriptive classifications independently of descriptive ones; that is, without affecting the representation of business objects and aspects in environments.

Let's take, for example, the (caricatural?) merging of information systems supporting a hotchpotch of providers classified as *Staff Provider*, *Foreign*, *HMO* (Health management organization), and *Self-incorporated* (figure 7-14).

At first, the objective is to integrate legacy components in order to consolidate and manage their references to externally defined entities through a single *Account#* anchor; a *Provider* generalization is created at that end. That generalization is not a blank one because overlaps (white triangle) must be consolidated and discrepancies ironed out, thus ruling out reversibility.

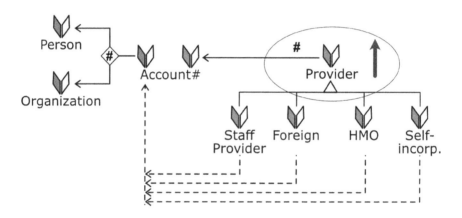

Figure 7-14. *Prescriptive (blue) Generalization*

Still, as such, it could remain an engineering development and not affect descriptive models.

Architectural issues arise when prescriptive generalizations (systems level) affect descriptive models, or when generalizations are used to consolidate descriptive models. The refactoring of legacy components (cf. chapter 14) illustrates the former issue.

Continuing with the merger example above, there are two approaches: a piecemeal one based on prescriptive models, and a global one driven by descriptive models.

A prescriptive approach would flesh out a ***Provider*** classifier with aspects associated with business functions managed at the enterprise level, like finance or Research and development (R&D). For example, all new business transactions could be factored out and handled through the existing anchor ***Contract#***. The specificity of foreign transactions could thus be managed through ***Contract#*** (e.g., ***Regulations, Trade Agreement***), making a ***Foreign*** subtype redundant.

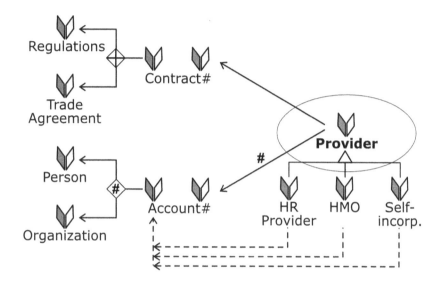

Figure 7-15. *Prescriptive Generalization with Descriptive Impact*

While a prescriptive generalization will, in all likelihood, entail changes in descriptive models, these changes will not amount to generalizations.

Descriptive Generalizations & Consistency

The generalization of descriptive anchors is arguably one of the primary challenges for enterprise architects, because comprehensive changes in enterprises' business and organization pull in two opposite directions:

- They entail the merging and consolidation of enterprises' symbolic representations.

- Expansion and the competitive drive tend to increase the specificity of business domains.

As already noted, the semantics of subtypes (descriptive or prescriptive) distinguish objects and behaviors:

• With objects, subtypes represent exclusive subsets of individuals that share the same identification mechanism (e.g., **Contract**).

• With behaviors, subtypes represent inclusive subsets of aspects (e.g., **Business Role**).

That difference identifies the two gears of architectural transformations: structural subtypes for changes affecting the coupling with environments, and functional subtypes for changes limited to organization and systems.

Taking, for example, a simplified merger of car-rental companies serving different market segments (figure 7-16):

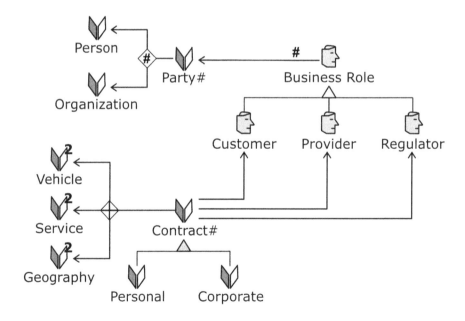

Figure 7-16. Generalization of Descriptive Models

- The anchor *Party#* is not affected.

- A functional (white triangle) generalization (*Business Role*) is introduced to factor out aspects shared by all agents identified in environments (*Customer*, *Provider*, *Regulator*).

- A structural (black triangle) generalization (*Contract#*) is introduced to consolidate the aspects of *Personal* and *Corporate* contracts managed by merged entities.

- The consolidation of rental conditions is done through powertypes (^{2}) for *Vehicle*, *Service*, and *Geography*.

The distinction between structural and functional generalizations makes possible a distinction between structural and functional consistency checks:

- Structural (or external) consistency: contracts are continuously and consistently identified before and after the merger.

- Functional (or internal) consistency: prior rental conditions can be unambiguously consolidated into new ones.

Enterprise architects can thus use abstraction levels to draw the line between enterprise and domain responsibilities; for example, a request for managed personal data will return the same records whichever level of description is used, general or specialized.

Process Consistency

Compared to architectural (or structural) consistency, which deals with the continuous anchoring of architectures to their environment, process consistency deals only with anchoring during the execution of processes.

To that end, assuming that business anchors are secure (i.e., checked for structural consistency), processes must be checked with regard to the integrity of objects and the semantics of aspects.

The execution of processes crisscrosses business objects, inducing concurrent accesses (cf. chapter 4). Typically, consistency can be managed at the object or process level. At the object level, integrity constraints are the responsibility of business domains; at the process level, business analysts (for business logic) and systems engineers (for process execution) segment execution units to limit the impact of constraints on resources and performances (cf. chapter 12).

For example, for a simplified *Take Reservation* process (wheel, red center) and corresponding activities (wheels, white center) for a car rental *request* (figure 7-17), two kinds of constraints should be considered:

- Context: the consistency of business objects pertaining to the request must be guaranteed independently of business processes (e.g., *Party#* and *Contract#*).

- Target: the state of business objects (or aspects) should be affected by the activities (e.g., *Reservation*).

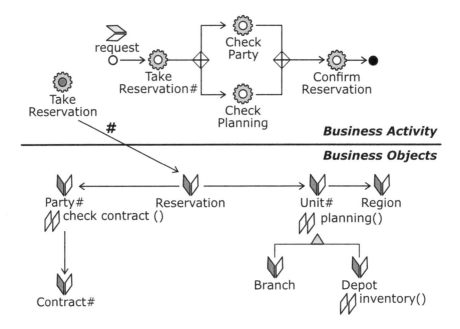

Figure 7-17. Business Processes & Anchors

Given the constraints on context, the objective is to design processes in a way that minimizes the impact of constraints on targets. That can be done with identifying connectors (#) tying processes to business objects (e.g., ***Reservation***). These identifying connectors between business processes and objects can be seen as the equivalent of the ACID (atomicity, consistency, isolation, durability) constraints used to guarantee the validity of database transactions. Process anchors are introduced when identifying connectors encompass multiple business objects (e.g., options trading).

Whereas the integrity of objects is checked with regard to process execution, the semantic consistency of processes is checked with regard to the activities concerned.

Given that processes are set across anchors and domains, they comprise aspects from a variety of domains, and there is a possibility of semantic overlaps. Yet, preventing homonyms in large organizations is neither a reasonable nor realistic option because, first, domains should be given a free hand with their business terms and, second, the number of awkward monikers would get out of hand. Moreover, preventing homonyms at the domain level will be of little help because functional consistency must be secured for processes (i.e., across domains).

As it happens, preventing homonyms in descriptive models may not be necessary because the issue can be handed over to prescriptive models to be handled using OO polymorphism.

Polymorphism is an OO mechanism that lets the same messages be interpreted differently according to context. For example, a request for "source" can refer to "cause," "origin," or "author," depending on the actual recipient, instances of event, transfer, or book, respectively. With polymorphism, interpretations will be left to the business context. Considering that OO is universally (if not uniformly) adopted by systems architects, polymorphism can be taken for granted in prescriptive models. As a corollary, homonyms can be seen as a purely descriptive issue that can be handled with thesauruses (cf. chapter 4).

Alignment Policies

If changes in architecture often aim to reduce the complexity of systems, business competition usually pulls it in the other direction. This pressure toward ever greater complexity is heightened as digital environments further business opportunities across domains. For enterprise architects, the objective is thus to deal with the growing complexity of business environments, while keeping the lid on the complexity of organization and systems.

As noted, specializations and neutral generalizations of anchors do not affect their complexity; therefore, the capabilities of supporting systems remain consistent. But strategic moves or disruptive changes in business environments call for more in-depth architectural transformations that affect the alignment of business objectives, organization, and systems.

For such transformations, the bottom line should be to maintain intrinsic architectural complexity: namely, the continuity and consistency of the identification mechanisms of anchors across descriptive and prescriptive models.

Patterns of Alignment

On that account, three basic patterns of alignment can be identified (figure 7-18):

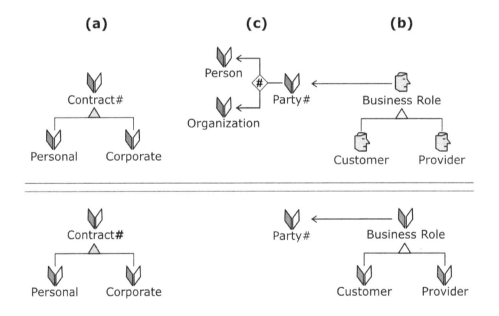

Figure 7-18. Patterns of Alignments

• Descriptive structural hierarchies (black triangle): for business objects defined and identified in environments independently of their representation in systems; e.g., for exclusive sets of accounts, **Personal** and **Corporate** contracts are uniformly identified as **Contract#** (a).

- Descriptive functional hierarchies (white triangle): for business objects defined and identified at the enterprise level independently of environments; e.g., non-exclusive **Business Role** of **Customer** or of **Provider** (b).

- Identifying association: to avoid the mix of generalization semantics in descriptive and prescriptive models; e.g., **Party#** is defined in both descriptive and prescriptive models, and identified in environments by an identifying reference to **Person** or **Organization** (c).

Applying these patterns of alignment to EA transformations can prevent unwarranted increases in architectural complexity.

Anchor Anti-patterns

Anchors can be seen as the cornerstones of enterprise architecture, hence the need to avoid flawed options (figure 7-19).

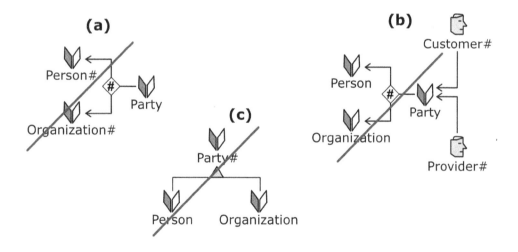

Figure 7-19. Anchor Anti-patterns

Coercive Anchors

Using homogeneous structural (i.e., identifying) hierarchies for EA anchors in descriptive models means that individuals in business environments can be continuously

and consistently identified across domains and levels of abstraction without the need
for extraneous routines. A typical benefit of using such hierarchies to anchor external
and internal identities is to reduce the complexity of security schemes for enterprises
immersed in digital environments.

By contrast (figure 7-19a), chaining enterprise representations to anchors fully
defined outside the enterprise could critically hamper the enterprise's capacity to
change. For example, were *Person* and *Organization* to serve as anchors, enterprise
representations would need to mirror their structures whether or not they would be
relevant.

Slack Anchors

Using functional (i.e., nonidentifying) hierarchies for business domain entities in
prescriptive models means that the semantics of features and operations (or aspects)
can be modified independently of their attachment to anchors. Setting identities in
descriptive models and roles in prescriptive ones combines a continuous and consistent representation of environments with a versatile and plastic architecture. That
combination of stability (environments) and agility (architecture) should limit the
complexity induced by changes; e.g., *Customer* and *Provider* are anchored to the
business environment through their *Party#* identity, but can be managed independently by domains.

By contrast (figure 7-19b), using *Customer#* and *Provider#* as anchors would be
pointless because there would be no continuously and consistently identified counterparts in the business environment. For example, individual *Person* or *Organization*
could be "Customer" and "Provider" simultaneously or could be neither — a scenario
which would counter the very purpose of anchors.

Hybrid Anchors

Besides the modeling issues (e.g., the meaning of inheritance), banning cross specializations or generalizations between descriptive and prescriptive models prevents the
mingling of externally defined issues with the ones managed at the enterprise level.

As an example, let's take *Person* and *Organization* (both defined by the business
environment) and assume a generalization as a *Party#* anchor (defined by enterprise).

As noted above, *Party#* is a hybrid representation, a business abstraction built
from physical and symbolic objects. Whereas such symbolic objects are the bread
and butter of abstraction in both descriptive and prescriptive models, the semantics
differ. Accordingly, it is difficult for prescriptive anchors to mirror their descriptive

counterpart (figure 7-19c); e.g., descriptive **Party#** represents managed instances of both **Person** and **Organization** as symbolic objects. Along that reasoning, the subtypes are misleading: they do not represent actual instances of business objects in the environment but subsets of representations within the enterprise. And that's not enough to serve as an anchor.

Summary

Descriptive and prescriptive models fastened through anchors can secure the continuity and consistency of representations of environments and systems. But models do not encompass the whole of enterprise representations, which calls for modeling extensions. The next chapter considers the merits and limitations of profiles and meta-models.

CHAPTER 8

Models, Meta-models & Ontologies

Data are digital objects devoid of context and, therefore, of meaning; information is data with context; knowledge is information with purpose

Enterprise architecture (EA) models can be summarily defined by their level (system or enterprise) and scope (environments or architectures). At the system level, anchors are introduced between descriptive and prescriptive models to secure the consistency of representations (cf. chapter 7). But at the enterprise level, there is no reason to assume that everything can be represented in models.

To begin with, the digital immersion of enterprises, combined with the integration of operational processes and business intelligence, calls for a differentiated yet consistent description of enterprises and environments, based on the levels introduced in part I:

• Physical environments and applications (data level)

• Processes and systems functionalities (information level)

• Business environments and strategies (knowledge level)

The distinction between data, information, and knowledge is usually overlooked at the system level because the focus is put on models; but this distinction comes front and center at the enterprise level.

As a makeshift, profiles and meta-models are introduced to extend the semantic capabilities of modeling languages. However, they fall short in bridging the conceptual gap between representations at the system (information) and enterprise (knowledge) levels.

Ontologies appear better suited to the conceptual integration of the whole range of representations pertaining to enterprise architecture:

• In principle: as hatched by early Greek philosophers, ontologies are meant to provide a systematic account of what can be known in a given domain of concern.

• In practice: Knowledge graphs, the jack-of-all-trades of Machine-learning technologies, are a direct implementation of ontologies.

The benefits of ontologies for conceptual representations, as well as concrete applications (e.g., smart human interfaces or data-mining), are especially relevant for enterprise architectures that are fully immersed in digital environments.

Patterns, Profiles & Meta-models

Just as models represent sets of actual instances that correspond to categories deemed relevant, meta-models represent sets of categories appearing in sets of models; e.g., a meta-category could represent all categories of interfaces supporting communication in natural language. Using the modeling paradigm introduced in part I, a simplified meta-model would look something like this:

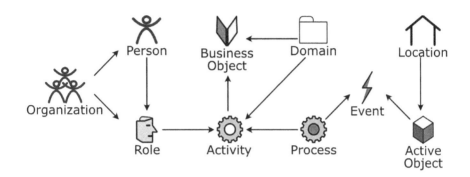

Figure 8-1. *A Simple EA Meta-model*

Meta-models can characterize models using any kind of criteria at any level of representation (figure 8-2): with the sky as the limit, some are effectively aligned with the models of concern (e.g., relational databases, a), whereas others are too abstract to be of any use (b, c).

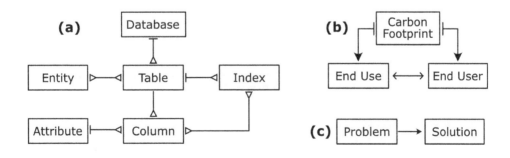

Figure 8-2. *Meta-models & the Limits of Abstraction*

For enterprise architects, the challenge is therefore to align meta-models with contexts and concerns. On that account, three different approaches can be considered: patterns, profiles, and meta-languages.

Patterns

Modeling patterns are typical, if basic, meta-models, as they are both abstract and pragmatic: abstract because their objective is to associate categories of problems and solutions independently of the actual issues at hand; and pragmatic when applied to software patterns, as demonstrated by the wide-ranging implementations of the Gang of Four's Design Patterns.

From the enterprise architecture perspective, four categories of patterns are especially relevant when defining transitions between Model-driven architecture (MDA) modeling layers (cf. chapter 3):

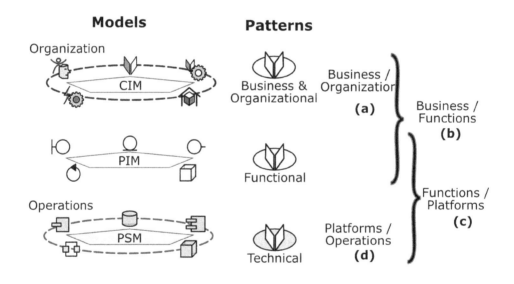

Figure 8-3. Modeling Patterns

• Organizational schemes with regard to business capabilities are represented by Computation independent models (CIM, a).

• Alignments of business processes and functional architecture are represented by Platform independent models (PIM, b).

- Design-mapping guidelines from functional architectures to technical platforms are represented by Platform specific models (PSM, c).

- Code generation targets technical and operational environments (d).

Patterns rely on abstractions for generic issues and policies, yet their effectiveness depends on the degree of homogeneity of representations. Given that proviso, patterns can be:

- Very effective within systems architectures, as patterns can be uniformly defined with systems-modeling languages (c, d)

- Helpful with well-defined issues, when patterns are set across boundaries and between organizations and systems; patterns are therefore expressed with heterogeneous modeling semantics (b)

- Mostly irrelevant when patterns have to match organizational solutions to the idiosyncrasies of business environments (a)

Leaving systems architecture patterns to systems architects, enterprise architects should focus on patterns that frame organizational problems with architectural solutions. The level of abstraction should be set by functional capabilities (cf. chapter 14).

Profiles

Patterns are at their best for well-identified and structured issues. By comparison, profiles, combined with stereotypes (cf. chapter 2), are better suited to specific issues that cannot be easily associated with generic constructs.

For that purpose, profiles employ stereotyped extensions (<<label>>) to customize models with regard to specific contexts or concerns; for example (figure 8-4):

- Business profile: to map enterprises' domains and activities to regulatory environments

- Functional profile: to implement an Enterprise resource planning (ERP) solution

- Technical profile: to deploy and operate home appliances

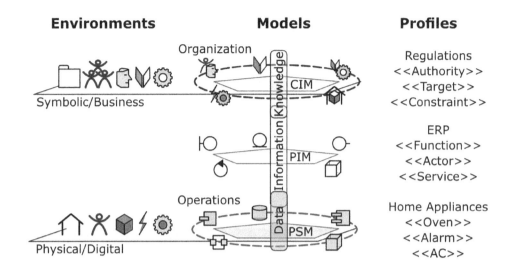

Figure 8-4. Typical Profiles

But stereotypes are just sets of characteristics; as such, they cannot be generalized or specialized, and are supposed to be loosely aligned with categories. It ensues that when profiles are included in modeling languages, stereotypes must be applied in a strictly additive manner in order to prevent confusion or conflicts with the semantics of the host languages.

Assuming the modeling languages are well-defined and homogeneous, stereotypes can be fine-tuned to avoid ambiguities or overlaps with the semantics of the enclosing language. But ambiguities or overlaps cannot be avoided if stereotypes are mingled with heterogeneous or fuzzy semantics. Moreover, the detrimental consequences of muddled meanings can be disproportionate due to a domino effect: any single discrepancy can trigger a cascade of associated misrepresentations.

The importance of homogeneous semantics for profiles can be illustrated by contrasting the effectiveness of Domain-specific languages (DSLs) in systems engineering with the confusing motley (around 230 and counting) of notional profiles aimed at enterprise architecture, as gathered by the Object Management Group (OMG).

DSLs are the tool of choice for Model-based systems engineering (MBSE, cf. chapter 14); they are used to knit profiles with models and are meant to support transformations and code generation. When based on established modeling languages (e.g., Unified Modeling Language), DSLs can neatly demarcate the semantic perimeter of a profile and thus limit inconsistencies. However, that's not the case for OMG's profiles, which rely on a meta-language.

Meta-languages

OMG's attempts to break out of systems' semantics using abstraction ladders and customized profiles (e.g., healthcare, finances, military, retail) are confronted with a practical pitfall: if abstraction scales (ladder perspective) and profiles (transverse perspective) cannot be neatly separated, semantics get mixed up and whole models get muddled.

Hence the need to establish a Chinese wall between meta-language constructs and domain-specific ones (figure 8-5):

- Meta-classes: used to characterize the semantic categories employed by the modeling languages

- Stereotypes: used to define lexical categories related to the targeted domain; e.g., regulation, maintenance, communication protocol, public administration

- Constraints: used to qualify meta-classes and stereotypes, depending on modeling languages, profiles, or patterns

Such constructs can be incorporated in modeling languages (a) or used to build meta-models (b). The same generic constructs can thus be used directly through modeling languages (solid lines) or indirectly through meta-models (dashed lines) as profiles (c), patterns (d), or both. Patterns could also be used to associate profiled issues with policies and strategies.

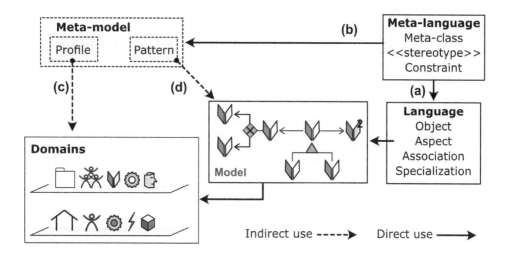

Figure 8-5. Direct or Indirect Use of Meta-languages

If defined independently of systems-modeling languages, tailored profiles, stereotypes, and constraints can help to upgrade systems modeling to the enterprise level; for example:

- Portfolio management: projects would be profiled with regard to business value, technologies, business and engineering risks, etc.

- Maintenance: architecture components would be profiled with regard to the type of component, nature of intervention, cost of failure, etc.

- Engineering: projects would be profiled with regard to functional requirements, organizational dependencies, technical environment, etc.

Nonetheless, using stereotypes to associate descriptive and prescriptive representations cannot bridge the conceptual gap between modeling semantics. A trivial example (figure 8-6) illustrates the difference between subtypes and stereotypes:

Cooking Appliance serves as an anchor between the descriptive model of actual appliances and the prescriptive model of surrogates. In the descriptive model (figure 8-6, left), *Cooker* represents all cookers, with subsets represented by *Slow Cooker* and *Pressure Cooker*.

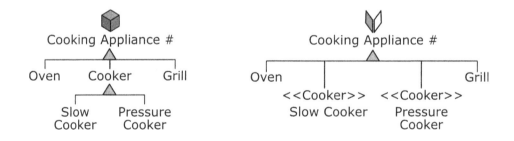

Figure 8-6. *Stereotypes are not Substitutes for Subtypes*

Usual OO prescriptive modeling would have mirrored the descriptive hierarchy, employing inheritance to set apart shared features from specific ones (cf.

chapter 7). Alternatively (figure 8-6, right), in order to tie the model to a broader business context, a <<*Cooker*>> stereotype could be employed to characterize the descriptions of **Slow Cooker** and **Pressure Cooker**. But using stereotypes instead of subtypes has more cons than pros:

- On the pros side, and assuming there is a thesaurus (cf. chapter 4), prescriptive stereotypes for **Slow Cooker** and **Pressure Cooker** could be associated with the concept of "Cooker" defined at the enterprise level, instead of a type of artifact defined at the system level.

- But on the cons side, **Cooker** as a prescriptive type (or class) would have to be waived - and with it the notion of **Slow Cooker** and **Pressure Cooker** as functional subsets. The waiver is necessary because maintaining both descriptions would induce confusion between the semantics of stereotypes and of type inheritance, as defined in prescriptive models.

That mismatch between subtypes and stereotypes is evidence of the broader limitations of profiles and meta-models when different levels of representation are concerned: whereas stereotypes can be used to associate systems representations with organization and contexts, they cannot deal with abstraction levels; conversely, meta-models can deal with abstraction levels but fall short in keeping track of contexts.

Ontologies

For all intents and purposes, meta-models mark the limits of systems-modeling languages in representing the semantic diversity of business and digital environments. Practitioners in business as well as information technology are already overcoming these limitations with technologies like Deep learning and Knowledge graphs, which have become ubiquitous at the boundaries of digital (data mining) and symbolic (smart assistants) enterprise architecture. As it happens, the formal foundations of these technologies have been there for some time; after all, Knowledge graphs are a realization of ontologies, a knowledge-representation paradigm devised by Greek philosophers 2500 years ago.

Information & Knowledge

As epitomized long ago by the telescopic observations of Galileo Galilei, theories and technologies often progress side by side, offering mutual and alternative cues and support. Something similar can be observed today, with Knowledge graphs and Machine-learning technologies hinting at a new understanding of data, information, and knowledge.

To begin with a formal point of view, information models can be defined in terms of knowledge representation. Taking a leaf from the pivotal work of Randall Davis, Howard Shrobe, and Peter Szolovits (cf. bibliography), we can determine that systems information models should include:

1. Surrogates: symbolic artifacts are used as substitutes for whichever *things* (actual or symbolic objects, events, or activities) are deemed relevant.

2. Ontological commitments: models are meant to define the categories of *things* that may exist in the domain under consideration.

3. Fragmentary theory of intelligent reasoning: models are meant to define what *things* can do or what can be done with them.

4. Medium for efficient computation: surrogates are meant to support operational processes.

5. Medium for human expression: symbolic representations must ensure clear, pertinent, and unambiguous communication between specific domain experts, on the one hand, and generic knowledge managers, on the other hand.

On that basis, the modeling of information systems appears as a special case of knowledge representation. Applying that reasoning to the representation of enterprise architectures would suggest an extension of these same five core components of models:

1. Surrogates: in addition to actual business surrogates associated with business processes, virtual ones should be introduced in relation to business intelligence.

2. Ontological commitments: besides the categories describing the sets of objects, events, or activities that pertain to actual business activities, additional dimensions are necessary to represent hypothetical or fuzzy classifications of environments and enterprises' strategies (e.g., Netflix's marketing profiles for suggested content).

3. Reasoning: compared to systems models, which are focused on legitimate or truth-preserving operations, other forms of reasoning should be supported, from modal logic to Machine learning.

4. Computation: applying different kinds of reasoning to different kinds of content may increase complexity by multiple orders of magnitude, which would require dedicated representations and processing capabilities.

5. Communication: smart interfaces are necessary to support knowledge-based exchanges and collaborations.

These extensions can be achieved with ontologies.

Knowledge & Ontologies

As the brainchild of classical philosophers, ontologies are meant to provide a formal and systematic account of what makes sense in a given domain of discourse; more precisely:

- Ontologies are structured sets of terms denoting cognitive representations.

- These representations can stand at different epistemic levels:

  - Terms or labels: items that represent nothing by themselves; e.g., "royalty", with quotation marks removing meaning from the word

  - Ideas or concepts: pure semantic constructs, defined independently of instances or categories; e.g., royalty (without quotation marks) gets its meaning back

  - Instances: identified (or named) objects or phenomena; e.g., United Kingdom

- Categories: sets of instances with shared features; e.g., kingdom

- Documents; e.g., Magna Carta

- Ontology as a discipline is a matter of philosophy, which means that ontologies are solely dedicated to the internal relevance and consistency of representations, and are not concerned with external validity or empirical purposes.

On that basis, models can be defined as subsets of ontologies that are built to serve specific purposes; e.g., analysis (descriptive), simulation (predictive), or design (prescriptive) (cf. chapter 3).

EA & Ontologies

Ontologies are usually implemented through a mixture of conceptual graphs and predicate logic, commonly known as Resource description frameworks (RDFs).

Cut to the bone, all graph-based representations (e.g., property graphs, conceptual graphs, semantic networks) are made of two kinds of nodes: one for concepts and the other for conceptual relationships. As explicitly stated in Charles Sanders Peirce's seminal work (cf. bibliography), both categories are meant to represent existential references: one for something that exists on its own (concepts) and the other for something that exists relative to something else (conceptual relationships).

As such, conceptual graphs are just grammars like the ones governing expressions in natural languages; they should not be confused with what is expressed, namely the ontologies using them to represent domain semantics. The ontological neutrality of conceptual graphs can be made explicit by marking the difference between generic and domain-specific nodes and relationships (figure 8-7):

- Conceptual nodes represent concepts specific to domains (rectangle, green).

- Conceptual-connection nodes represent relationships with semantics specific to domains (e.g., **Order** cannot be defined independently of **Menu** and **Customer**) (circle, green).

- Syntactic-connection nodes represent relationships with neutral semantics (e.g., **Part** can be understood independently of its context, in this case, **Menu** and **Dish**) and should be applied uniformly across domains (circle, blue).

- Subtyping connectors with neutral semantics should be applied uniformly across domains (triangle, blue).

- Reference connectors are relationships without semantics.

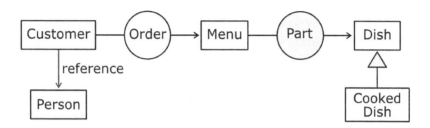

Figure 8-7. Conceptual Graph Cut to the Bone

Setting apart neutral constructs is necessary if conceptual graphs are to be used to integrate modeling languages and thesauruses into ontologies. Accordingly, the juncture between corresponding representations should rely on the uniform understanding of the core modeling syntax defined for models (cf. chapter 3).

In addition to achieving consistency, maintaining a clear distinction between modeling languages and ontologies sets up the basis of functional interoperability with other tools (figure 8-8):

- Lexicons, for terms in use within or outside the enterprise

- Directories, for facts: instances of symbolic and physical objects, events, or activities in environments, the enterprise, or systems

- Thesauruses, for concepts supporting the enterprise's understanding of environments, objectives, and assets

- Categories, for descriptive, predictive, and prescriptive enterprise models

- Document management systems (DMS)

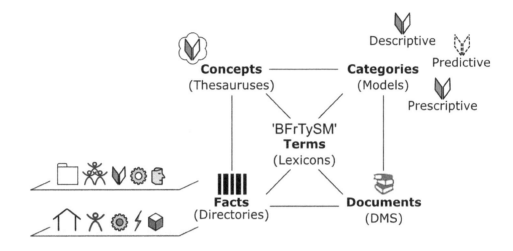

Figure 8-8. Ontologies & Enterprise Knowledge

Finally, a comprehensive integration of knowledge with regard to source (e.g., corporate, institutional, scientific) and nature (e.g., markets, regulations, systems) opens the door to a combination of different levels of reasoning; typically (figure 8-9):

- Information: truth-preserving operations applied uniformly across representations

- Knowledge: modal or fuzzy logic or nonparametric statistics applied to domain-specific targets

- Data: Machine learning

Ontologies can then be used to manage all knowledge related to enterprises' environments, objectives, and assets.

Architectures & Knowledge

Enterprise architectures are characterized by the merging of physical artifacts, organization, and symbolic representations, and by the necessity of continuous adaptation. That double specificity of enterprise architecture is compounded by the digital

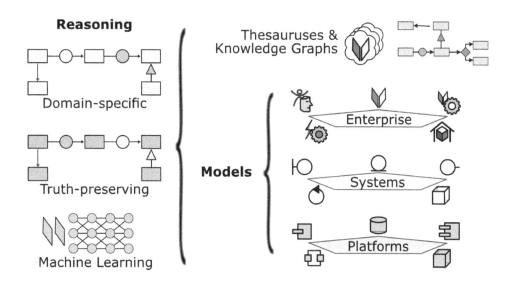

Figure 8-9. EA & Ontology

transformation, which unifies the representations of physical, symbolic, or organizational components, as well as the exchanges between them and environments. Assuming that ontologies satisfy the first imperative and provide an integrated representation of business environments, organization, and a mix of symbolic and physical artifacts, the question is how an extensive and consistent ontological representation would help with the second imperative; namely, the continuous adaptation of architectures to changes in environments (cf. chapter 3).

From Data to Information

The immersion of enterprises in digital environments opens the gates to an extensive and continuous flow of unstructured data, devoid of customary marks for context (e.g., institutional, professional, corporate, social, personal), scope (business, organization, systems, platforms), or time frames (e.g., operational, tactical, strategic). How these flows are sorted, processed, and used becomes a primary concern of enterprise governance.

As it happens, data analytics, information modeling, and knowledge management have long been carried out as separate undertakings, but without a conceptual distinction between data, information, and knowledge. That confusion puts enterprise architects in a dilemma:

On the one hand, enterprises' competitive edge increasingly depends on the accurate, reliable, and continuous processing of massive inflows of raw data. Since making sense of data is pointless without fusing it with operations, a tight integration is needed between decision-making and the processing of data flows, information, and knowledge.

On the other hand, the ubiquity of digital synapses connecting every corner of social activity (there is nowhere to hide) has induced a forceful and overarching wave of regulatory initiatives focused on protecting the privacy of personal data. Enterprises are thus compelled to make a statutory distinction between business data that is legitimately modeled and managed by information systems, and personal data, which is protected by privacy regulations.

Assuming that regulatory compliance is better managed at the enterprise level, enterprise architects become the gatekeepers of choice, letting in only the data with sanctioned representation. This authorized data can be used to:

- Update managed surrogates related to business activities or systems operations (e.g., customer records or banking transactions)

- Make adjustments to digital, logical, or conceptual information models

- Amend or extend corporate knowledge

Yet, keeping privacy data out of systems representations doesn't mean such data can't be used at the enterprise level; on the contrary, its role as a direct source of knowledge is boosted by the spread of Deep-learning technologies. Observed data could therefore be (figure 8-10):

- Used to feed, update, or refine analytic models

- Sanitized (e.g., anonymized or converted into pseudonyms) and kept for later use

- Deleted as noise or in compliance with regulations

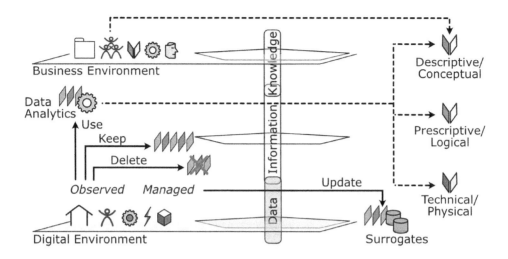

Figure 8-10. *Data (dotted line) & Information (dashed line) Flows*

The distinction between data and information thus appears necessary as well as relevant. Drawing a line between them is necessary because privacy regulations call for Chinese walls between observations and representations. It is also relevant because the transformation of raw data into modeled information is at the nexus of learning processes.

From Information to Knowledge

Compared to models, the primary benefit of ontologies is to bridge the conceptual gap between systems and enterprise architectures. But the benefits are not limited to the conceptual representations; they also apply to functional and physical ones. The possibility of well-defined associations between architecture layers and external contexts removes many of the provisos mentioned above about profiles: given the conceptual graphs' distinction between neutral and specific semantics, stereotyped extensions can now be formally checked for consistency with the semantics of the host modeling languages. The practical consequence for EA is to pave a conceptual path between systems models (information) and the representation of environments (knowledge).

The range of potential benefits can be typified by profiling contexts according to the way they affect enterprise governance (figure 8-11):

- Institutional contexts: set by regulatory authorities, these contexts are steady, with changes subject to statutory procedures (e.g., United States (US) Food & Drug Administration (FDA), European Union's General Data Protection Regulation (GDPR)).

- Professional contexts: agreed upon between parties (e.g., enterprises, unions, governments), these contexts are steady, with changes subject to negotiated procedures (e.g., US National Retail Federation (NRF)/National Council of Chain Restaurants, UML, International Organization for Standardization (ISO))

- Corporate contexts: defined by the enterprise, changes are subject to internal decision-making processes (e.g., SysML, IBM, SAP, Microsoft)

- Social contexts: defined by usage, these contexts are volatile, with changes subject to factors that could be both periodic and predictable, as well as continuous and erratic (e.g., YouTube blogs).

- Personal contexts: mark the fundamental divide between collective and individual entities and phenomena. Individual facts (e.g., a candidate's resumé or CV, a research paper, social behavior) cannot be assessed directly, whether it is due to limitations of computation (statistics work on populations), law (privacy regulations), or logic (personal motives are veiled).

Such profiles that cross governance contexts with enterprise architecture layers can significantly enhance the transparency and traceability of enterprise decision-making (cf. chapter 10).

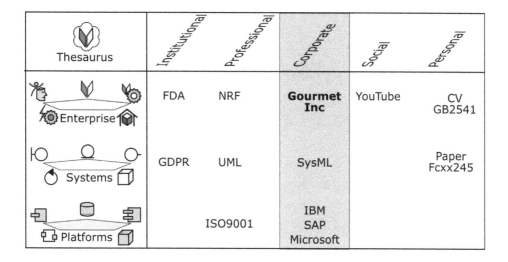

Figure 8-11. Profiled Environments for a Diner

Closing the Learning Loop

Supporting continuous and consistent adaptations to changing environments is one of the primary purposes of enterprise architecture, and it cannot be done without actionable information (i.e., knowledge). Given that, in competitive environments, knowledge is a fleeting matter to be constantly refreshed, enterprises' success depends on the ability of their organization and systems to learn; i.e., to continuously adapt enterprises' objectives, representations and decisions depending on their effectiveness. That ability can directly benefit from the integration of knowledge processing with enterprise architecture (figure 8-12):

• Knowledge graphs and ontologies can be used to bring together the representation of facts (data); models (information); and concepts, patterns, and profiles (knowledge).

• Requirements analysis can be combined with data- and process mining to adapt information models.

• Truth-preserving operations can be combined with Knowledge graphs to improve information and business models.

• Deep learning can be combined with statistics to translate implicit knowledge into explicit knowledge.

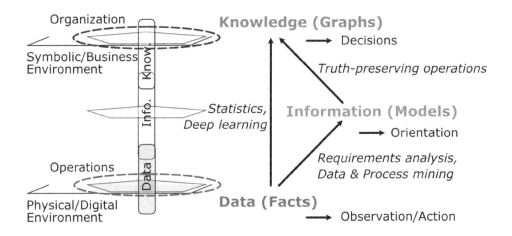

Figure 8-12. Data, Information & Knowledge

That knitting of enterprise, systems, and platforms layers, on the one hand, with the thread of knowledge, information, and data, on the other hand, can transform enterprises into learning machines. This corroborates Stafford Beer's conceptualization of firms as viable systems whose sustainability depends on the integration of their nervous system (*The Brain of the Firm*) with their information-processing capabilities (cf. chapter 15).

Beer's vision has renewed relevance with the immersion of systems with smart brains in digital environments:

• Data: at the physical level, digital interfaces ensure the direct and immediate observation of facts and the execution of actions.

• Information: at the logical level, models provide orientation maps of situations and policies.

• Knowledge: at the business level, decision-making is supported by facts, maps, profiles, and graphs.

Looking ahead, chapter 9 will consider how ontologies can support knowledge-able architectures, and chapter 10 will consider the consequence of that integration for decision-making processes.

Knowledgeable Architectures

Adding knowledge through observation, reasoning, or belief

Overview

To take advantage of their immersion in digital environments, enterprises have to differentiate between data (observed in environments), information (structured data with semantics), and knowledge (information put to use). As explained in the previous chapter, ontologies can be used to iron out discrepancies between corresponding representations. But beyond the interoperability of symbolic representations, what is at stake is the enterprise's ability to learn from observations (data), reasoning (information), and experience (knowledge).

At the system level, the semantic interoperability of modeling languages involves two basic transitions: between conceptual and logical models, and between logical and physical models. As noted in chapter 8, the latter transition is fully set within the semantic confines of systems architecture and is essentially a matter of systems and software-engineering expertise. That's not the case for the former transition, in which the specifics of business objectives and enterprise organization must be mapped to the generics of functional and technical systems architectures.

At the enterprise level, ontologies have to bring together the semantics of business and organization, on the one hand, with the semantics of systems and engineering, on the other hand. Chapter 8 explained that this integration can be done in terms of concepts (driving knowledge), categories (defining information), and facts (observed through data). This chapter examines how representations of environments, organization, and systems can become actionable maps that weave together enterprises' actual and symbolic artifacts and assets. The next chapter will consider the benefits of a comprehensive and integrated mapping of data, information, and knowledge for decision-making processes.

Enterprise & Thesauruses

The primary objective of ontologies is to bring together different kinds of representations. But the benefits of ontologies go beyond that, because they can frame the contents of thesauruses and models not only with regard to the categories represented, but also with regard to the nature of the representations. For example, considering Washington, D.C., ontologies can frame the names used (e.g., "Washington, D.C.," "Washington," "D.C."), associated facts (e.g., the location of the US federal government), the categories considered ("Washington" may denote a state, city, district, or the government officials working there), and concepts behind the categories (e.g., administrative division, capital city). Moreover, ontologies can inform the actuality, likelihood, and modalities of all the aforementioned (e.g., the representations and rationales of two chess players, each devising their next moves, taking into account what they think their opponent is planning, and what they think their opponent will think of what they're planning). Although these distinctions are of limited use at the system level, they take center stage for enterprises' business plans, scenarios, and/or strategies.

Models & Beyond

For ontologies to ensure interoperability between representations at the system and enterprise levels, all contents must be characterized with regard to the capabilities (lexical, syntactic, semantic, pragmatic) of the languages used to express them (cf. chapter 8) (figure 9-1):

- A syntactic core must be common to all models and ontologies across domains.

- All lexical items must be indexed across domains independently of modeling languages.

- Domains' semantics must be defined in thesauruses, possibly but not necessarily in relation to modeling languages.

- Domains' pragmatics (how semantics are used in practice) are defined in thesauruses independently of modeling languages.

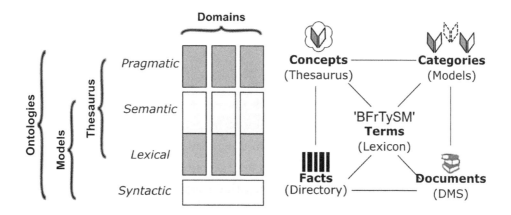

Figure 9-1. Languages & Ontologies

Semantic interoperability (between modeling languages) coupled with conceptual interoperability (between all lexical, pragmatic, and semantic entries in thesauruses) can then support functional interoperability between systems modeling, knowledge management, and decision-making:

- Systems modeling: all items in models can be clearly associated with an ontological representation; but not vice versa, because some parts of an enterprise's conceptual realm are not modeled, now or ever.

- Knowledge management: there is a built-in and principled traceability between facts (observed through data), categories (used by models and profiles, and defined by concepts), and the nature of reasoning (inductive or deductive, and generic or specific to the domain).

- Decision-making: integrated loops can be designed between observations and actions (facts), orientation (categories and profiles), and individual or collective knowledge that supports decision-making (concepts and policies).

That interoperability serves two main purposes of enterprise architecture (figure 9-2):

- Aligning enterprise organization with business objectives, typically by using concepts, profiles, patterns, and predictive models to define descriptive ones

- Mapping organization and business processes to systems functional architectures, typically using functional and technical profiles to translate descriptive models into prescriptive ones

Interoperability

Compared to the semantic interoperability of modeling languages, conceptual interoperability (between models and thesauruses) may be of limited consequence for systems given the homogeneity of architectural representations. But that is not so for enterprises trading in digital environments. Their systems become open to business

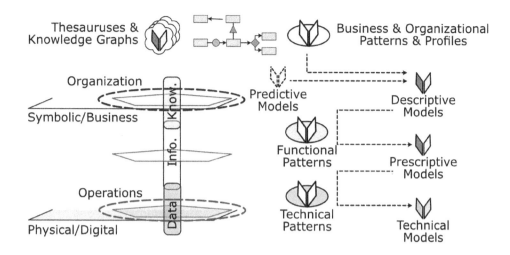

Figure 9-2. Systems & Business Meanings

flows bearing a plurality of semantics without the filter of interfaces, which were previously used to deal with the diversity of formats and made redundant by the generalization of the digital one.

To begin with, enterprise architects have to define the organization and business processes that can best support enterprise business models, taking into account both profiles and business intelligence. To that end, they can use:

- Profiles (cf. chapter 8): to frame the whole range of enterprise environments and objectives

- Predictive models: to figure out business objectives, prognoses, and strategies

- Descriptive models: to define business domains, organization, and processes

In conjunction with thesauruses, ontologies provide the semantic glue between these models and the reasoning capabilities of the Knowledge graphs needed to put information into business use.

Thesauruses

If representations are to be managed separately across organizational units, over time, and depend on relevant contexts and purposes, thesauruses must be clear about the nature of entries (figure 9-3):

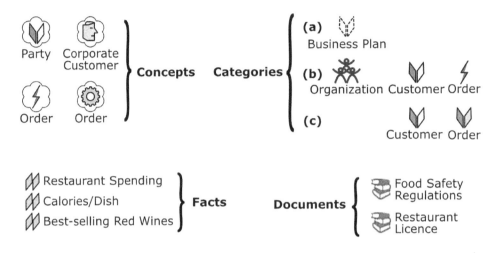

Figure 9-3. Sample of Thesauruses' Entries for a Restaurant

- *Concepts* are meant to support the definition of business objectives, models, plans, or strategies independently of their actual realization. They can be used to analyze requirements (e.g., **Order**), consolidate organizational structures (e.g., **Party**), or introduce new roles (e.g., **Corporate Customer**).

- *Facts* are data sets representing the state of objects or phenomena (e.g., statistical series for **Restaurant Spending**, **Calories per Dish**, or **Best-selling Red Wines**).

- *Documents* are symbolic containers of contents identified as a whole independently of their format (e.g., **Food Safety Regulations**, **Restaurant Licence**).

- *Categories* are symbolic descriptions used to build virtual (a), descriptive (b), or prescriptive (c) models; e.g., **Business Plan** (virtual), **Organization** (descriptive), **Customer** and **Order** (both descriptive and prescriptive).

Compared to lexicons or glossaries, thesauruses are not limited to semantic interoperability between modeling languages (cf. chapter 7). They can also support conceptual interoperability between epistemic levels; i.e., the nature of what is known: concepts, categories, and facts. For example, a thesaurus may simultaneously manage entries for:

- *Customer*: as a concept (defined in a business environment), a business entity (category defined at the enterprise level), and a software component (category defined at the system level)

- *Order*: as a business event (category defined at the enterprise level) or an active software component (category defined at the system level)

Moreover, in contrast to lexicons and glossaries, that kind of conceptual interoperability is a built-in capability of thesauruses. Since these connections between entries are not defined piecemeal by knowledge engineers but are generated by semantic engines, they can be rigorously managed and will not get jumbled up. Thesauruses could thus support effective and traceable reasoning.

Connectors

Assuming that Knowledge graphs encompass all the specifics of modeling languages (cf. chapter 8), thesauruses can bring under a common roof the whole range of concepts, categories, facts, and artifacts pertaining to enterprise governance, independently of their origin or scope, or whether they are represented in systems.

But reasoning out all of the thesauruses' contents cannot be achieved without upgrading core modeling constructs. This upgrade is required in order to introduce epistemic levels (concepts, categories, facts, documents) into modeling references:

- Realization: for references set across epistemic levels

- Association: for references set within epistemic levels, at the same level of abstraction

- Analogy: for references set within epistemic levels, at different levels of abstraction

As figure 9-4 shows, nondescript (or flat) *references* (a) are used between documents and other entries; e.g., between ***Best-selling Red Wines*** or ***Kitchen Organization*** to ***Food Safety Regulations***.

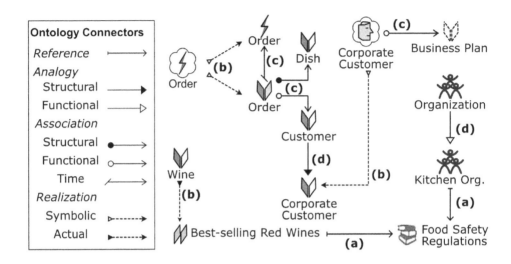

Figure 9-4. Adding Epistemic Levels to References

Realizations (b) are used to connect entries across epistemic levels. For example, the aims associated with the concept of ***Corporate Customer*** are meant to be realized by a ***Business Plan***; the concept of ***Order*** can be represented by descriptive (event) and prescriptive (active entity) categories; and ***Best-selling Red Wines*** (identified by producer and year) are instances of ***Wine*** (with designations by grape or region).

Associations (c) are used for structural, functional, or temporal relationships between homogeneous entries; i.e., entries set at the same epistemic level. Their syntax and semantics are meant to be directly aligned with modeling languages (cf. chapter 7), ensuring that thesauruses and models are congruent. For example, associations can be made from ***Order*** (active prescriptive entity) to ***Dish*** (structural), to ***Customer*** (functional), or to ***Order*** (time association with the corresponding descriptive event).

Analogies (d) are used to represent structural or functional similarities within epistemic levels. The objective is to link different levels of generalization or specialization independently of the semantics of modeling languages. For example, analogies can be made between ***Corporate*** and ***Corporate Customer*** (structural), or between ***Organization*** and ***Kitchen Organization*** (functional).

These generic connectors within and across epistemic levels of representations are meant to support conceptual interoperability at the enterprise level. They should also subsume the more specific connectors defined for models; e.g., composition and aggregation (cf. chapter 2), or <<include>> and <<extend>> (cf. chapter 13).

EA & Ontologies

At the enterprise level, thesauruses ensure a comprehensive and consistent symbolic representation of environments, organization, and systems. At the system level, models add the engineering perspective; namely, how symbolic representations can be used to design, build, and operate actual systems.

Chapter 7 described how anchors, both descriptive (enterprise representation) and prescriptive (enterprise and systems representation), provide a modeling bridge. This bridging role relies on the working assumption that all of enterprises' symbolic representations (business, organization, systems) are conceptually homogenous. Now, with thesauruses at hand, that assumption can be relinquished.

Conceptual Interoperability

Enterprise architecture is sometimes understood as a management nirvana, where systems architectures and abstract representations of business could go hand in hand. Yet, as illustrated by the hotchpotch of enterprise architecture blueprints, the difficulty is to find the proper level of representation between concrete and fine-grained descriptions, on the one hand, and abstract and coarse-grained ones, on the other hand. The former is prone to complexity traps; the latter, to detachment from actual architectural concerns. In between, enterprise architects must find a level of representation that secures a common and unambiguous understanding of what must be shared between business analysts and systems architects. Such a juncture can be materialized by a conceptual equivalent of modeling anchors; namely, a necessary and sufficient set of concepts shared between the representations of business, organization, and systems:

• Object: anything with a perennial identity

• Phenomenon: a change in the state of an object or activity

• Time: the intervals between phenomena

- Identity: a unique biological, social, or designed characteristic of individual objects or phenomena

- Actuality: the physical or symbolic nature of objects or activities

- Behavior: actions performed or events generated by active objects

- Collection: an object managing a set of objects or phenomena with identities of their own

These concepts provide a formal and compact kernel (cf. annex B) that supports the whole of EA's symbolic representations:

- Entity: an object with business relevance

- Agent: an object with identity and behaviors; agents can be individual or collective, actual (e.g., person) or symbolic (e.g., enterprise) identity

- Event: a phenomenon with business relevance, meant to be observable (e.g., a change in agents' expectations)

- Activity: a symbolic description of an agent's behavior

- Organization: a collective entity — both active (i.e., with behavior) and symbolic (i.e., defined by consensus or statute by an external agent)

- Objective: a symbolic representation of the state of an object, phenomenon, or expectation

- Process: the actual execution of activities

- Role: what agents may or should do as defined by a collective entity

- Surrogate: a symbolic object meant to reproduce the state of identified actual objects or phenomena, either instantly (or synchronously) or with delay (or asynchronously)

The aim of the kernel is not to enter into a definition game but to employ Occam's razor and cut definitions to unambiguous and effective assertions, which could be easily extended and/or qualified according to business and technical contexts.

The kernel, implemented with the OWL Web Ontology Language, could thus be used to support open and actionable specifications of enterprise architectures.

Open Models

As already noted, thesauruses encompass concepts that may or may not be modeled. But if these concepts are to serve as modeling roots, continuity must be achieved with the modeled saplings that could eventually grow into systems' artifacts. To that eventuality, a mechanism securing semantic consistency should be available between thesauruses and descriptive and prescriptive models. Open models can provide that mechanism.

SOLID Principles

Open models (figure 9-5) are defined according to the SOLID design principles — a pillar of the Object-oriented (OO) paradigm introduced by Robert C. Martin (cf. bibliography).

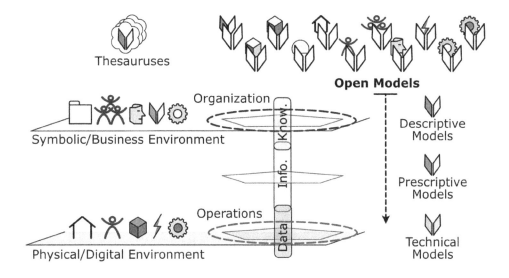

Figure 9-5. Open Models

The acronym stands for:

• **S**ingle responsibility principle (SRP)

• **O**pen/Close principle (OCP)

• **L**iskov substitution principle (LSP)

• **I**nterface-segregation principle (ISP)

• **D**ependency-inversion principle (DIP)

These principles can be directly applied to descriptive and prescriptive representations of enterprise architecture:

Single responsibility principle: descriptive business entities must have only one reason to change.

Open/close principle (figure 9-6): descriptive business entities are open for specialization but closed for modification to ensure the neutrality of transformations (cf. chapter 7); e.g., **Customer** can be further specialized as **VIP** and **Standard**, but **Organization** and **Person** cannot be merged into **Customer**.

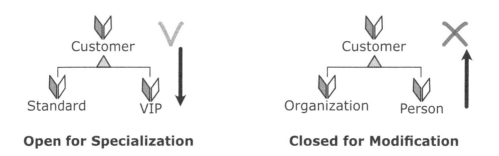

Open for Specialization   **Closed for Modification**

Figure 9-6. Open/Close Principle

Liskov substitution principle (figure 9-7): the sets of identified individuals should not depend on the level of abstraction; e.g., individuals within **Party** identified as

Business Partner (a) should coincide with the ones identified as ***Customer*** and ***Provider*** through ***Contract*** (b). LSP ensures that business entities are consistently managed at the enterprise as well as domains level.

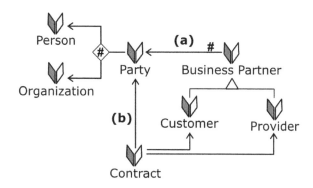

Figure 9-7. Liskov Substitution Principle

Interface-segregation principle (figure 9-8): aspects (or interfaces in OO parlance) are semantically and functionally homogeneous, such that all features are meaningful without regard to the context of use; e.g., since having a name and address doesn't require the documentation of a ***date of birth*** or a ***credit rating, date of birth*** and ***credit rating*** should be defined as separate aspects. ISP prevents semantic overlaps between domains, even when common subsets of individuals are targeted.

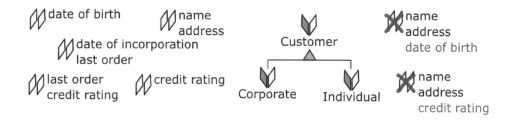

Figure 9-8. Interface-Segregation Principle

Dependency-inversion principle: combines OCP and LSP, such that the semantics of higher (enterprise) levels are defined independently of those at lower (domains) levels. This distinction ensures that domain semantics are consistently but not necessarily uniformly defined, which is typically the case for accounting entities and operations.

Applying SOLID principles to descriptive and prescriptive models serves two key EA purposes:

- Establishing a principled distinction between concerns and responsibilities at the enterprise, business domains, and systems levels

- Ensuring the continuity and consistency of these representations without impairing the autonomy of decision-making at the corresponding levels

Moreover, extending the scope of OO principles to the whole of enterprise modeling means that benefits can be leveraged further across functional and technical architecture layers, making the most of the maturity of design patterns.

Open Models & Business Patterns

Attempts to emulate the conceptual soundness and practical effectiveness of design patterns at the business level have produced an open-ended catalogue of problems to pair with solutions. And there is a good reason for the disappointing outcomes: contrary to well-trodden software engineering problems, business ones are set by shifting circumstances and competitive pressure. By nature, successes are singular, innovative, and different from standard solutions.

Open models are meant to set apart business and functional issues: the former, specific; the latter, generic. SOLID principles should thus be applied to make sure that the specifics of business solutions (e.g., credit rating) don't interfere with the generic functional ones (e.g., authorizations).

Instead of unyielding templates made of fully defined objects and features, business patterns should come as core structures to be fleshed out with customized aspects, according to clear rationales (figure 9-9).

For business process modeling, open models can help to deal with complexity by replacing procedures with constraints and rules that are attached to business patterns and execution units. The collaboration between processes, as well as their shared access to business entities, could thus be set apart from business logic and specified at the architecture level, without using pseudo-programming languages (cf. chapter 12).

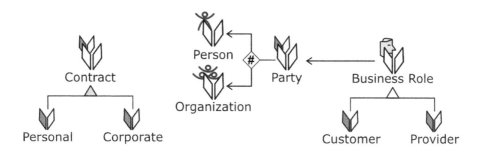

Figure 9-9. Sample Roots of SOLID Business Patterns

For systems modeling, open models can serve as the upper level of model-based systems engineering, helping to redeem the conceptual discrepancies between Computation independent (CIM) and Platform independent (PIM) models (cf. chapter 14).

At the enterprise level, the benefits of the conceptual integration of business and systems perspectives are compounded by their corresponding digital integration.

The Digital Integration of Business & Systems

The integration of business and engineering representations constitutes a key success factor for enterprises competing in digital environments:

At the technical level, software agents, smart or otherwise, are spreading into every nook and cranny of business processes, calling for a tight integration of business and engineering processes.

At the enterprise level, the time frames of business (environments) and engineering (systems), once aligned periodically, must now be continuously realigned lest enterprises relinquish their awareness of business changes.

As a consequence, enterprises must balance two contrary momentums:

- A top-down momentum, fed by anticipations, organization, and business objectives: it relies on models and pivots on information systems.

- A bottom-up momentum, fed by observations in digital environments: it relies on data analytics and pivots on knowledge management.

To balance these two opposing forces, governance can take advantage of the traceability and transparency of environments, objectives, and engineering representations:

- Open models: between engineering and business objectives (figure 9-5)

- Ontological connectors: between the objectives and realizations of enterprise (thesauruses) and systems (models) (figure 9-4)

- Profiles, including stereotypes and patterns: for "canned" knowledge about statutory, business, or technical environments (cf. chapter 8)

But competition in digital environments calls for more than alignment with shifting environments; it also requires an ability to learn from experience.

Learning Systems

Knowledge Architecture

Taking a leaf from Spinoza, one can argue that enterprises expand their knowledge (or learn) in three ways:

1. Through senses: learning occurs by applying data mining and statistical methods to facts observed at the digital level, or as information through applications.

2. Through reasoning: learning occurs by processing information, as defined by modeling categories.

3. Through judgment: learning is carried out by people and organizations that put information to use as knowledge.

That tripartite understanding of learning parallels the distinction between data, information, and knowledge. The corresponding pairing between cognitive activity (senses, reasoning, judgment) and resources (data, information, knowledge) allow for a double helix of self-reinforcing learning processes (figure 9-10):

- Integration of learning modalities: data analytics (senses), knowledge management (reasoning), and individual or collective decision-making (judgment)

- Integration of learned contents: digital models (data), logical models (information), conceptual models (knowledge), and returns on experience with data observations

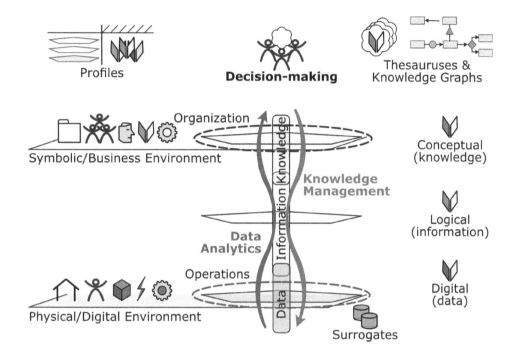

Figure 9-10. Knowledge-driven Architecture

Last but not least, that twofold processing of data (from operations) and knowledge (from organization) can be weaved into the digital fabric of systems, providing enterprise architectures with built-in proactive capabilities.

Pushing Knowledge Boundaries

While an intrinsic EA learning capability can clearly be decisive, its actual benefits depend on what can be learned. Taking a cue from the often quoted distinction made by the former US Secretary of Defense Donald Rumsfeld, we can understand learning to be about:

1. Known knowns (KK): Making better use of what is already known; e.g., more timely and targeted actions

2. Known unknowns (KU): filling the blanks circumscribed by what is already known; e.g., exploring new opportunities

3. Unknown unknowns (UU): mapping hypothetical territories; e.g., conjuring up the representations behind the decision-making of business competitors

These distinctions are especially relevant for enterprises engaged in competitive environments, where success depends on unexplored opportunities and unprecedented courses of action.

On that count, Machine-learning (ML) technologies are shaking up knowledge grounds, breaking boundaries, and opening doors to the unknown unknowns. Summarily, ML technologies operate on three levels:

1. Traditional Machine learning uses symbolic representations and rules to reproduce human expertise.

2. Supervised Deep learning (DL) uses neural networks to reproduce cognitive processes, and profiled data samples to train systems through examples.

3. Reinforcement learning (RL) replaces profiled samples and training with extensive raw inputs and statistical inference.

While implementations, especially the Deep-learning variants, combine a wide range of established technologies (e.g., modal logic, game theory, nonparametric statistics), their main characteristic is their ability to extract implicit knowledge from raw data and morph it into symbolic representations.

These technologies already make up the nuts and bolts of business intelligence, but their broader significance for enterprise architecture is an open issue (cf. chapter 16). Based on game theory's basic distinction between zero- and nonzero-sum situations, ML can be employed in three basic contexts (figure 9-11):

• One-sided (no identified parties) issues make up the bulk of ML applications, continuing the traditional operational research on the symbolic side of knowledge (KK), or defining new frontiers with pattern matching on the nonsymbolic side of knowledge (KU).

- Multisided, zero-sum issues entail fully assessable outcomes, enabling improvements based on comparisons. Given symbolic representations, ML can rely on computation and reasoning (KK); otherwise, it relies on statistics (KU).

- Multisided, nonzero-sum issues result in open-ended and multidimensional outcomes that cannot be assessed unequivocally. With symbolic representations (KU), qualified assessments — and therefore learning — can be achieved with supervised Deep learning; otherwise (UU), Reinforcement learning is necessary.

	Symbolic Representation	Nonsymbolic Representation
One-sided Tasks	Operational Research (KK)	Pattern Matching (KU)
Zero-sum Issues	Computation, Reasoning (KK)	Statistics (KU)
Nonzero-sum Issues	Supervised Learning (KU)	Reinforcement Learning (UU)

Figure 9-11. Enterprise Learning Capabilities

If only to provide guidelines, that taxonomy can be aligned with EA concerns: operations and business intelligence (one-sided), systems (zero-sum), and enterprise (nonzero-sum).

On that basis, the use of ML at the enterprise level is meant to be collective and detached from domain-specific concerns, with rationales and outcomes embodied in organization and systems. As a consequence, the issue of knowledge traceability (why is that true?) is compounded by one of organizational accountability (who contributed?). Both issues will be considered in the next chapter.

CHAPTER 10.

Enterprise Architecture & Decision-making

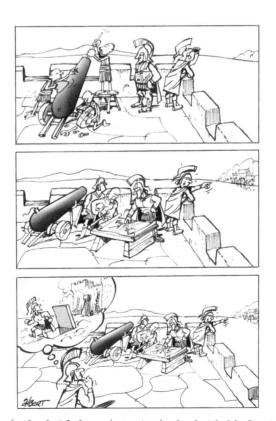

Operations (to be decided now); tactics (to be decided before it's too late); strategy (to hedge your bets)

Decision-making (DM) is often presented as a sequence of predefined tasks (e.g., analyzing the situation, identifying the problem, defining the objectives, assessing alternative options, committing to a solution, implementing the solution). That paradigm may be effective with well-identified problems that can be handled in isolation through detailed steps. But procedures are of little use with continuums of intricate issues, because the complexity of cross dependencies will increase exponentially with the number of steps, not to mention the number of iterations. That's precisely the challenge for enterprise architects.

Overview

Enterprise architects can be seen as fair brokers between business and systems stakeholders, with enterprise architecture (EA) decisions set in terms of the optimization of business value and quality of service, under constraints set by architecture assets and systems sustainability (figure 10-1).

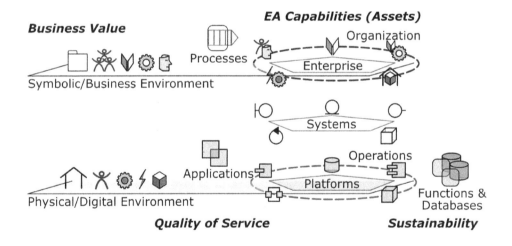

Figure 10-1. What is at Stake

Since enterprise architecture is by nature transverse, DM cannot be confined to organizational hierarchies. Instead, it should be seen as a balancing act between concerns (e.g., business vs. systems) and responsibilities (e.g., operational vs. strategic), which should be defined and decided as required. Decision-makers need to consider (figure 10-2):

• What decisions to focus on: business, organization, systems, or platforms

• How decisions should be carried out: planned (procedure) or unplanned (ad hoc)

• Where decisions should be implemented: platforms, systems, or organization

• When decisions should be carried out: instantly, scheduled conditionally, or scheduled unconditionally

• Who makes the decisions: individuals or collective units

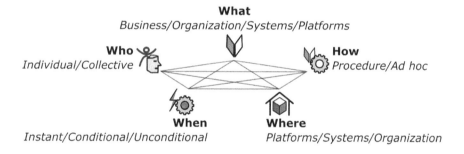

Figure 10-2. *Decision-making & Organization*

At the enterprise level, those aspects of decision-making can be detailed along three dimensions: processes, planning, and knowledge.

Decision-making Processes

Compared to its brick-and-mortar counterpart, which designs structures that are meant to remain constructed for long intervals, enterprise architecture is a work in progress to be carried out over the life cycle of enterprises. Accordingly, DM processes need to be supported by actionable and up-to-date representations of business objectives and architecture assets.

Mapping Value to Assets

Whereas business value and assets are meant to be assessed by business and systems stakeholders, respectively, the role of enterprise architects is to mark out the value chains in between.

The aim of value chains (cf. chapter 4) is to chart the contributions of supporting activities to the delivery of a valuable product or service to market. Reset in digital environments, value chains could thus uncover the path of added value across contributing assets.

As it happens, the digital transformation could undermine the relevance of value chains:

- The ubiquity of software components fused with business processes could blur the lines between primary and supporting activities and meld them together.

- Because changes in digitized activities are by nature routine and opportunistic, value chains could become chronically unstable and consequently redundant.

Yet, these issues can be fixed if generalized and homogeneous digital flows are used to link business activities and enterprise capabilities, with the organization serving as a bridge (figure 10-3):

- Business activities would be typified in line with organizational patterns by roles, objects, activities, locations, and processes.

- Supporting capabilities would be assessed at organizational, functional, and operational levels.

- Contributing assets could then be identified and crossed with supported business activities, reinstating some sort of value chain.

Such a mapping would significantly enhance the transparency of decisions and the traceability of contributing assets across enterprise, systems, and platforms. Yet,

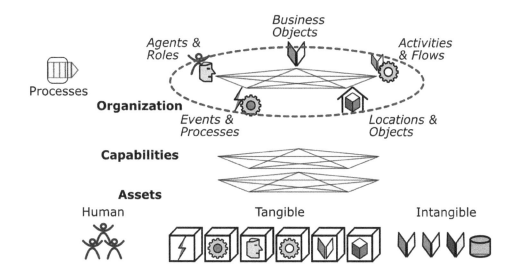

Figure 10-3. Value Chains & Assets

while mapping value chains to systems architecture capabilities would help to assess the contribution of tangible assets, human and intangible ones — people skills, organization, information, and smart components embedded in business processes — would mostly be ignored. Taking these assets into account calls for their integration into decision-making loops.

Observation-Orientation-Decision-Action (OODA) Loop

The OODA loop is a well-known decision-making paradigm developed in the 60s by Colonel John Boyd (cf. bibliography), based on his experience as fighter pilot and military strategist. Its renewed relevance for today's operational DM comes from the correspondence between the seamless integration of IT systems with business processes, and fighter jets' command and control processes.

Enterprises immersed in digital environments have to continuously align their business plans with facts on the ground. Their success comes from readiness, proactive undertakings, and the ability to subsume and subvert adversaries' time scales, both defensively (to force competitors out of favorable positions) as well as offensively (to get a competitive edge) — hence Boyd's reference to dogfights between fighter aircrafts.

The benefits of the OODA loop appear clearly when set in the context of enterprise architecture (figure 10-4):

1. Observation: changes in business and digital environments are monitored (and their reliability assessed) at the digital (data mining) or business (business intelligence) level.

2. Orientation: models and Knowledge graphs (cf. chapter 9) are used to assess changes with regard to enterprise objectives, organization, and systems.

3. Decision: policies are defined or updated, and decisions made regarding organization, systems, or platforms.

4. Action: decisions are implemented in terms of processes, functions, or applications.

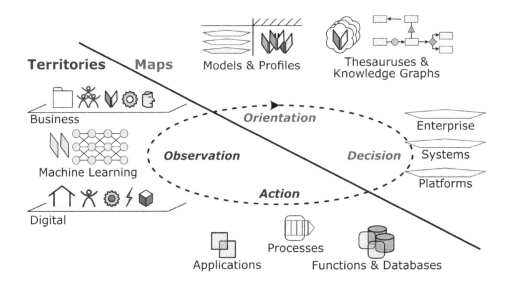

Figure 10-4. OODA Loop & Supporting Environment

The supporting environment of DM processes can then be defined in terms of territories and maps (cf. part I).

Regarding territories, the tight integration of systems and knowledge architectures means that data, information, and knowledge can be traced specifically to their sources in environments (observation); moreover, their relevance can be determined for applications, processes, or functions (actions). Depending on their characteristics (e.g, reliability and shelf-life) and timeline for use (instant or scheduled), data, information, and knowledge can be assessed either as resources to be consumed directly or as assets to be managed.

Regarding maps, DM can rely on the distinction between actual and virtual representations, taking advantage of their semantic interoperability (orientation) and alignment with systems architecture layers (decision). These representations ensure the traceability of policies at the system as well as enterprise levels, for physical environments and tangible assets, as well as for business environments and intangible assets.

Actionable Maps

In order to manage the resulting intricacies, the stages in decision-making loops should be crisscrossed with the targeted contexts materialized by the engineering workshops for enterprise, business domains, business applications, and systems (cf. chapter 3) (figure 10-5).

In the *enterprise workshop*, decision-making is driven by changes in business environments and pertains to business models and objectives. Each step in the loop covers a different aspect of a decision:

1. Observation: Uncovering business opportunities

2. Orientation: Assessing business opportunities with regard to business objectives

3. Decision: Committing resources to changes in organization and processes

4. Action: Achieving changes in organization and processes

In the *domains workshop*, changes can arise from decisions made for the whole enterprise or from more specific objectives. In both cases, decisions are supposed to impact a number of applications that rely on the models of the relevant domains:

1. Observation: Using data mining to analyze specific business segments

2. Orientation: Using business intelligence to assess the functional feasibility and expected benefits of the segments under consideration

3. Decision: Commiting changes in the functional architecture

4. Action: Developing, integrating, and testing functions

In the *applications workshop*, changes can arise from decisions made at the functional level or can be initiated by organizational units, business or otherwise. Developments are supposed to be self-contained.

1. Observation: Collecting users' requirements

2. Orientation: Assessing the engineering feasibility and the development options; e.g., Agile or phased (cf. next part of this chapter)

3. Decision: Picking a development model

4. Action: Developing, integrating, and testing self-contained applications

In the *systems workshop*, changes arise from decisions made by business or systems units. Operational changes can potentially be felt across business processes.

1. Observation: Collecting operational requirements and process mining

2. Orientation: Assessing the operational feasibility and the configuration of resources to be deployed in order to support business processes, given the existing organization and the expected quality of service

3. Decision: Determining operational configurations

4. Action: Deploying applications and running acceptance tests

Backing up DM processes with actionable maps enables direct and fine-grained traceability between issues (business, organization, and systems) and policies. Instead of procedural schemes that use predefined one-size-fits-all activities (e.g., define, gather facts, reflect, assess, decide, plan, implement) to attach projects to artifacts, decision-making can be seamlessly integrated into work units and targeted changes without being frustrated by cumbersome appendages (cf. chapter 14).

Enterprise
1. Business opportunities
2. Business assessment
3. Resource commitment
4. Realization

Domains
1. Business intelligence
2. Functional assessment
3. Functional commitment
4. Development, integration, tests

Applications
1. User requirements
2. Project assessment
3. Development model selection
4. Development, integration, tests

Systems
1. Operational requirements
2. Operational assessment
3. Configuration
4. Deployment and acceptance

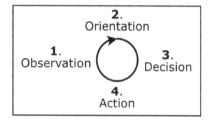

Figure 10-5. Actionable Maps

Planning: Time & Uncertainty

For enterprise architects, decisions are framed by two kinds of horizons: external ones, set by regulatory, business, or technology environments; and internal ones, set by enterprise objectives, strategies, organization, and systems.

Enterprises used to be comforted by a vertical and stable market organization and the specificity of business channels, on the one hand, and the hard-wired physical boundaries of their systems, on the other hand. That security gave planners more latitude with external (business) and internal (engineering) time frames, such that they could be defined, monitored, and/or managed separately, and aligned periodically or episodically.

But the digital transformation has leveled the usual statutory, seasonal, or business-specific landmarks (e.g., fiscal year, holidays, national boundaries), as demonstrated by privacy regulations (which apply to everybody everywhere), the importance of social media networks (for business-to-consumer activities), and just-in-time supply chains (which rub out seasonal or scheduled set pieces).

To keep in touch with shifting markets and floating time scales, projects' portfolios can no longer be simply organized and carried out top-down over predefined time frames. Lest they lose their grip on shifting markets, enterprises have to knit together top-down preparedness with bottom-up awareness. Moreover, DM processes have to ensure the continuity of time frames as well as a seamless integration of feeds from digital (data) and business (information) environments.

Motives & Time Frames

All things considered, decisions are commitments, and planning requires arranging their realization over time. Given that environments will not wait for EA plans to be completed, enterprise architects must keep track of motives (why commitments are needed) and time frames (how the timing of commitments must be determined). The motives of commitments can stem from external or internal changes (figure 10-6):

External motives can be sourced in the symbolic/business or physical/digital environments:

- At the symbolic/business level, decisions can be motivated by institutional or regulatory changes, agreements with external organizations, or initiatives taken by competitors. Such changes are conveyed as information or knowledge and can thus be directly acted upon.

- At the physical/digital level, decisions can be motivated by actual observations of changes in external objects, activities, or expectations. Such changes are conveyed through data, which must be processed into information before it can be acted upon.

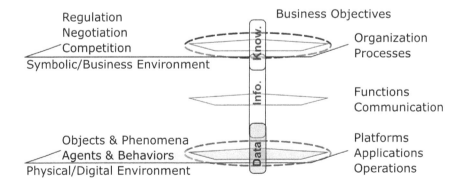

Figure 10-6. Motives for Decisions

Internal motives, whether primary (or intrinsic) or induced by external changes, can be associated with changes in:

• Business objectives

• Organization or processes

• Systems functions or communication architecture

• Platforms, applications, or operations

Keeping tabs on motivations is clearly a prerequisite for the traceability of DM, and these tabs can also serve to characterize the timing of DM steps (figure 10-7):

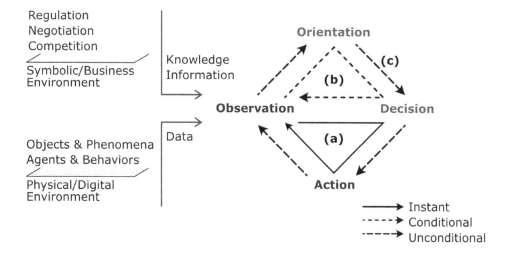

***Figure 10-7.** Timing of Decisions*

• Instant decision-making can be carried out without orientation; that rules out the direct use of raw data, whose meaning must first be assessed. That kind of decision is typically triggered by anticipated changes in business environments (a).

- Conditional decision-making is contingent on the availability of reliable information, and may thus require repeated observation and orientation. That's typically the case with periodic statistical series (b).

- Unconditional decision-making can be set by exceptional circumstances (e.g., regulations or hostile takeover), or in accordance with business agreements or corporate policies (c).

Considering the intricacy of the root causes of changes in environments, and the pressure from competitors, the difficulty is to balance the reliability of assessments (which is supposed to increase with time and information) against the benefits of commitments (which are supposed to decrease over time, if postponing decisions give competitors more leeway).

Uncertainty, Causality & Risks

To get a competitive edge in digital environments, enterprises have to read through a massive and continuous flow of raw data — a task that involves three basic undertakings (figure 10-8):

1. Reducing uncertainty (observation): facts are not manna from heaven ready to be observed but have to be mined from qualified data.

2. Determining causal chains (orientation): while predicate logic and statistical inference may suffice with single root causes, they may lose their way in causal mazes.

3. Managing risks (decision): since business competition is by nature a time-dependent, nonzero-sum game, DM processes must weigh orientations with a dynamic assessment of risks, and balance business value with sustainability and architecture assets.

Not by chance, these objectives can be neatly aligned with the triad of data (quality and descriptive statistics), information (logic and statistical inference), and knowledge (time-dependent risk assessment).

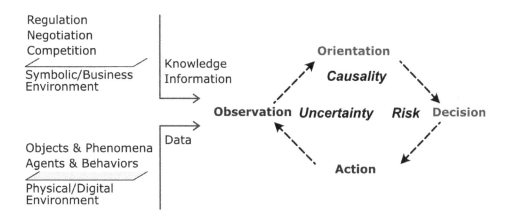

Figure 10-8. Uncertainty, Causality & Risks

At the enterprise level, the relationship between time, the reliability of information, and causal chains, allows for a dynamic integration of DM processes and knowledge-based enterprise architecture (cf. chapter 9). That understanding of DM integration sheds a new light on the distinction between operational, tactical, and strategic decision-making (cf. illustration introducing this chapter):

• Operational: observed data can be directly mapped to information and put to use as knowledge, thus allowing for routine decision-making (e.g., weapons must be kept ready).

• Tactical: partial or imperfect information can be improved with additional data until causal chains are secured. Risks are managed through traceability, and the timing of decisions will depend on a cost/benefit assessment of improving traceability (e.g., delaying a decision until more can be known about the approaching army will leave less time to act).

• Strategic: unreliable or insufficient relevant facts and doubtful causal chains prevent cost/benefit assessments within the targeted time frame. Whenever such decisions must be taken and changes committed to, risk-management schemes are introduced to cover for ill-fated turns of events (e.g., escape route for a defeated army).

While operational and tactical decision-making are supposed to be the preserve of systems and business units, the digital transformation is amalgamating the stakes and spreading the hazards — as illustrated by the range of potential consequences of a data breach, from regulatory sanctions for noncompliance to damage to customers' trust. Enterprise architects must therefore marshal overlapping DM levels, and the best way to do that is through the smart use of data, information, and knowledge to support decisions.

Knowledge & EA Decision-making

For enterprises competing in digital environments, decision-making is all about reading changes and taking chances; that can be achieved through a dynamic management of knowledge to support traceability and assessment.

Decision Trees & Knowledge Graphs

Taking a leaf from Judea Pearl's The Book of Why (cf. bibliography), causation can be understood through three modalities of knowledge:

1. Seeing: observing regularities and associations

2. Doing: trying out relationships between causes and effects by acting on the former and observing the latter

3. Imagining: modeling causes, effects, and relationships

That understanding of knowledge as a dynamic combination of actions and representations is of particular relevance for enterprise architecture considering its mix of physical and symbolic structures, in continuous exchange with digital environments. For decision-makers, that understanding of knowledge induces a blending of reality with causality:

• Reality: perceived through past and present digital observations from environments and systems

- Causality: expressed as symbolic representations (in predictive, descriptive, and prescriptive models) of why things did or didn't happen, do or do not happen, should and should not happen, and may or may not happen

With actions set at the juncture of facts and representations, their execution also affects the representations themselves, and therefore knowledge (as per the second point in the list above). Critically for decision-making in digital environments, knowledge becomes a dynamic (or time-related) factor because it is affected by actions; thus knowledge can:

- Increase (as a result of more data)

- Decrease (as a consequence of fewer business opportunities)

- Be drastically transformed by the consequences of actions that induce a shift of explanatory models (e.g., following a split with a partner)

It ensues that sorting out causes (expressed as information or knowledge) and effects (observed as data) can only be attempted with time serving as a referee. But then, there is a caveat: if symbolic representations are works in progress for both inputs and outcomes (as is the case with nonparametric statistical models), nothing can be assumed upfront about where to draw the line between data and information. Only actions, and therefore time, can set apart models from facts, and give causal credit to the former.

For enterprise architects, the difficulty is to manage the shifting overlaps between concerns, and thus between related causes and effects. To that end, setting aside labelling controversies (e.g., operational, tactical, or strategic), decisions should be ranked according to the status of supporting causal chains (figure 10-9):

1. Identified causal chains are built on well-defined options, reliable data, and clear relationships. At this level, causal chains are characterized by a degree of uncertainty that can be measured, allowing for direct decision-making, typically with decision trees.

2. Questioned causal chains keep the first level's assumptions about business perspectives and commitments made about organizational options. However, they

question the validity of representations and causal relationships and, consequently, the adequacy of the decision trees used at the first level. Statistical inference is typically used to assess predictive and descriptive models in relation to data from environments and operations.

3. Subsumed causal chains deal with the merits of the enterprise's expectations and objectives in relation to its business and physical environments. Causality takes a back seat as they are subsumed into modal logic or Game theory. Decisions are framed by Knowledge graphs and Machine learning (cf. chapter 9).

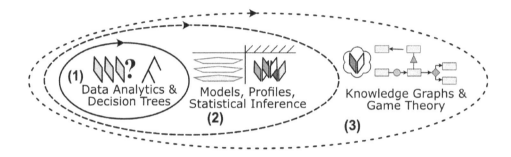

Figure 10-9. Shifting Causality for Decision-making

Taking advantage of the integration of systems- and knowledge-architectures, these tiers of causation can be inserted into DM loops, enabling feedbacks between data and business understanding, on the one hand, and enterprise architecture and information systems, on the other hand (figure 10-10):

- Data understanding: data analytics combines statistics and Deep learning to monitor physical environments and operations.

- Business understanding: business intelligence combines thesauruses and Knowledge graphs to support individual and collective DM.

- Information systems: models are assessed with regard to business objectives.

- Architecture profiles and patterns are amended or updated.

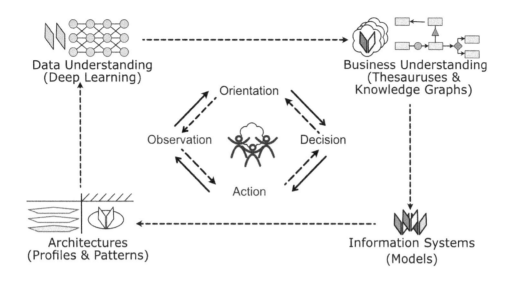

Figure 10-10. Decision-making & Knowledge Chains

Ontologies provide a comprehensive and consistent framework supporting the integration of the whole range of EA representations (data, information, knowledge), as well as associated processing (statistics, logic, Knowledge graphs). Taking advantage of that integration, decision-making can leverage the benefits of Machine learning across enterprises' systems and organization.

Causal Chains & Traceability

For EA decision-makers, the main issue is the integration of heterogeneous objectives, constraints, and time frames into a consistent causal model. Considering the dynamic nature of enterprise governance in digital environments, such integration would not be possible without feedback and self-improving mechanisms.

Machine learning (ML), broadly defined as the self-improvement capability of systems (cf. chapter 16), has become the cutting edge of information technology (IT). Given more credence by the universal relevance of software across economic, social, and political activities, ML technologies have spread across systems, enterprises, and environments.

For enterprise architects, ML's potential benefits can be found all along the DM loop:

- Observation: data mining (for facts) and process mining (for operations) pave the way for a digital osmosis between systems and environments.

- Orientation: ML can be used to identify latent developments (e.g., competitors' schemes) or emerging patterns (e.g., consumers' tastes) from environments, or to improve maps' relevance and reliability.

- Decision: ML can be used to assess the validity of policies in relation to observations and orientations, to amend existing policies, or to devise new ones.

- Action: process mining and data mining can also be used ex post to assess and improve operational effectiveness.

At the system level, ML could help to elicit causal chains from implicit yet well-circumscribed knowledge (cf. chapter 9). But at the enterprise level, decision-making involves a wide array of overlapping rationales and open-ended knowledge.

For EA decision-making, the traceability of causal chains (how decisions are assessed) is thus compounded by their accountability (who contributed to the assessment).

Yet, putting off decisions until explicit and comprehensive causal chains are secured would clearly lead to paralysis, especially for EA decisions, which are by nature subject to shifting and multidimensional factors, and rely on collective and implicit knowledge. Instead, enterprise architects should lay the groundwork supporting reliable timelines for all resources that could improve knowledge until the last responsible moment.

Assessment & Improvement

Given that EA decision-making is a continuous activity, carried out in changing environments and supported by partial and imperfect information, transparency and traceability must be explicitly managed:

- Assuming that transparency is going to improve with time, explanatory charts detailing causes, motivations, and effects should be padded with blank spaces and margins for further adjustments and justifications, with some decisions left open, pending latent information or implicit knowledge.

- Traceability should be handled in terms of alternative scenarios, with default options or exit pathways pointing to latent or patent representations; i.e., implicit or explicit knowledge.

Traceability can thus become an inherent part of decision-making, and thus of assessment and timing.

With regard to assessment, the objective is to improve the supporting data, information, and/or knowledge. To that effect, the proprietary nature and the availability of pricing references in environments should be taken into consideration:

- Data resources are generally nonproprietary; they are commonly traded and priced directly as raw commodities or as refined products bought from data factories.

- Information, understood as a combination of data and models, can be open source (free to use), proprietary (traded and priced), or exclusive (to be priced internally).

- Knowledge, understood as actionable information, constitutes an exclusive but elusive success factor; as such, it epitomizes enterprise architecture's intangible, invaluable and priceless assets.

With regard to timing, improving the information behind a decision can proceed until the "last responsible moment," when delaying a commitment would reduce the range of options or the expected returns.

But, as noted before, the digital flattening of business and systems perspectives, and the ubiquity of smart technologies in business processes, are blurring the lines: for enterprise architects, the difficulty is to determine the costs and benefits of improving the traceability of decisions.

If enterprise architects were to assess exclusive information and knowledge resources using internal prices, they would face a circular quandary: such prices do not reflect circumstances in environments but are corporate instruments whose purpose is to assess the contribution of internal resources. Using internal prices to justify decisions could introduce circular causal chains, because the assessment of options would make use of administered (as opposed to market-defined) values, which are themselves based on implicit choices. It would muddle the traceability of the whole process. That difficulty points to an intrinsic caveat in measuring knowledge as a given asset: being by nature contextual and defined by purpose and circumstances, knowledge must be constantly renewed if it is to support decision-making in changing environments.

Learning & EA Decision-making

Sustained performances in changing environments are conditioned by enterprises' ability to learn, not only from their environment but also from the way decisions are made and carried out. The paired helix of learning modes and resources (senses/data, reasoning/information, judgment/knowledge), introduced in the previous chapter, lays the groundwork for Reinforcement learning (RL). Assuming that learning is driven by purpose, harnessing DM processes to that learning loop (cf. chapter 8) will set the loop in motion.

Organization & Learning

DM capabilities can be bolstered by improving the quality of data, the traceability of reasoning, and the accountability of judgments. Some improvements can be obtained directly by investing in resources (see above), and others, through a more effective integration of the learning loop. Last but not least, ML technologies are pushing knowledge frontiers further by extracting new explicit representations from environments' raw observations.

  Improvements in learning capabilities can be aligned with operational, tactical, and strategic DM levels (figure 10-11):

- Investing in the quality of data will improve *operational* DM as well as the reliability of information models (a).

- Improving reasoning capabilities and traceability will enhance *tactical* DM and improve judgment capabilities (b).

- Integrating organization (for accountability) and systems (for traceability) will improve *strategic* DM (c).

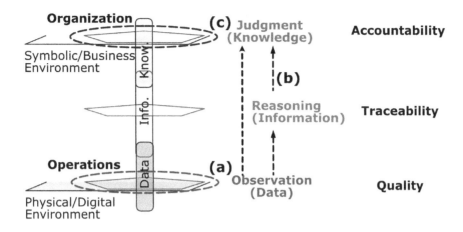

Figure 10-11. DM Capabilities: Operational (a), Tactical (b), Strategic (c)

Yet, as would be expected, improvements in decision-making processes for business domains or systems architecture do not translate easily at the enterprise level.

Issues of integration and traceability are not so much specific to EA as they are a direct consequence of the extensive employment of Deep-learning technologies focused on nonsymbolic knowledge — which is by nature difficult to elicit. The lack of traceability is a technical issue for decisions about systems or business domains. But it takes on a new significance at the enterprise level because judgments there entail values and beliefs (which are often implicit), and rely on collective knowledge and consensus. Improving decision-making at the enterprise level thus appears to be a matter of organization and collective knowledge.

Even with comprehensive and reliable causal chains, on the one hand, and explicit individual contributions, on the other hand, accountability at the enterprise level is essentially an organizational issue: when organizations as a whole know more and better than their individual members, the net collective additional knowledge is bound to be implicit — an unfathomable alloy of team spirit, culture, and leadership.

That makes the DM organizational improvements a complement to the operational ones, with collective learning mirroring Machine learning.

ML technologies are at their best when harnessing knowledge from massive and anonymous data; successful organizations accomplish something equivalent with the skills and experience of individuals. Both can also improve their learning capability: machines with Reinforcement learning, and organizations through collaboration.

But the significance of collaboration at the enterprise level goes much further than reinforcement; thus collaboration:

- Constitutes the hub of collective knowledge and decision-making

- Oils the gears between people and systems

- Knits the threads of traceability and accountability

Moreover, collaboration is necessary for DM when dealing with nonzero-sum issues and with open-ended options weighted by social values (cf. chapter 9).

Enhancing Collaboration

Organizations are symbolic systems, combining authority structures and collaboration mechanisms. Assuming that the former is embodied in the latter, the objective is to determine how collaboration can enhance collective knowledge and decision-making. On that account, a primary distinction should be made between three levels of collaboration:

- *Personal* collaboration is carried out between identified individuals, in person or through communication channels.

- *Functional* collaborations are personal collaborations carried out within socially-defined contexts (e.g., a committee) or objectives (e.g., a project team).

- *Organizational* (or institutional) collaborations are carried out between collective entities through representatives and documents.

As conclusively set forth by psychologist Robin Dunbar (cf. bibliography), personal and group collaborations correspond to human cognitive levels; one is set for around 10 trusted personal contacts, and the other, for around 150 untested social ones. Arguably not by chance, those numbers broadly square with empirical studies of personal and network clusters in professional and social contexts.

From a knowledge perspective, the cognitive levels of collaboration should be aligned with individual or collective reasoning and judgment capabilities. From a decision-making perspective, they should be aligned with the personal and functional levels of accountability.

The integrated systems and knowledge architectures described in chapter 9 can then ensure a clear functional autonomy between judgment, to be carried out at the organizational level, and observation and reasoning, supported by systems.

On the one hand, the traceability and accountability of decisions will be backed by the differentiation of reasoning capabilities (figure 10-12):

• Truth-preserving operations, supported by unified syntax and logic

• Domain-specific semantics

• Epistemic dimensions, for hypothetical representations and modal logic

• Models and profiles, for canned (sanitized, packaged, and reusable) knowledge

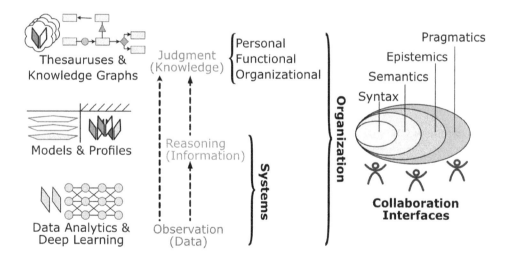

Figure 10-12. Knowledge-driven Collaboration

On the other hand, collaboration will benefit from the transparency of DM interfaces. They could be structured according to the nature of resources (data, information, knowledge), roles and accountability (systems or people), kind of collaboration (direct or mediated), and DM capability (observation, orientation, decision, action).

In between, collaboration interfaces can take advantage of the structure of ontologies (syntax, semantics, epistemics, and pragmatics) to match resources (data, information, knowledge) with reasoning capabilities and purposes.

Backed by that integration, the benefits of Artificial intelligence and Machine-learning technologies could be leveraged from the operational bottom (data mining) to the organizational top (natural-language interfaces).

Agility & Sustainability

Finally, EA decision-making should be assessed with regard to its impact on enterprises' agility and sustainability. The former attribute is driven by business opportunities; the latter, by long-term expectations and plans.

To begin with, enterprise architects are not directly concerned with decisions that can be confined to business or technical domains, as long as there is no impact on the coupling between enterprise architecture and its environments (cf. chapter 3); for example:

- Limited changes to organization or operations

- Changes to business aspects or rules

- Technical changes to software designs or platforms

- Stand-alone applications

Issues arise in enterprise architecture when there are changes in the structure of representations and associated processes; for example:

- Representation of new categories of business or physical objects

- New synchronization constraints on the representation of business or physical objects

- New business processes or new synchronization constraints on the execution of processes

EA decision-making must then balance agility with sustainability in order to manage systems complexity (cf. chapter 7). That's made possible by actionable maps; i.e., the integrated representation of engineering processes and architecture capabilities (figure 10-13).

On the architecture side, the learning loop feeds DM processes with data analytics (brown, upward arrow) and knowledge management (green, downward arrow).

On the engineering side, the workshops distribute the work units according to target and purpose: enterprise governance (a), applications development (b), domains (c), and systems operations (d).

Decisions driven by *agility* take advantage of the versatility and plasticity of systems, enabling the development of new applications with limited changes to architectures. However, there is a proviso: adding variants inevitably increases the overall complexity of a system. These decisions put the focus on changes in Computation independent models (CIM) that can be directly implemented in Platform specific models (PSM) and are not meant to interfere with strategic orientations.

Decisions driven by *sustainability* look for congruence between new business developments and planned architectural ones. The risks are missed business opportunities and/or the enterprise's weakened competitive edge. These decisions focus on changes in CIM and Platform independent models (PIM) that are in line with strategic orientations.

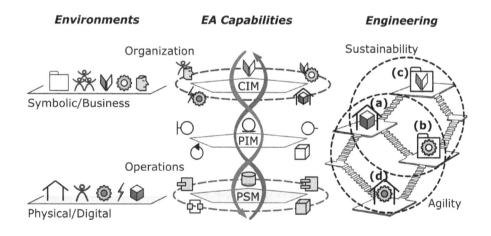

Figure 10-13. Balancing Agility & Sustainability

Coming up, Part IV will consider the solutions; i.e., how the decision-making framework can be implemented by enterprise architecture engineering.

PART IV

Enterprise Architecture Engineering

As a discipline, enterprise architecture (EA) has to cope with a problem of perspective: while a plurality of professionals is now ready to admit that EA goes well beyond information technology (IT), the digital transformation is nonetheless erasing most of the distinctive traits of systems. That apparent confusion about the scope of EA can be cleared up if a distinction is made between platforms (technical architecture), systems (functional architecture), and organization (enterprise architecture), with information providing a symbolic glue between these layers.

Apart from enabling a principled mapping of enterprises' environments, objectives, and assets, such layering — combined with mirrored symbolic representations — is at the core of enterprises' ability to adapt their structures in line with changing environments.

As expounded in part III, symbolic representations at the enterprise level combine systems-oriented languages like the Unified modeling language (UML), and business processes ones, like Business process model and notation (BPMN). The pairing is supported by a mix of thesauruses and networks that target business contexts, and ontologies that support the integration of the whole of data (digital environment and operations), information (systems), and knowledge (business environment and organization). That integration of representations with enterprise architecture provides the matrix of EA engineering.

Requirements are where changes are first spelled out. Consequently, requirements are also where enterprise and systems concerns should be set apart and their respective footprints detailed in terms of applications, systems, and organization (chapters 11 and 12).

With enterprise architecture concerns properly identified, and requirements refactored accordingly, Use cases provide application-modeling interfaces between environments and enterprise architectures (chapter 13). Projects can then be organized with regard to scope and objectives, and development models chosen, to ensure that changes across architecture layers and business domains can be continuously and consistently carried out without hampering enterprises' activities. Two basic development models should be considered: iterative solutions (e.g., Agile), when conditions about shared ownership and continuous delivery can be met, and model-based schemes otherwise (chapter 14).

CHAPTER 11.

Taxonomy of Requirements

Requirements stem from partial & biased expectations

Marking both the entry point and the direction of engineering processes, requirements have to meet conflicting constraints: at the very beginning, nothing should be taken for granted about forms or semantics. Nevertheless, some engineering options must be decided upfront regarding the organization and planning of projects. Such options may be of limited consequence at the application level, but not necessarily so at the system level, and definitively not at the enterprise level.

For enterprise architects, the primary objective is therefore to determine upfront the scope and ramifications of requirements without having to delve into the particulars of business domains.

Requirements' Capture

Initial errors are expansive and they may put whole ventures on the wrong path; this is especially so for ventures set at the enterprise or system levels, which are characterized by intrinsic complexity and uncertain perspectives. Since dealing comprehensively with these issues at the inception may not be cost-effective or even feasible, basic and robust criteria should be met to sort out the requirements pertaining to enterprise architecture.

Discovery: Principles & Illustration

Requirements can be expressed in a number of ways:

- Formal language (e.g., maths or logic): possibly shared by business analysts, systems architects, and software engineers

- Domain-specific language (e.g., law, accounting, or insurance): not necessarily familiar to IT architects and software engineers

- Natural language (e.g., media or games): supposedly common to all contributors to EA modeling, yet with business idiosyncrasies unfamiliar to IT architects and software engineers

When formally expressed, requirements can usually be assessed according to their architectural footprint; otherwise, some kind of transcription into a commonly accepted form is necessary (cf. chapter 14). In any case, the first step is to ensure the continuity of requirements with systems' existing functionalities; i.e., to sort out possible attachments with those business objects or processes already supported by systems architecture. Such attachments should meet two conditions:

- Requirements should remain tied to actual concerns: trying to apprehend them at a higher level would put the cart of architecture before the horse of applications, and so would go against the very purpose of the capture and analysis of requirements.

- Requirements should refer to models if and when necessary: although many applications can be developed directly, from requirements to code, the ones pertaining to enterprise architecture capabilities are supposed to be modeled.

Mapping new requirements to existing objects or functionalities would help to determine the footprints and primary responsibilities of requirements:

- Business perspective: stakeholders set the objectives; analysts define the objects and activities; users describe what is expected from supporting systems

- Systems perspective: analysts specify the functionalities of supporting systems; architects consolidate the already supported functionalities with new ones to be developed; engineers design and develop the new ones

- Project perspective: project managers bring together business value and time to market, on the one hand, with engineering constraints and development costs, on the other hand

A fabled taxonomy of Jorge Luis Borges can illustrate the discovery of requirements. The Celestial Emporium of Benevolent Knowledge, whose rationale and purpose have unfortunately been lost, divided animals into fourteen categories. These categories can be usefully applied to enterprise architecture:

1. Those that belong to the Emperor: business objectives

2. Embalmed ones: mothballed requirements made obsolete by changes in organizational or technical contexts

3. Those that are trained: additional requirements to existing applications

4. Suckling pigs: additional requirements to projects still under development

5. Mermaids: enticing requirements with no clear purpose or stakeholder

6. Fabulous ones: ambitious requirements waiting for a technological break-through or a dream team

7. Stray dogs: requirements with a clear purpose but without an identified stakeholder

8. Those included in the present classification

9. Those that tremble as if they were mad: shifting requirements that change when reviewed

10. Innumerable ones: growing requirements that multiply when reviewed

11. Those drawn with a very fine camel-hair brush: requirements expressed with a graphical modeling language

12. Others: requirements that cannot be expressed in terms of symbolic contents

13. Those that have just broken a flower vase: requirements associated with recent failures

14. Those that from a long way off look like flies: vexing clouds of unclassified requirements that keep coming and going

Except for the 11th and 12th items (and, of course, the 8th), this list can be re-grouped into five meta-categories:

• Business objectives (not to be confused with business requirements) that may be supported by functional requirements (1)

- Requirements under the authority of a unique owner or stakeholder (7)

- Requirements affecting applications under development or already deployed (3, 4)

- Mothballed requirements (2, 5, 6)

- Requirements pending classification (9, 10, 13, 14)

Setting aside business objectives (which are not directly considered for engineering), requirements already assigned (supposedly with proper classification), mothballed ones (without need of classification), and pending ones (to be classified later on, once the taxonomy under consideration is stabilized), the immediate objective is to align the remaining core requirements with current architecture capabilities.

Architecture-based Taxonomy

Classifications are meant to serve a purpose: for requirements, in general, that should be to identify footprints and stakeholders; for enterprise architecture, in particular, footprints and stakeholders should be defined through maps and territories (cf. part I).

Regarding maps, the granularity of requirements should be aligned with the representations of business objects or activities that are already supported by systems and, consequently, with business-domain boundaries. That alignment of requirements' items with business boundaries would serve to identify owners or stakeholders.

Regarding territories, not all requirements can be unequivocally attached to symbolic representations, or even to business domains. Some requirements pertain to applications set across domains, whereas others deal with technical issues that cannot be assigned to specific business stakeholders.

That classification, which tallies with the modeling paradigm introduced in chapter 3, is often expressed in terms of functional vs. nonfunctional requirements, which can be further refined (though labels may vary) into four basic categories when users' experience (direct or indirect) is taken into account (figure 11-1):

- Business (or process) requirements deal with organization and business processes independently of the part played by supporting systems. They are transcribed as descriptive models and may affect enterprise architecture capabilities.

- Functional requirements deal with the part played by supporting systems in the realization of business requirements. They are transcribed as prescriptive models and may affect systems functional capabilities. Application requirements are the part specific to business domains; i.e., not shared at the architecture level. As such, they can be developed directly without being translated as prescriptive models.

- Nonfunctional requirements encompass Quality of service (QoS) and technical requirements. QoS requirements deal with users' experience independently of business (or symbolic) contents and technical solutions. Technical requirements deal with the implementation of systems' functions and applications independently of business (or symbolic) contents and users' experience. Nonfunctional requirements are transcribed as technical models and may affect platforms capabilities.

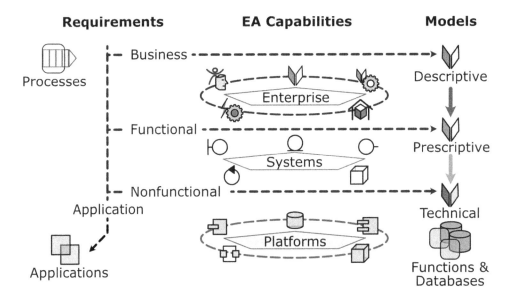

Figure 11-1. Taxonomy of Requirements

However useful these categories may be to help map requirements to architecture capabilities, understandings often differ, notably in the context of digital environments. Complementing the process/application view of requirements with references to both descriptive (for processes) and prescriptive (for applications) models may help to avoid confusion (cf. chapter 7).

EA-driven Requirements

As far as EA is concerned, the primary objective is to characterize requirements with regard to environments and organization.

Requirements in Digital Environments

With the digital intermingling of business processes and IT, two established distinctions are losing relevance: first, between the layers of processes and applications and, second, between users and systems.

Before the digital era (figure 11-2, left), processes neatly distinguished between people with roles defined by organization (or users), applications run by supporting systems, and users' interfaces embedded in applications.

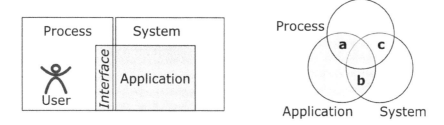

Figure 11-2. Before (left) and After (right) the Digital Transformation

Nowadays (figure 11-2, right), the digital flattening of exchanges between enterprises and environments means that nondeterministic operations (e.g., heuristics, fuzzy logic, learning) that used to be the prerogative of users can now be carried out by digital brains set in applications (a), user interfaces (b), or functions carried out by systems somewhere in the Cloud (c). As a consequence, instead of identified and steady systems with clearly defined boundaries, requirements may have to consider a miscellany of proxies with blurred identities.

Such merging of business logic, decision-making, and smart systems often translates into hybrid requirements, inducing foggy interfaces and lacking traceability. Given the ubiquity of digital agents across environments and systems, these issues may become critical and should be dealt with explicitly by adding an organizational dimension to requirements.

Requirements & Organization

As commonly understood, functional requirements cover business concerns (domains, objects, events, activities) as well as the part of the corresponding processes supported by systems (roles, locations, processes). That distinction also broadly matches the one between computation and Platform independent models introduced in part I.

Yet that understanding is set at the systems level, where business processes are aligned with systems capabilities; it bypasses the enterprise level and the role of organization as a buffer between business environment and systems. Such overlooking of organizational issues is typified by approaches to business-process modeling that mix business logic with control over the execution of processes (cf. chapter 4). In these approaches, business logic is a matter of computation better dealt with independently of organization, and control logic is a matter of organization (for roles and authorizations) and systems (for the execution of transactions). Blending both kinds of requirements binds changes in business rules (e.g., credit rating) to systems capabilities (e.g., communication channels).

From an EA perspective, overlooking the role of organization in requirements (figure 11-3a) can significantly hamper architectures' versatility (ability to change processes without changing architecture) and plasticity (ability to change architecture without impacting processes).

The drawbacks of overlooking organization are compounded by the immersion of enterprises in digital environments, because traditional systems boundaries, which are often made obsolete by the ubiquity of digital flows, have to be redefined relative to enterprise organization. Hence the need to set apart the requirements pertaining to organization (figure 11-3b) from the ones directly associated with systems capabilities (figure 11-3c).

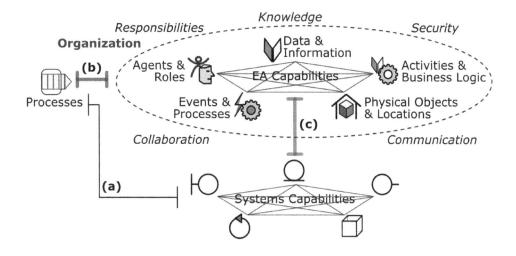

Figure 11-3. *Organizational & Functional Requirements*

Concerning organization, the focus should be on harnessing processes and EA capabilities; for example, enterprise architects should focus on how:

- Responsibilities are defined such that they combine roles, information, and activities

- Information is built from data and put to use as knowledge

- Security and confidentiality can be taken into account globally across capabilities

- Communication requirements combine physical (locations) and functional (roles) dimensions

- Collaboration requirements combine business logic and the execution of processes

More specifically, if organizations are to serve as buffers between environments and systems, requirements must be explicit about agents' roles and responsibilities, on the one hand, and the abilities and activities of people and systems, on the other hand. That should imply:

- A conceptual distinction between categories of agents identified at the enterprise level (people, organizational units, systems, devices), roles in organization (what agents are meant to do), and actors identified by systems (or roles enacted in processes)

- A triple functional distinction between granted (for agents) and required (for roles or actors) abilities associated with activities, communication abilities (natural, symbolic, or digital), and decision-making capabilities

- A logical distinction of digital contents depending on their nature (data, information, or knowledge) and modus operandi (e.g., truth- preserving operations, heuristics, learning)

Nonfunctional Requirements

Requirements can also bypass organizational aspects and be directly expressed using descriptive and prescriptive models (cf. chapter 7).

Systems architects would then take responsibility for nonfunctional requirements: technical ones (between functions and platforms capabilities) and constraints on the Quality of service (between applications and platforms).

Regardless of definition games, the meaning of nonfunctional requirements is straightforward when taken literally: nonfunctional simply refers to items that cannot be associated with functional requirements. Thus, as should be expected for leftover categories, the outcomes are by nature irreducible to definitions and can only be determined by concrete circumstances. For requirements, it means a mixed bag of overlapping items in the confines between (figure 11-4):

- Application requirements (functional); e.g., high-frequency trading orders must be executed in less than half a second

- Quality of service (nonfunctional); e.g., users' average waiting time should be less than 30 seconds

• Technical requirements (nonfunctional); e.g., the server's time response should be less than 3 seconds

It must be stressed that the line between functional and nonfunctional requirements can only be drawn case by case, because it depends on whether they directly affect users' experience or are solely the concern of architects and engineers.

Technical requirements are by nature defined and implemented at the systems and platforms levels. By contrast, QoS involves users' experience and is consequently better managed at the enterprise level — if only because it cannot be specifically assigned to one business domain or implemented by one technical platform. That course of action is reinforced by the digital transformation and the possibility for these requirements to be uniformly expressed between domains and implemented across architectures.

Moreover, a number of transverse issues (e.g., privacy and security) are best dealt with through organization at the enterprise level, and consequently should be put under the aegis of enterprise architects.

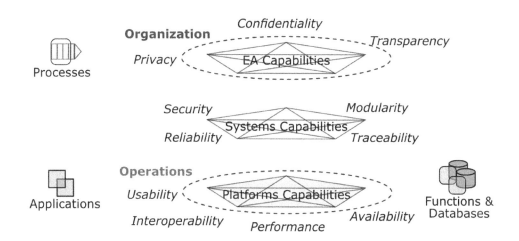

Figure 11-4. Nonfunctional Requirements

Metrics of Requirements

Measurements are not facts but observations defined by perspectives and purposes; consequently, they are contingent on the conceptual and technical apparatus used to get them. At the system level, three basic dimensions should be considered for measurement:

- the business value of new applications,

- the size and complexity of the functionalities to be supported by systems, and

- the development work effort.

On the one hand, business value, whether assessed locally by business units or in light of broader objectives set at the enterprise level, is the preserve of business stakeholders. On the other hand, estimations of development costs are the preserve of systems architects and software engineers. In between, enterprise architects should lay the groundwork for consensual decision-making, balancing business value, functional scope, and development costs. For that purpose, both parties must agree on a double gauge: first, for the intrinsic size and complexity of the business issues and, second, for the expected contribution of supporting systems. Descriptive (or Computation independent) models are well suited for the former aspect, whereas prescriptive (or Platform independent) models incorporate both aspects — although the specific contribution of systems can be factored out given the intrinsic size and complexity of the business aspect (figure 11-5).

Based on our modeling paradigm (cf. chapter 2), descriptive models can be assessed with regard to:

- Organizational complexity: estimated by the dependencies between enterprise capabilities (figure 11-5a)

- Domain complexity: estimated by the number of business objects, aspects, and partitions (figure 11-5b)

- Process complexity, due to business logic: estimated by the number of symbolic boundaries (roles), functional execution units, and functional variants (figure 11-5c)

- Process complexity, due to the control of execution: estimated by the number of synchronized boundaries (events), synchronized execution units, and synchronization variants (figure 11-5d)

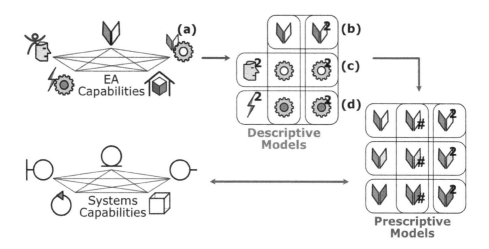

Figure 11-5. *Requirements' Metrics*

As pointed out in chapter 3, prescriptive models represent IT artifacts, in contrast to descriptive models, which represent business environment and processes. While there is no reason to assume that systems should mimic environments, the representations of anchors in both representations must be aligned, which means that corresponding prescriptive metrics can be directly derived from (but not equated with) descriptive ones. For prescriptive models as a whole, the difference stems from anchors' constraints (#), additional business objects, execution units, and aspects introduced at the system level. Adjusted prescriptive models could then serve as a basis for the assessment of the development work effort, taking into account targeted and engineering environments.

These three metrics (descriptive, prescriptive, work effort) could then be used to adjust the scope and schedule of new developments with regard to business revenues and returns on assets.

Requirements & Engineering

The term "requirements engineering" is misleading because it introduces a confusion between business needs, formally documented or not, and their realization as software components, at the application or system level. That confusion is especially detrimental for enterprise architects, whose job description is based on the distinction between enterprise and systems.

Sorting out mixed concerns should thus be a priority for enterprise architects: when presented with new ventures, they must determine upfront if the proposed changes should take place under or above the floor separating systems and enterprise architectures (cf. chapter 3). Assuming proper mappings of architectures, enterprise architects could ignore:

- Changes in operations that do not affect enterprise organization or systems functional architecture

- Changes in IT architecture or software design that do not affect the coupling between systems architecture and environments

- Stand-alone applications

Conversely, enterprise architects should focus on:

- Changes in organization, even if there is no immediate consequences for systems architecture

- Changes in business domains induced by changes in business environments or enterprise objectives

- Changes in systems and business processes induced by changes in domains and applications

In theory, one would expect architecture floors to be clearly set between systems (for shared functions) and platforms (for specific applications), and requirements to be easily assessed as described above. In practice, requirements can seldom be neatly framed, if only because the outlines of systems architecture and component designs often reflect systems' legacies with different life cycles. The difficulty could be managed by organizing requirements with regard to decision-making processes (cf. chapter 10) and engineering workshops, introduced in chapter 3 (figure 11-6):

• Enterprise: for requirements concerning organization and processes

• Domains: for requirements concerning shared business objects and functions

• Application: for requirements concerning the development of applications

• Systems: for requirements concerning operations and QoS

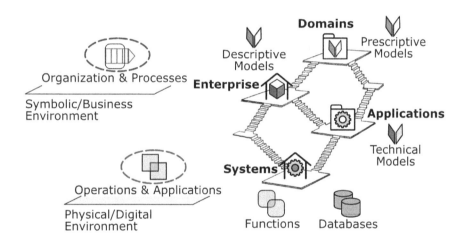

Figure 11-6. Drawing the Line between Applications and Architecture

The next chapter considers how requirements can be sorted out as to be aligned with the respective concerns of business domains and enterprise architectures.

CHAPTER 12

Enterprise Architecture Requirements

To continuously anchor enterprise architectures to their environment,
each requirement unit must meet Aristotle's classical three unities of drama:
a single action, executed at the same place, within the same time frame

In theory, enterprise architects would get requirements from customers neatly packaged according to scope (application or system) and stakeholder (specific or shared) (cf. chapter 11):

- Business functions shared across domains

- Business applications specific to domains

- Quality of service (QoS) expected from all applications

- Technical implementations

In practice, enterprise architects are more like gardeners, growing an assortment of plants according to differing soil type, changing seasons, and the vicissitudes of weather.

While the digital transformation is bound to facilitate changes and iron out discrepancies between business processes and supporting systems, it also undermines technical and customary fences used to set apart systems, organization, and environments. Thus, if change is to be the name of the game for enterprise architects, requirements should first be organized with regard to their impact on the edges of systems architecture; in particular, locations, roles, and events.

Architecture Edges

As the embodiment of an enterprise's identity, systems used to come with tangible boundaries, where requirements could be clearly posted. But the digital transformation is erasing the confines of systems and, consequently, changing the meaning of locations, agents and roles, and events and time frames (figure 12-1).

Locations

Locations are where processes are executed, with resources directly and immediately available. As far as enterprise architecture (EA) is concerned, requirements may address physical, functional, and organizational locations:

- Physical locations: for activities that are supposed to be executed within the same time frame (or controlled by a single clock), with all active (people, systems, devices) and passive resources (buildings, furnitures) immediately available; this implies synchronous communication channels (physical or digital)

• Functional locations: for symbolic activities defined independently of physical locations, yet within the same address space, with all symbolic resources immediately identifiable and available

• Organizational locations: for activities that are supposed to be executed within the same customary context (enterprise units or external organizations), with all relevant identified agents and roles consistently defined

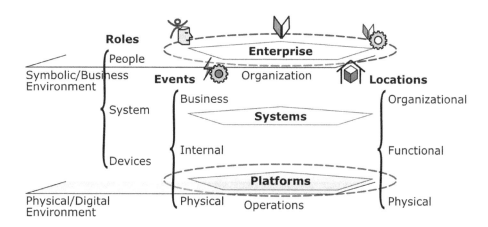

Figure 12-1. EA's Edges

These distinctions are especially relevant if virtual capabilities are to be defined, managed, and used as services independently of their location in the Cloud.

Agents & Roles

Roles are set at the boundaries between enterprises and systems, and their significance for EA is reinforced by the immersion of enterprises in digital environments; for example:

• Compliance with privacy regulations cannot be achieved without a built-in distinction between managed (e.g., customers) and unmanaged (e.g., mined identities) roles.

- The dismantling of physical boundaries, the generalization of digital identities, and the spreading of smart software agents put roles front and center for issues of confidentiality.

From the perspective of enterprise architecture, requirements should therefore be explicit with regard to:

- Roles defined at the business level should be fulfilled by people whose identity is defined by external organizations, people acting as individuals (e.g., chef) or as representatives of collective entities (e.g., food safety regulator).

- Roles defined at the systems level (actors in UML parlance) should be fulfilled by actual (e.g., user) or symbolic (e.g., banking service) agents.

- Roles defined at the physical level are typically fulfilled through the Internet of things (IoT); e.g., rice cooker.

That distinction is necessary if organizational aspects (or roles) are to be defined and managed at the enterprise level independently of functional (systems) and technical (applications) ones.

Events & Time Frames

From the EA perspective, events can be seen as the dynamic equivalent of roles:

- Roles are tied to identified external entities (agents); events are associated with external phenomena — namely, changes in the state of objects, processes, or agents' expectations.

- Roles are defined by the enterprise's organization and are enacted as actors (in UML parlance) in processes; events are defined by the enterprise's business concerns and carried out as transitions between the states of processes' execution.

The architectural significance of events is also reinforced by the digital transformation, which redraws the lines between external (environments) and internal (systems) events. The need for explicit requirements can be illustrated by IoT, which cuts the characteristics of events to the bone in order to make use of faster, yet cheaper, communication channels.

Enterprise architects must consequently characterize events according to their nature and impact:

- Business events are symbolic and sourced in the environment, which implies a role (e.g., customer) and a symbolic representation (e.g., reservation). They can be directly and immediately taken into consideration.

- Internal events are symbolic and sourced in the enterprise, which implies a symbolic representation (e.g., invoicing) but rules out business roles.

- Physical (or digital) events are nonsymbolic and sourced in the environment, which implies a physical agent and location (e.g., change in ambient temperature). They must be processed (or interpreted) before being taken into consideration.

That taxonomy of events also determines the enterprise's basic time frames:

- Business time frames; e.g., regulatory delay for the notification of a data breach

- Internal time frames; e.g., interval between customer surveys

- Physical time frames; e.g., clocks

The necessity of explicit requirements with regard to the customary or statutory nature of events can be illustrated by the European Union's General Data Protection Regulation (GDPR). By introducing legal constraints on the notifications of changes in personal data, regulators appear to put internal events on the same standing as statutory ones. However, without a built-in distinction between observed data (external events) and managed information (internal events), regulatory compliance would coerce an amalgamation of systems- and enterprise-architecture timescales, which would be defined externally by GDPR.

Anchoring Requirements

Once the edges (roles, events, locations) of requirements are established, enterprise architects should sort them out on a need-to-know basis.

Process Archetypes

Set across different business entities and domains, business processes have to rely on architectures' resources and mechanisms. By that account, six basic archetypes can be identified (figure 12-2):

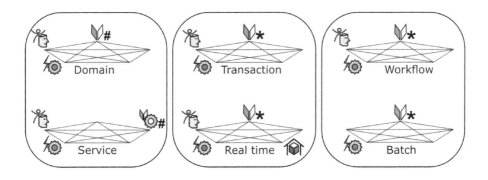

Figure 12-2. Process Archetypes

- Processes centered on specific domains or services should be seen as EA primitives; i.e., processes tied to a single architecture anchor (#), which are persistent for domain-based processes and transient for service-oriented ones (figure 12-2, left).

- Transactional and real-time processes involve shared access to a number (*) of anchors; the former through asynchronous interactions with environments, and the latter through synchronous ones (figure 12-2, center).

- Workflows and batch processes involve shared access to a number (*) of anchors; the former controlled by internal (or systems) events and the state of computations, and the latter only by the state of computations (figure 12-2, right).

Assuming that business logic has been factored out (cf. chapter 4), enterprise architects should try to align the requirements of business processes with these archetypes.

Anchors & Aspects

With processes attached to EA anchors, requirements must detail the aspects involved (cf. chapter 7). And when processes are set across domains, requirements should be explicit about their semantics; that can be achieved with thesauruses (cf. chapter 9).

If EA anchors are meant to be shared between organizational units over open-ended periods of time, there is no reason to assume that aspects and semantics would be uniformly defined and/or remain so. As a way to secure the continuity of representations while enabling changes in semantics, requirements should maintain a distinction between structural and functional aspects; the former, for continuity, and the latter, for variability.

Names may differ (e.g., aspects, features, functions, behaviors, interfaces), but the intent remains the same: assuming a consistent and continuous identification of business entities, beholders (domains or processes) should be given a free hand with the meanings and usages of their pick of aspects. For that to be achieved, requirements should set apart the identification and structure of business entities, on the one hand, and their features and associated semantics, on the other hand (figure 12-3).

First, the backbone of the process should be built (cf. chapter 7), which would tie business processes (e.g., **Book Tour**) to EA anchors (e.g., **Customer Account**). Compared to anchor references, which secure the integrity of the business entities identified at the architecture level, functional references to other business entities (e.g., **Railway, Car, Airline, Hotel**) must ensure the consistency of aspect semantics (a).

Then, using composition (black diamonds) or aggregation (white diamonds), backbones should be fleshed out with business entities identified (#) by processes (e.g., **Reservation**) and associated activities (e.g., **Book Transit, Book Lodgings, Bill Customer**).

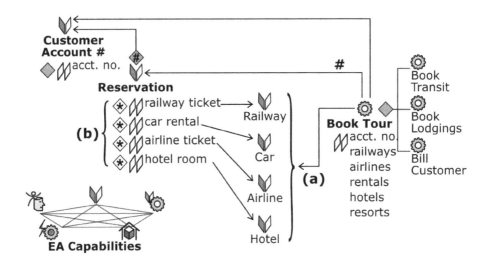

Figure 12-3. EA View on Process Requirements

With a secure architectural backbone, the structural (e.g., ***acct. no.***) and functional (b) aspects of process requirements can be added iteratively.

Execution Units

Requirements should also be transparent about shared access without enterprise architects having to know the details of business operations. To that end, execution units must be defined at the architecture level and anchored to business environments independently of the specifics of applications.

As defined by the Business process model and notation (BPMN), business processes are built from "elementary activities (or tasks) representing single units of work that cannot be broken down to a further level of business process detail." Such a cursory definition falls short of addressing architectural concerns, because it ignores the critical architectural distinction between the business content of activities and the way it should be executed at the system level.

Something more thorough is clearly needed for the definition of processes' execution units, and Aristotle's classical three unities of drama fits the bill:

Unity of action (roles): execution units should have one main course of action initiated by a single primary role (e.g., ***Customer #***), with all resources identified (e.g., ***Book Tour, Reservation***). Subplots, if any, can summon the collaboration of secondary actors, providing a return to the main plot once completed; that condition guarantees that all possible execution dependencies are identified.

Unity of place (locations): execution units must be run in a single location (e.g., *Cloud Services #*), where all resources (e.g., *Book Tour, Reservation*) can be obtained directly and immediately, so as not to depend on communication capabilities between locations. That is a necessity if functional architectures are to be defined and managed independently of technical ones.

Unity of time (events): execution units must be timed in relation to a single event (e.g., *Customer Request #*) and, consequently, to a single time frame, within which accesses to resources can be synchronized. That is necessary if the innards of business logic and the synchronization of business processes are to be managed independently of communication channels and mechanisms.

Not by chance, Aristotle's three unities neatly coincide with the edges defined above: roles, locations, and events.

That's the principle; in practice, it is difficult to align execution units (determined by roles, events, and locations) with functional ones (determined by business context and business logic). Taking a data breach as an example (figure 12-4):

• Execution units are determined by the data controller being aware (a) of the event (b) and its location (c), and by the time constraints on notification.

• Functional units are determined by the format and nature of the targeted data (d), and by the assessment of privacy risks (e).

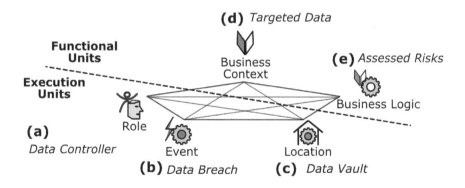

Figure 12-4. Illustration of Aristotle's Rule of Three Unities

Given that requirements are set at the very beginning, neat definitions of execution and functional units cannot be assumed; more often than not, requirements will mix constraints and conditions pertaining to both aspects.

For enterprise architects, the difficulty is therefore to sort out the threads of execution at the enterprise level without delving into the specifics of business requirements.

Sorting Out Requirements

Rules make up the bread and butter of requirements, and range from a disorderly mixture of roles, events, objects, and operations, to a neat arrangement in terms of structural, functional, and QoS constraints. A refactoring of rules can thus be used to sort out requirements' threads with regard to EA. That can be best achieved with regard to the rules' footprint, triggering, and the variants (or partitions) involved.

Rules' Footprints

The architectural footprint of rules can be defined by their triggering conditions, what is evaluated (rule's domain), and what is affected (rule's co-domain). On that basis, a distinction can be made between:

- Homogeneous rules: triggered, evaluated, and executed on the same side of the environment/EA divide

- Heterogeneous rules: set astride EA edges, with a possible mix of business complexity and architecture capabilities

Homogeneous rules, which are evaluated and executed on the same side of the divide, should not affect the tie-up (or coupling) between systems and their environment; for example (figure 12-5):

- Data analytics: for rules used to build business (or symbolic) views of environments (e.g., market demographics) without a direct impact on systems' representations (figure 12-5a)

- Regulations: for rules governing business environments (e.g., food labeling); possibly used by business intelligence (figure 12-5b)

- Business logic and computation rules: meant to be applied to enterprises' symbolic representations without affecting them (e.g., audit rules) (figure 12-5c)

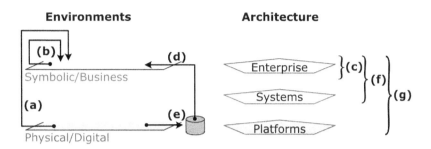

Figure 12-5. Rules' Footprint

By contrast, the footprint of heterogeneous rules straddles the fences between enterprises and environments:

- Input/Output rules: to log external events (figure 12-5e) or to notify internal ones (figure 12-5d)

- Application rules: combine the complexity of business domains with the constraints of systems functional architecture (figure 12-5f)

- Technical rules: combine functional complexity with the constraints of QoS (figure 12-5g)

Refactoring rules with regard to their footprint on the environment/architecture divide helps to map requirements to EA capabilities.

Rules' Triggering

Untangling rules can be seen as a prerequisite of requirements analysis, especially if their impact on enterprise architecture has to be identified.

First to consider is the unity of time: the triggering conditions of rules should be used to determine the architectural impact of requirements' threads; i.e., the changes, other than updates and computation, induced across the EA divide.

For rules triggered by internal (or systems) events:

- Asynchronous changes in the business environment; e.g., an overdraft generating a notification

- Synchronous changes in processes; e.g., a timer triggering an audible signal

For rules triggered by digital (or physical) events:

- Asynchronous changes in the business environment; e.g., an unusual connection generating a notification

- Synchronous changes in processes; e.g., a forcible entry triggering an alarm

For rules triggered by business (or symbolic) events:

- Asynchronous changes in expectations; e.g., private data should be provided when requested

- Synchronous changes in processes; e.g., the number of operating checkout terminals is determined by management

It must be remembered that, as far as enterprise architects are concerned, the objective is not to specify the rules but to check their consistency with architecture capabilities without having to consider their business content.

Partitions

Partitions define variants and are consequently at the core of rules and, more generally, requirements.

As logic expressions, partitions can be organized in a decision tree (figure 12-6):

1. Structural partitions are set once and for all; e.g., string or trebuchet catapults.

2. Phased partitions are nonstructural, with changes subject to events and sequencing constraints, e.g., a catapult can be idle or armed

3. Functional partitions reflect differences in the state of surrogates independently of events; e.g., chariots with or without scythes.

4. Analytical partitions are defined on data independently of the specific states of instances; e.g., chariots scheduled for maintenance based on statistical inference.

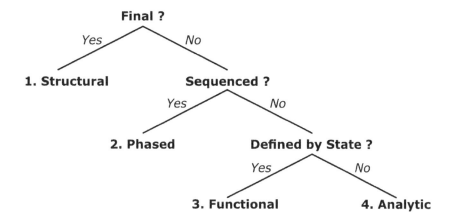

Figure 12-6. Partitions

When applying partitions to rules, enterprise architects must set apart the rules pertaining to the structural integrity and functional consistency of business entities independently of their use by business processes; for example:

- Integrity constraint: invoices are identified by customer and vehicles

- Structural partitions: circuits of electric cars must be checked after 1000 miles

- Functional partitions: customers with payment arrears cannot make reservations

- Functional constraint: vehicle repairs requiring imported parts must be invoiced using the previous day's currency rates

The objective is to obtain rules that can be evaluated upfront, so that their impact on architectures could be determined independently of the execution of processes.

To that effect, EA visibility on the course of action should be limited to partitions that can be decided upfront, together with triggering conditions; i.e., on roles, events, business entities, and activities. For example:

- Roles (authorizations): only managers can modify customers' credit ratings

- Business entities (organization): cars must be checked when transferred between rental locations

- Events: requests from VIP customers should be given priority

- Activities: technical problems affecting security on checked cars should be notified immediately

By contrast, business-specific rules should not be considered; e.g., car check-ins must record date, time, and staff identity.

From a broader perspective, rules should be formulated in a way that would help systems architects to decide between design options, typically:

- Events vs. data: should systems behavior be driven by changes in business context (as signaled by events from users, devices, or other systems) or by changes in symbolic representations?

- Activities vs. data: should systems behavior be governed by planned activities or by the states of business objects?

- Activities vs. events: should systems behavior be governed by planned activities or driven by changes in business context?

Taking out business logic from the factors that determine processes' execution would also help with assessing feasibility and QoS.

Quality of Service

QoS requirements directly affect users' experience yet are meant to be met independently of specific business domains or applications (cf. chapter 11). As a corollary, these requirements will often be mixed with organizational and business-specific considerations. So, in the case of GDPR, customers should be notified of any data breach targeting unencrypted data within 72 hours.

The aim should therefore be to refactor rules to set apart architectural issues (typically, performance, reliability, or confidentiality) so that they could be matched with architecture capabilities.

However, even without considering the legacy of systems (cf. chapter 14), the complexity of rules often means that their refactoring fails to fully separate business from architectural issues, leaving enterprise architects to sort out the respective stakes and options. Organizing requirements around domains or services may help.

Domains & Services

Besides changes brought about through business processes, requirements may also target EA capabilities as a whole, either to consolidate changes in business domains, or to carry out long-term transformations of shared assets and mechanisms.

Domain-driven Requirements

As illustrated by Customer relationship management (CRM) systems, the representations of business entities stand front and center among enterprises' assets; requirements should therefore guarantee their continuity and consistency. That issue is best ascertained through the Domain-driven design (DDD) approach.

A brainchild of Eric Evans (cf. bibliography), DDD replaces a process perspective with a domain one, and carries on with engineering directly from the complexity of business logic. Requirements are organized in terms of conceptual domains (for business entities, the equivalent to anchors) and bounded contexts (for business semantics, the equivalent to aspects). A ubiquitous language is meant to deal with the semantic overlaps between bounded contexts and to support shared access to business entities.

The relevance of the DDD approach comes from its analysis of domain complexity and shared access; yet despite the significance of these issues for enterprise architecture, they are not dealt with accordingly:

- The enterprise-modeling conundrum (cf. chapter 8) is simply overlooked, and the conceptual and semantic discrepancies between business and systems representations are supposed to be unified through a high-level ("ubiquitous") programming language.

- Mirroring that modeling shortcut, there is no room for a distinction between organization, systems, and software, and consequently between business and engineering processes.

- Object-oriented design is used as an engineering bypass between business domains and systems applications, avoiding possible modeling gaps. The implicit assumption is that symbolic representations of business processes and systems components can be aligned through programs; i.e., the distinction between enterprise and systems architectures can be overlooked.

For enterprise architects, the priority is to reinstate explicit requirements instead of programming proxies; that can be achieved with a service-oriented approach.

Service Perspective

Enterprise architecture's primary objective is to manage the coupling between business processes and architecture capabilities. As detailed above, part of that undertaking can be achieved with tailored requirements, either through their anchoring to domains or through the unraveling of the rules and constraints tying processes and domains. Both options come with provisos:

- Domain-driven design bypasses enterprise architects and tasks software engineers with solving the issue.

- The refactoring of rules cannot fully contend with mixed business and systems complexities.

Given the limits of the separation-of-concerns approach, service-oriented solutions can be seen as the divide-and-conquer alternative: instead of being solved at the architecture level, the issue of shared business entities and collaboration mechanisms is handed over to functions shared across the architecture.

Compared to DDD's focus on domains, Service-oriented architectures (SOA) wrap together access to shared entities with all associated capabilities deemed necessary. Such a wrapping of services can be summarily identified by architecture layers: technical, functional, or business.

What is commonly known as Enterprise service bus (ESB) regroups a number of mainstream collaborative solutions at the technical (or platform) level. Positioned on middleware between systems architecture and component design, ESB solutions are part and parcel of systems technical architecture. Their impact at the enterprise level (organization and business processes) is mainly felt through feasibility and QoS requirements.

Service-oriented architectures can be seen as ESB, which has been upgraded to the functional level, in order to fully describe systems through their functionalities independently of their technical realization. Such services can thus be used as markers of architectural boundaries for both business and engineering processes:

- Business processes: collaborations can be defined and managed independently of what happens at the technical level for applications.

- Engineering processes: the design and implementation of services can be detached from the business requirements expressed by domains.

Services can thus serve as templates for architecture-driven requirements, providing a level of indirection meant to detach organization and business processes, on the one hand, from architecture capabilities, on the other hand (figure 12-7):

- What (messages): services only deal with symbolic objects, and can thus be described as aspects.

- Who (customers): services don't have to know about agents and roles because they only deal with symbolic customers.

- How (contracts): services are meant to be purely declarative, which means that expected outcomes and business logic should be specified independently of the way they are to be executed.

- When (policies): for business logic, the way services are executed should be specified in terms of rules and constraints, as if the execution were timeless.

- Where (endpoints): access to services are defined in terms of capabilities of communication channels.

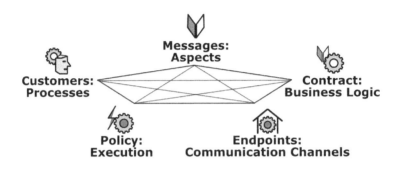

Figure 12-7. Services & EA Capabilities

Besides the clear benefits of SOA, expressing requirements in terms of services could help to clarify possible misgivings between business and systems stakeholders, with enterprise architects serving as brokers.

From Requirements to Projects

Managing EA Requirements

All in all, the schemes mentioned above could be used to manage EA requirements in relation to the nature and time frame of changes (figure 12-8):

- DDD can be instrumental in the long-term planning of business domains (enterprise architecture)

- The refactoring of rules (R2) is a necessary yet insufficient undertaking when sorting out the issues pertaining to organization and business processes (enterprise capabilities)

• SOA should serve as a template for requirements set at the business-process level, with services used to hide combined business, functional, and technical complexities (systems capabilities)

• The alignment of requirements defined at the application level (e.g., identification) with ESB technologies can be used to iron out technical discrepancies and smooth the refactoring of legacy systems (platforms capabilities)

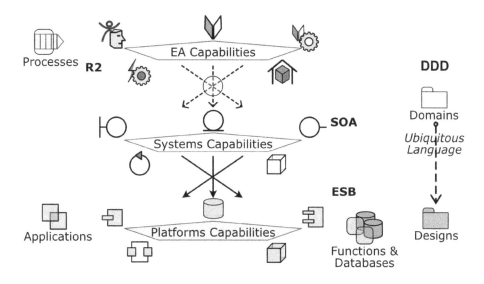

Figure 12-8. Architectural Perspectives

It must be noted that these different ways of dealing with requirements serve different purposes over different time frames; they can thus be carried out iteratively and independently in order to provide a sound basis for projects' planning and development.

The Rationale behind Engineering Processes

To paraphrase Albert Einstein, the only reason for processes [time] is so that everything [events] doesn't happen simultaneously. Regarding systems engineering, processes are introduced when outcomes or activities must be differentiated due to business, organizational, or technical constraints. On that account, there are two basic development models: one for differentiated engineering activities, and the other for undifferentiated ones.

Still taking a cue from Einstein (and Occam before him), one can suggest that systems engineering should be made as simple as possible. The simplest process is a single work unit, with the same activity (or group thereof) carried out repetitively by the same fully empowered agent (or group thereof), until a well-defined outcome can meet customers' expectations; otherwise, work units have to be differentiated to take dependencies into account.

It ensues that, notwithstanding the variety of development methods and tools, systems-engineering processes can be neatly regrouped into two categories (figure 12-9), iterative or phased:

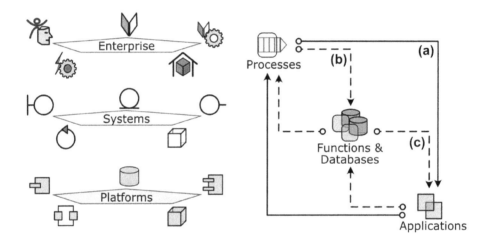

Figure 12-9. Systems Engineering: Agile (solid lines) or Model-based (dashed lines)

- Iterative development models, typically Agile, should be the default (Occam's) option when there are no cross dependencies; i.e., when a single stakeholder can take responsibility (organization), there is no impact on functional architecture (systems), and there are no constraints on deliveries (platforms) (a).

- Phased development models, typically Model-based system engineering (MBSE), is necessary when the development or deployment of applications (c) is conditioned by the development of architecture functions (b).

Since EA is meant to deal with large and complex organizations, it's safe to assume that both development models will be needed. And since engineering leaves no room for faith and dogma, interoperability should be a primary concern.

Picking Development Models

Beyond the perennial nature of change and the need to maintain business efficiency, changes at the enterprise level encompass a whole range of structural, organizational and cultural dimensions, set across different time frames, and involving a plurality of stakeholders. The challenge for EA engineering can only be met through workflows that combine phased and iterative schemes; the former dealing with architecture-based functions, and the latter, with business-specific applications. The refactoring of requirements should thus support clear and easy decision-making guidelines regarding (figure 12-10):

1. Agile development, for stand-alone developments free of cross dependencies

2. Model-based developments, possibly in conjunction with Agile ones, for requirements with system-level dependencies

3. Workflows combining Agile and Model-based developments, for requirements with enterprise-level dependencies

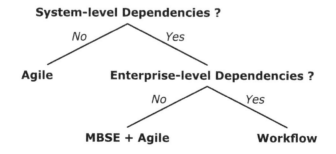

Figure 12-10. How to Pick a Development Model

The choice between Agile and phased development models is often presented as a binary one, overlooking the diversity and specificity of engineering issues in large and complex organizations. The next chapter will focus on the benefits of Use cases for dealing with EA separation of concerns, and chapter 14 will concentrate on Model-based engineering processes.

CHAPTER 13.

Enterprise Architecture & Use Cases

*Business cases are not meant to be executed; Use cases may or may not
be directly supported by systems; System cases are directly supported
by systems according to Aristotle's classical three unities of drama*

Things may happen by chance but won't last without a reason. That could be the twofold motto for both applications and architectures; the former, chasing business opportunities, and the latter, trying to milk perennial assets. But there are two caveats: to keep up with digital environments, enterprises have to change more than their application spots; but too many changes may turn architectures into cluttered shambles. Thus, the challenge for enterprise architects is how to transform a plurality of emerging trends into agile, consistent, and sustainable structures.

Planning for Change

Planning is the bread and butter of architecture, in general; this is even more true for its enterprise embodiment, considering its constant focus on change. Once requirements are refactored in line with the distinctive aims of enterprise architecture (EA) (cf. chapter 12), projects in the enterprise portfolio should be planned with regard to responsibilities, scope, and sequencing constraints.

Responsibilities

Change is challenging, especially for organizations: handing over the management of changes to an additional and dedicated structure may be self-defeating if change is meant to be a built-in capacity of the organization as a whole. Instead, enterprise architects should be seen as fair brokers between business and systems stakeholders at the enterprise level, and business analysts and development teams at the application level.

Such a loose definition of enterprise architects is deliberate and serves a double purpose:

- It will facilitate the integration of EA responsibilities in existing organizations, without causing misunderstandings or frictions.

- It will enable a smooth evolution of EA responsibilities as enterprise architectures evolve.

The same approach to this job description is applied to those of other contributors simply defined as business analysts, systems architects, software engineers, and systems administrators.

Scope & Schedules

As demonstrated by Waterfall development models, embarking on sizable and complex projects on the assumption that detailed scope and schedules can be set upfront may be very hazardous. Conversely, dealing iteratively with projects' scope (or space), schedules (or pace), and development steps (or paths) may lead into quagmires when different contexts, time frames, and stakeholders are involved.

In principle, projects can span three different time frames:

- Business: set by market moves and enterprise business plans

- Systems: set by organization and technologies

- Engineering: set by development constraints and the availability of resources

In practice, the objective of planning should be to avoid overlaps and to try to wrap engineering time frames into business and systems ones, thus paving the way to dynamic adjustments of scope, schedules, price, and quality.

For projects set at the enterprise level, decision-making processes (cf. chapter 10) will help to dynamically adjust the expectations and commitments of business analysts and systems architects regarding the scope and schedule of organizational and systems changes. These adjustments will determine the leeway allowed to projects' schedules at the system level (figure 13-1).

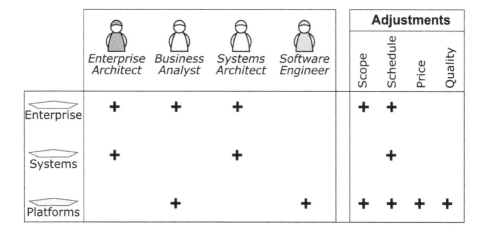

Figure 13-1. *Parties & Adjustments*

Once the scope and schedule of changes at the architecture level are set, business analysts and applications' development teams can proceed with adjustments of scope, schedule, price, and quality.

Such adjustments could bring mutual benefits through a more effective use of resources (reduced engineering costs) and a faster adaptation to market moves (increased business value). Price could also be used to compensate for unbalanced benefits of adjustments to scope or schedule.

Quality, summarily defined as the probability that nothing will go amiss during a product's life cycle, is set on two dimensions:

- Product (or intrinsic) quality is determined by the resources, time and engineering skills invested in the process and its supporting environment, with well-understood relationships between means and ends.

- Functional (or external) quality is contingent on the reliability of requirements and the stability of the business environment, both subject to uncertainties.

Compared to product quality, an engineering variable that can be managed in line with the criticality of applications (e.g., medical devices), functional quality is directly affected by the expected shelf-life of applications. Nonetheless, when business value is not affected by delays, more time given to decision-making will usually improve products' functional as well as product quality.

Given that projects managed independently at the application level offer more latitude for direct negotiation and win-win adjustments between business stakeholders and development teams, such projects should be the default option. Accordingly, enterprise architects should try to organize projects in order to circumscribe responsibilities to well-identified business units.

Development Steps

Beyond the open-ended list of labels given by methodologies to boxes and arrows (e.g., requirements, specifications, design, high level, low level, detailed), the question is basically the same: how many steps and intermediate outcomes are necessary between the inception of a project and its completion?

In a lean, just-in-time, and frictionless pure software realm, the answer would be none — a scenario that would minimize the waste of time and/or resources. Assuming projects are free of organizational, functional, or technical dependencies, developments could be carried out directly from processes to applications through iterations combining requirements, development and tests, and deployment (figure 13-2a). Decision-making (cf. chapter 10) could also be streamlined between enterprise workshop (for business objectives and systems constraints), applications workshop (for users' requirements), and systems workshop (for deployment).

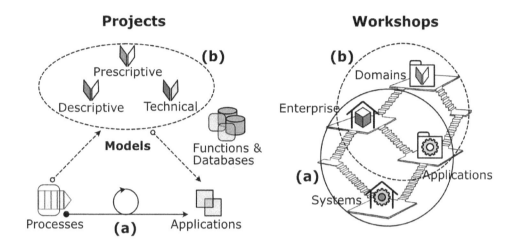

Figure 13-2. Direct (solid line) & Phased (dashed line) Development Models

That straightforward development model is not limited to stand-alone applications. It can also pertain to applications relying on systems functions, providing that requirements are stable — a condition that can be expected if functions are supposed to be shared across the architecture. In that case, EA frameworks (cf. chapter 5) should secure easy access to all relevant resources, preferably through agreed-upon models (cf. chapter 7). Such a development model, typical of business-driven requirements, can also be applied to architecture-driven projects; for instance, to Quality of service (QoS) developments.

By contrast, a phased development model (figure 13-2b) characterizes architecture-driven projects, with intermediate outcomes or milestones used to manage organizational, functional, or engineering dependencies. Assuming an architecture framework, development teams would collaborate through the exchange of models: descriptive or Computation independent (from the enterprise workshop), prescriptive or Platform independent (from the domains workshop), and technical or

Platform specific (from the applications workshop). These issues will be detailed in the next chapter.

Alignment of Expectations & Commitments

Assuming requirements are properly refactored (cf. chapter 12), the role of EA is to organize projects across workshops and to manage their progress, while taking into account changes in environments and agendas. For that to be possible, the parties concerned need to share a common understanding of the projects' outcomes and work units, without having to dig into the specifics of business contents or engineering works.

That kind of conceptual flyover, connecting business analysts with systems architects and software engineers, can be achieved with user stories and Use cases (figure 13-3):

- User stories, a companion technique of Agile methods, are meant to handle requirements' capture. They are at their best for self-contained projects, providing that direct collaboration can be attained between users, business analysts, and development teams.

- Use cases (UC), the entry point of the Unified Modeling Language (UML), put the focus on the part played by supporting systems; the objective is to detail what happens between systems and environments.

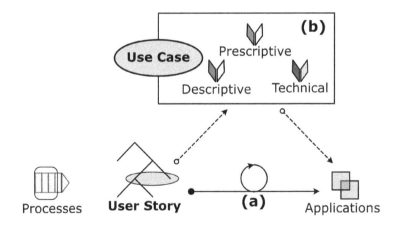

Figure 13-3. User Stories' (a) & Use Cases' (b) Development Models

The complementarity between user stories and Use cases — the former focused on business requirements, the latter on functional ones — can be used to integrate iterative (a) and phased (b) development processes.

User Stories & Iterative Development

Iterative development models can be seen as the archetype of lean processes, as they are meant to do away with the waste of intermediate artifacts, physical or otherwise. Beyond the specifics of Agile methodologies, iterative development models can be characterized as:

- Made up of the same generic engineering activity or a combination of basic ones

- Being performed repetitively by the same organizational unit, which is empowered with full responsibility from inception to completion

- Made up of iterations guarded by a set of invariants, with the iterations being carried out until a specific exit conditions can be met

Projects meeting these conditions should constitute the elementary units of EA engineering.

Agile Development Principles

The Agile development model, as pioneered by the eponymous Manifesto, enumerates twelve principles: ten are relevant and beneficial to all projects independently of engineering objectives and circumstances; two are contingent on demanding prerequisites:

- Early and continuous delivery of valuable software to customers

- Collective decision-making and responsibility of parties (typically business analysts and software engineers) throughout the project

These two conditions induce far-reaching consequences that characterize iterative developments:

- They should not depend on cross dependencies between business units; otherwise, collective decision-making and responsibility would be impracticable

- There should be no milestones or intermediate outcomes; otherwise they would prevent continuous delivery

As a corollary, iterative development models are at their best for complex and self-contained projects that could benefit from direct and continuous collaboration. But they fall short when teams cannot be given full responsibility over the exploration of problem spaces, the choice of development paths, and the pace of deliveries.

Enterprise architects should therefore try to dodge these hazards and design projects in order to make the best of each development model.

User Stories & Models

User stories are literal descriptions of actual users' operations, expressed in their own language, natural or otherwise, independently of supporting systems and development models. Stories are meant to be told before being written, and that's their underlying rationale: expressing requirements as narratives that weave circumstances, roles, events, operations, and outcomes.

Combined with backlogs (a management tool handling prioritized lists, cf. chapter 14), users' stories constitute the cornerstone of Agile projects and enable straight iterative development without the need for any intermediate artifacts other than code. Although EA should not be concerned with the nuts and bolts of self-contained developments, their outcomes are not necessarily specific to business domains and may contribute to architecture capabilities. In that case, their objectives and schedules should be managed at the enterprise level in conjunction with those of phased engineering projects.

User stories (figure 13-4), like any other kind of requirements, should be anchored (#) to business entities already managed at the enterprise level, whenever they can be identified (cf. chapter 12). Taking advantage of the iterative nature of developments, such attachments can be introduced progressively with managed business entities (a), other modeled objects (b), or with terms only defined in enterprise thesauruses (c). With ontologies providing a conceptual integration of thesauruses and models (cf. chapter 9), most attachments could be managed through automated indexing tools.

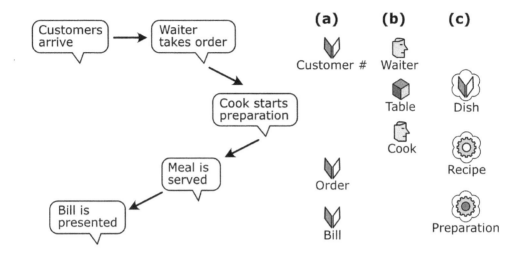

Figure 13-4. User Story & Model

User stories are not models, which are deemed superfluous in iterative developments. However, they, like requirements in general, can be drafted to uncover alignments with enterprise architecture (cf. chapter 12); for example:

- Roles, events, objects, operations, and locations mentioned in stories could be linked to corresponding capabilities, as defined by the enterprise's organization.

- Activities could be redefined with regard to Aristotle's three unities for action, place, and time (cf. chapter 12).

That divide between stories and models, and the semantic bridge spanning it, mark the preserve of enterprise architects. From that dividing point, user stories can be either:

- Developed as self-contained projects, below the radar of enterprise architects; or

- Mapped to broader business objectives and systems functional architecture, with their engineering managed as part of enterprise architecture

User & Business Stories

Given that user stories and broader business objectives are both set on the periphery of systems models, established modeling schemes of generalization and specialization (cf. chapter 8) are of little use in bridging the gap between concrete and specific stories, on the one hand, and abstract and comprehensive business objectives, policies, and strategies, on the other hand. Enter ontologies, which are meant to support the whole range of the enterprise's symbolic representations.

Taking stories literally, ontologies can be used to connect the narratives of users with the plots of business strategies; for example (figure 13-5):

- Making direct references to current prescriptive (e.g., *Bill*) or descriptive (e.g., *Customer Profile*) representations

- Using thesauruses to link concrete semantics (e.g., *Cook dish*) to general ones (e.g., *Molecular Cooking*)

- Linking concrete practices (e.g., *Customer complains*) to business strategies (e.g., *Customer Loyalty Program*), which are represented by Knowledge graphs

- Using partitions (e.g., *Dishes & Wines* is a cross between categories) to support decision-making (e.g., *Suggest wine*)

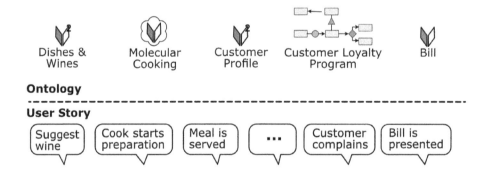

Figure 13-5. Mapping User Stories to Strategic Business Plots

The transparency and traceability of EA decision-making can be critically enhanced by bringing the semantics of user stories, and consequently of business processes, under a comprehensive conceptual canopy covering business as well as systems perspectives. Yet, more can be achieved if the mapping of user stories to business models and policies can be mirrored with corresponding changes in systems models.

To that end, some kind of Application modeling interface (AMI) — an equivalent to the Application programming interface (API) — could be devised in order to bind business processes to the models of supporting systems independently of engineering solutions. That can be done with Use cases.

By introducing UC, enterprise architects could manage and assess changes across maps (objectives or models) and territories (processes or enterprise), providing for (figure 13-6):

- The continuity and consistency of user stories with regard to enterprise objectives (a)

- The traceability of changes in business processes, as implemented by systems (b)

- The continuity and consistency of enterprise decision-making with regard to organization (c) and systems (d)

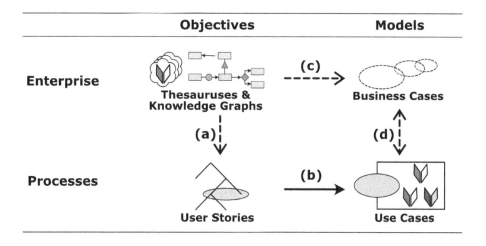

Figure 13-6. Traceability (solid line) & Consistency (dashed lines)

The next sections examine the role of Use cases as hubs between requirements and systems, and between systems and organization.

Use Cases & Models

As already noted, Agile development models fall short when conditions about collective responsibility and continuous delivery cannot be met, which is often the case for architecture-based projects. That limitation is sometimes seen as a matter of scale, to be dealt with by scaffolding Agile projects with procedures. But that understanding is misleading because architectures are not defined by size but by complexity, especially at the enterprise level, where systems' complexities are compounded by business ones. Alternatively, the procedural harnessing of Agile projects can be replaced by UCs serving as Application modeling interfaces between Agile and phased systems-engineering processes.

Use Cases as Application Modeling Interfaces

First devised by Ivar Jacobson before being integrated into UML, UCs are meant to describe what happens between users and systems in a simple and intuitive modeling language, with straightforward mapping to systems models.

Strictly speaking, a Use case can be defined by:

- A primary actor, possibly seconded by contributing (or secondary) ones

- A triggering event, possibly qualified by its features and/or conditions attached to the primary actor or context

- A set of interactions, possibly empty (e.g., batch application), and some expected outcome

Although such a bare-bones definition covers only part of what can be done with Use cases, it provides a clear, simple, and robust description:

- Clear and simple: while UCs can be fleshed out with detailed conditions and interactions, these details are not necessary to the core definition and can thus be postponed without impairing the relevance of the initial description.

• Robust: since the validity of the core definition is not contingent on conditions and refinements, simple and solid UCs can be defined and endorsed early in the process, before being further enriched iteratively.

Use cases are by nature two-sided:

1. As black boxes, they handle the users' perspective (descriptive or prescriptive models) but hide the corresponding implementation in systems.

2. As white boxes, they handle the systems perspective (prescriptive or technical models).

Use Cases as Black Boxes

On the *user side* of the box, UCs are specific, concrete, and focused on interactions with systems; they can be introduced directly, extracted from requirements, or serve as modeling extensions of user stories.

When rooted in user stories (figure 13-7), episodes supported by systems are marked as Use cases (represented by ellipses) in enterprise thesauruses, whether or not they are to be modeled as such; for example:

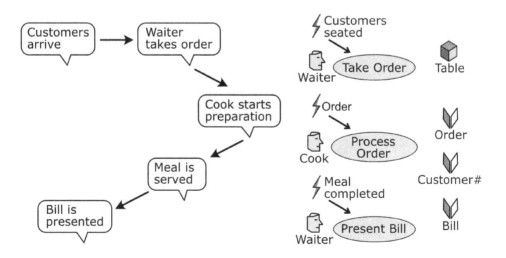

Figure 13-7. From User Story to Use Cases

- Three UCs are defined from the user story above (figure 13-4): *Take order*, *Process Order*, and *Present Bill*.

- Each UC is triggered by a single event (*Customers seated*, *Order*, or *Meal completed*), and a primary actor (*Waiter* or *Cook*).

- These UCs are tied to the enterprise architecture through the persistent anchor *Customer#* and business objects *Order* and *Bill*.

It must be stressed that whatever their source (defined directly or derived from requirements or user stories), Use cases should not be set across (but may encompass) units of space, action, and event (cf. chapter 12). Maintaining the integrity of these units will guarantee the continuity and consistency of Use cases serving as Application modeling interfaces between business and systems sides.

Use Cases as White Boxes

On the *system side* of the box (figure 13-8), UCs can be detailed through established modeling languages; typically with UML diagrams for activities (business logic), classes (business objects), sequences (execution of UCs), and states (execution control).

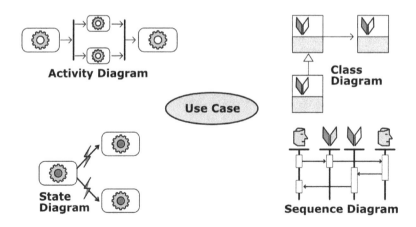

Figure 13-8. The Systems Perspective of Use Cases (UML Diagrams)

Use cases' duality (business and systems) and versatility (coarse- and fine-grained descriptions) makes them the tool of choice for enterprise architects. They can be used as black boxes to wrap all kinds of projects, and as white boxes to detail the footprints of architectural ones, setting the groundwork for Model-based systems engineering (cf. chapter 14).

Use Cases & Value Streams

Value streams can be understood as the operational counterpart of value chains (cf. chapter 4); i.e., the description of steps realizing value chains. The distinction often introduced between the business and engineering aspects of value streams is especially relevant for EA, because it makes explicit the difference of nature between business and systems architectures, even if the discrepancies can be ironed out with Agile projects. But when the difference can't be overlooked, it constitutes a major issue for EA that must be accounted for. To that effect, Use cases can serve as crossroads, associated with business streams when handled as black boxes, and to engineering streams when handled as white boxes.

Use Cases' Scenarios & Dependencies

Iterative development models build programs by increments, starting with typical scenarios in user stories and carrying on with alternative execution paths. Given that a number of operations (e.g., identification, authorization) are bound to appear repeatedly in different scenarios, not to mention stories, their specifications must be consolidated across scenarios and their development factored out. Whereas Agile project teams use ad-hoc dynamic lists (or backlogs) to iteratively define and rank the corresponding work units, such schemes are contingent on teams' autonomy and collective responsibility. When that's not possible (i.e., when some coordination is needed between different teams or organizational units), variants and dependencies must be explicitly documented and backlog mechanisms extended in order to operate at the architecture level (cf. chapter 14).

With Use cases, variants and dependencies are documented with extension points and <<include> and <<extend>> connectors.

Extension points (diamonds) are branching conditions that can be directly defined from structural and functional partitions (cf. chapter 12). The connectors

<<include>> and <<extend>> are used for conditional and unconditional bindings, respectively. For example (figure 13-9):

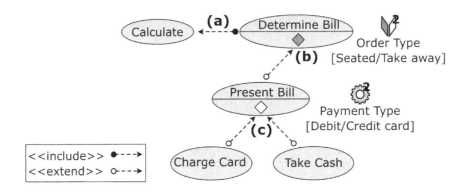

Figure 13-9. Use Cases: Extension Points & Connectors

• ***Determine Bill*** always includes ***Calculate*** (a).

• ***Present Bill*** extends ***Determine Bill*** only for seated customers (b). The extension point is structural (black diamond) because it's set upfront by the context (***Order Type***).

• ***Charge Card*** and ***Take Cash*** extend ***Present Bill*** depending on customers' choice of payment (c). The extension point is functional (white diamond) because it's set during execution (***Payment Type***).

Although there is no general consensus about the semantics of Use cases' connectors, unambiguous semantics are needed for their use at the architecture level if models are to support collaboration between teams over time. That can be achieved by applying the semantics of composition and aggregation, already defined for models (cf. chapter 2), to the control of UC execution:

• <<include>> can be understood in terms of composition: the included UC is controlled (or identified) by the thread of the one making the inclusion.

- <<extend>> can be understood in terms of aggregation: the extending UC can be executed (or identified) on its own.

It must be noted that the semantics of connectors have no bearing on the semantics of the UCs themselves; instead, they only pertain to the execution of UCs in the processes considered. The semantic neutrality of connectors has clear benefits:

- *Modularity*: the semantics of UCs should not be affected by the context of their utilization.

- *Complementarity*: the mapping between user stories and UCs must be maintained independently of the development model, Agile or phased. Such a mapping of user stories into uncommitted systems' facades marks a point of departure for enterprise architects, who can decide whether such facades remain simple post-its or become openings on engineering processes that link user stories to systems architectures.

- *Separation of concerns*: the neutrality of connectors means that functional architecture can be discussed and assessed by enterprise and systems architects without having to consider the business-specific contents of UCs.

Use Cases & Architecture

The role of Use cases can be generalized as an Application modeling interface between business requirements and architecture functional capabilities. To that end, the management of changes in EA should rely on uncommitted modeling or development methods. Use cases positioned between enterprise organization and architecture functional capabilities can achieve such neutrality (figure 13-10).

Given that requirements are anchored to business entities and process-execution units, both identified at the architecture level (cf. chapter 12), the objective should be to align corresponding Use cases with architecture functional capabilities in accordance with the Model-View-Controller (MVC) pattern (cf. chapter 5):

- Model/Entities: persistent and shared execution

- View/Boundaries: transient and local execution

- Controller: transient and shared execution

- Services: instant and shared execution

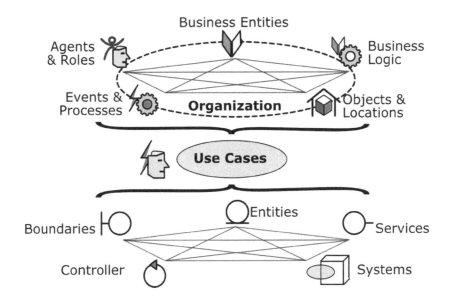

Figure 13-10. *Use Cases as a Functional Bridge between Enterprise Organization*
& Architecture Functional Capabilities

Functional dependencies between Use cases, represented by <<include>> and <<extend>> connectors, could thus be checked against architecture capability independently of the specifics of their business contents; for example (figure 13-11):

- ***Take Order*** initiates an execution thread (#) identified by a request from a primary actor (a)

- ***Take Order*** includes ***Read Customer*** record (b)

- ***Check Account*** extends ***Take Order*** for some customers with a functional dependency: the thread is given with a customer's name and returned with authorization (c)

- **Plan Delivery** extends **Take Order** with a functional dependency: the thread is given with the customer's address and returned with time (d)

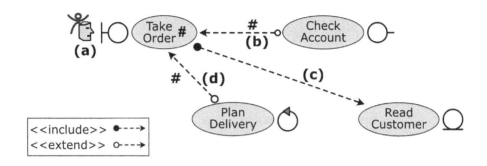

Figure 13-11. *Use Case & Systems Functional Capabilities*

The MVC-pattern family (there are several variations) takes on a new dimension with the digital transformation. As systems morph into networks of agents of a diverse and even undecided nature, enterprise architects can no longer rely on stable and well-defined categories of gatekeepers (e.g., thin or fat client, web browser) to maintain the integrity of systems. Instead, enterprise architects should consider functional agents with behaviors characterized by contracts and policies — something that can be done with Use cases serving as transitions between requirements and architectures' capabilities.

Business Processes & Architectural Changes

While Use cases provide the transparency and traceability of changes at the system level, enterprise architects should also consider how to integrate systems' and organizational changes, and how to align them with long-term business objectives.

Business Process Models

Compared to Use cases, which are focused on the interactions between systems and environments, Business process models (BPM) put the focus on organization (cf. chapter 4). If that makes BPM the preferred approach on the business side, it also comes with a double caveat:

- Changes in supporting systems have to be carried out either wholly for entire processes, or piecemeal for self-contained applications. Neither option is in keeping with a continuous and consistent adaptation of enterprise architectures to their environments.

- Such models are built on the assumption that processes (and implicitly, organization) can be designed independently of systems architecture capabilities. That assumption, which may be pertinent to architectures built from scratch and deployed in one move, is at odds with the ongoing modernization of legacy systems and the digital integration of business processes and supporting systems.

To overcome these drawbacks and be yoked to enterprise architecture, BPM must be anchored to business entities and execution units identified at the architecture level.

But BPM, in general, and Business process model and notation (BPMN), in particular, suffers from a flattened perspective that makes no distinction between the details of business logic and the control of business processes. This amalgam prevents principled and modular adjustments between processes and architectures:

- On the business side, the difficulty is dealing with the complexity of specific activities and rules without having to use pseudo-programming languages. A distinction between architectural mechanisms and business logic would reduce complexity, if only through greater transparency.

- On the systems side, the mix of architectural and business concerns impedes the separation of shared business functions (ideally supported through a Service-oriented architecture) from domain-specific applications (e.g., developed from user stories).

For enterprise architects, the objective should therefore be to set aside those BPMN core constructs that can be aligned with modeling anchors (cf. chapter 3) (figure 13-12):

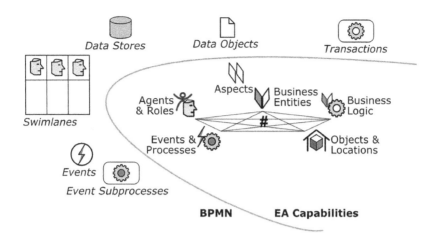

Figure 13-12. *Mapping BPMN to EA Capabilities*

• Business entities are not directly represented by BPMN; they can be referenced through the alignment of aspects with BPMN data and flow objects

• Activities can be directly mapped to BPMN transactions

• Process-execution states can be associated with event subprocesses

• Events can be directly mapped

• Roles can be mapped to organizational swimlanes defined by BPMN

These constructs can be used to define the architectural backbones of Business process models. Their mapping to enterprise architecture could then be carried out at the modeling and conceptual levels. For the former, backbones could be anchored to systems models. For the latter, the terms used in BPM could be indexed in thesauruses; more generally, processes' components could be mapped to business patterns, policies, or strategies defined in ontologies (cf. chapter 9).

Allowing for one step further on the path to the integration of BPM with enterprise architecture, Use cases open the door to a selective approach that sets apart what should be known (the capabilities needed to support business processes) from what can be hidden under the architecture floor (the sequence and details of activities).

Business Processes & Use Cases

Activities and flows in BPMN and UML diagrams are defined imperatively; i.e., expressed as sequences of operations and exchanges. By contrast, Use-case diagrams are declarative: the <<include>> and <<extend>> connectors put constraints on execution without specifying the sequences or the nature of the flows exchanged. It ensues that, as far as EA is concerned, business processes can be reduced to Use cases that are set in swimlanes associated with primary actors. The specifics of activities and business logic would be masked, as well as the details of data and control flows. Instead, UC connectors could be supplemented with communication semantics derived from data and control flows. While details may vary, communication semantics should be clear about the changes in the state of objects, processes, or expectations induced by the exchanges (figure 13-13):

- Data flow: no change; e.g., the message exchanged between **Take Order** and **Read Customer** has no consequence (a)

- Asynchronous control flow: change in environment or systems representations; e.g., the message exchanged between **Take Order** and **Plan Delivery** creates an expectation for the former and induces a commitment from the latter (b)

- Synchronous control flow: coupled change in environment and systems representations; e.g., changes induced by the message between **Take Order** and **Check Account** are supposed to be immediate (c)

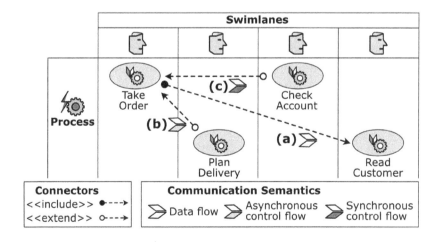

Figure 13-13. UC View of a Business Process

In accordance with the neutrality noted above, the types of connectors and the attached communication semantics should be defined independently; the former dealing with the channels, and the latter, with the contents. Their pairing is therefore a matter of design; e.g., using <<extend>> connectors with asynchronous communication is often presented as best practice.

Use Cases & EA Changes

Since swimlanes are defined by the organization, their alignment with Use cases introduces a mapping mechanism between systems- and enterprise-architecture capabilities. Similarly, the association of swimlanes with locations does the same with operations, mapping technical architecture capabilities with physical environments.

Use cases could thus be used to bring together the business and engineering aspects of changes (figure 13-14):

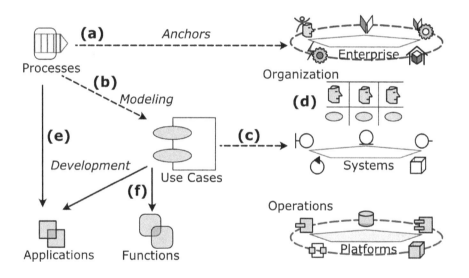

Figure 13-14. Use Cases as Hubs of Changes

Business objectives: changes in business processes are mapped to EA anchors (a), modeled through Use cases (b), and aligned with systems' capabilities (c) and organization (d).

Engineering processes: corresponding developments can be carried out directly through autonomous projects (e) or through as Use cases (f).

The remaining issue is the conceptual integration of changes in organization and systems with business models and objectives.

Typical Cases

At the system level, Use cases seem to be the tool of choice for a continuous and consistent integration of heterogeneous requirements into engineering processes. What is missing at the enterprise level is a mapping of architectural changes to business objectives, policies, and strategies.

Since these mappings are shared by executives and stakeholders across organizations and over time, they are generally formulated in terms of abstractions set across a range of diverse dimensions: unspecific scales (e.g., general, detailed, more detailed), data modeling (conceptual, logical, physical), decision-making (strategic, tactical, operational), etc. For enterprise architects, the challenge is to define actionable junctures between business expectations and their realization through EA engineering.

Extending the semantics of Use cases provides a way to identify and manage business shifts that emerge bottom-up from environments, and to integrate them with business policies and strategies that are planned top-down.

Taking a cue from Alistair Cockburn's seminal work (cf. bibliography), Use cases can be characterized with regard to execution and modeling level (figure 13-15):

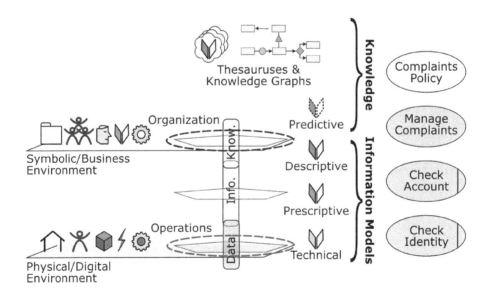

Figure 13-15. Typical Cases

- Business cases (green background) are meant to fulfill broadly defined objectives. As such, they are not supposed to be executed and are not limited to information models (descriptive or predictive), but can rely on knowledge (thesauruses, Knowledge graphs, and/or predictive models); e.g., ***Complaints Policy***.

- Use cases (orange background) are meant to describe what happens between enterprises and business environments. As such, they are supposed to be executed, and thus should only reference information models (descriptive or prescriptive); e.g., ***Manage Complaints***.

- System cases (orange background, slashed ellipse) are the parts of Use cases directly supported by systems; therefore, they should only rely on prescriptive or technical models. Some system cases correspond only to symbolic activities (e.g., ***Check Account***), whereas others are also tied to physical ones (e.g., ***Check Identity***).

The semantics of <<include>> and <extend>> connectors are not affected for Use cases and system cases, which are both meant to be executed in reference to information models. Taking the example of basic authentication and authorization operations (figure 13-16):

- ***Open Session***, ***Check Identity***, and ***Manage Session*** are shared at the enterprise level (prescriptive models)

- ***Open Session*** and ***Check Identity*** are specific to platforms (technical models)

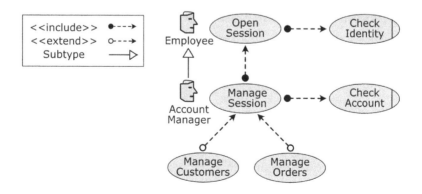

Figure 13-16. Use & System Cases

Use cases can thus be decomposed into system cases until they meet Aristotle's condition of three unities.

Conversely, given that the <<include>> and <extend>> connectors are defined in terms of execution, they cannot be used with business cases, which are not supposed to be executed. The issue then is to determine how business objectives are realized by architectural changes represented by Use cases.

The Case for Abstraction

The relationships between business processes and strategies, or between systems and enterprise architecture, are often expressed in terms of abstraction; the somewhat logical corollary is that concrete descriptions of the ways processes should realize strategies, or systems should support enterprise objectives, are bypassed. But to ensure the continuity and consistency of EA changes, charts need to be more specific about what lies between actual and virtual representations.

As far as modeling is concerned, the meaning of abstraction depends on context:

• For descriptive representations, abstraction is applied to instances of objects and behaviors, sorting them into categories by taking away features deemed to be irrelevant.

• For prescriptive representations, abstraction is applied to specifications, factoring out shared features (generalization) or adding new ones (specialization).

That semantic distinction may seem academic, but it's not because descriptive models are used to decide between shared entities and shared functions in prescriptive models. To understand that point, it must be reminded that the assignment of capabilities between structures and processes is a major architectural issue; for enterprise architecture that is done through the mapping of objects and behaviors identified in descriptive models into the system components of prescriptive models that implement both structures and functions:

• For descriptive entities (representing objects), the issue is to factor out shared structures, as well as common behaviors, in order to determine their counterparts in systems (as represented by prescriptive models). That can only be done through abstraction.

- For descriptive functions (representing behaviors), there are no "things" to factor out: prescriptive descriptions can be fully defined in terms of composition or aggregation of operations, and there is no need for abstraction.

On that account, Use cases, which represent systems' behaviors, can be combined and mapped to functions without the need for abstraction, even if abstractions are used to describe associated events, actors, and business entities; for example, *Employee* and *Account Manager* (figure 13-16).

Still, business cases introduce a dilemma: on the one hand, they are not meant to be executed, which suggests some higher level of abstraction. On the other hand, they rely on more than information models, such that abstraction semantics cannot be consistently applied across symbolic representations. The discrepancies of abstraction semantics between systems and business models raise the broader issue of the representation of business objectives.

Aligning Architectural Changes with Business Objectives

Business objectives can be defined in terms of goals or changes: goals rely on abstractions to bring together actual and virtual representations, and changes describe the path of planned realizations. Business cases illustrate the difference.

Abstraction vs. Realization

Business cases appear to be abstract by construction as well as by purpose:

- Construction: like abstract descriptions of objects, which cannot be realized (or instantiated), business cases are not supposed to be executed.

- Purpose: business cases are introduced to describe broader objectives and policies detached from immediate and concrete circumstances or implementation.

The apparent parallelism of business cases to the abstraction of objects would suggest applying to business cases the <<generalize>> connector, added by UML to the initial pair of <<include>> and <<extend>>.

Accordingly, Use cases would inherit whatever is defined by business cases. Yet that comes with a double caveat, for construction as well as purpose:

- Construction: as noted above, the semantics of abstraction differ between objects and behaviors; that discrepancy would be compounded if inheritance were applied to the aspects of business and Use cases (actor, event, activities) beyond the limits of information models, i.e., with different semantics.

- Purpose: the raison d'être of business cases is to set broader conceptual references, not to support the reuse (or inheritance) of properties or operations.

Resorting to <<generalize>> connectors between Use cases and business cases would therefore be doubly confusing: first, with regard to what the former inherits from the latter, and then, with regard to what pertains to enterprise and systems architecture, respectively.

Instead, representations should be explicit about the epistemic difference between objectives (business cases) and their realization (Use cases); the former relying on a mix of knowledge and information, and the latter, fully expressed through information models (cf. chapter 9). For example (figure 13-17):

- *Manage Complaints* is a Use case extending *Manage Customers* (a)

- *Manage Complaints* realizes the business case *Complaints Policy* (b1), which itself implements *Food Safety Regulations* (b2)

- *Manage Complaints* can thus combine specific resources (e.g., *Incidents Index*, c) with the ones associated with *Complaints Policy*, including data about *Risks* (d) and algorithms for *Compensation Assessment* (e).

- *Manage Complaints* can then include *Assess Compensation* (f) and execute the assessment using all the resources of its augmented context.

Representations from models and thesauruses can thus be combined without ambiguity into case diagrams, with arrangements of prospective and actual descriptions shifting over time.

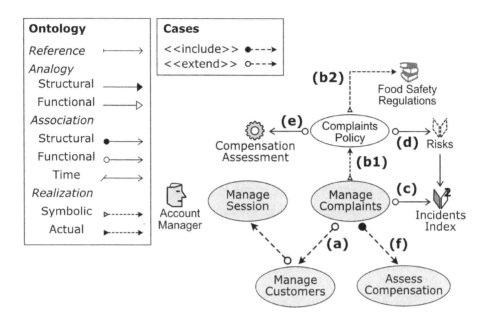

Figure 13-17. Business Cases (green) & Use Cases (orange)

Changes & Decision-making

EA change management can be seen as the yin to the decision-making yang, as suggested by the tight integration of architectural changes with the Observation-Orientation-Decision-Action (OODA) loop (cf. chapter 10):

- Regarding observation and orientation, enterprises immersed in digital environments have much to learn through a dynamic reassessment of changes in objectives and realizations.

- EA decisions are multifaceted and structured. Some parts are due for immediate execution, while others are commitments, possibly conditional, that will be carried out at a later date (fixed or not) — a scenario that entails planning and monitoring.

More fundamentally, dealing with changes in terms of objectives and realizations comes as a bottom-up complement to top-down decision-making, assuming a pragmatic attachment to the shifting reality of environments.

Taking advantage of a comprehensive and consistent representation of environments, organizations, and systems, roadmaps of objectives and realizations could be charted through business-, Use-, and system cases. These roadmaps could then be combined with strategy and policy profiles targeting environments, organizations, and systems architectures (cf. chapter 8).

Enterprise architects could then build dashboards to manage changes according to their source and nature, and their sway on enterprise governance (figure 13-18).

Institutional changes that are not decided at the corporate level should be managed separately. For example, changes in the Food and Drug Administration (**FDA**) regulations would be managed at the enterprise level through a **Complaints Policy** defined as a business case, in association with changes in the social environment, represented by a predictive model of exposure to **Risks** (figure 13-18a).

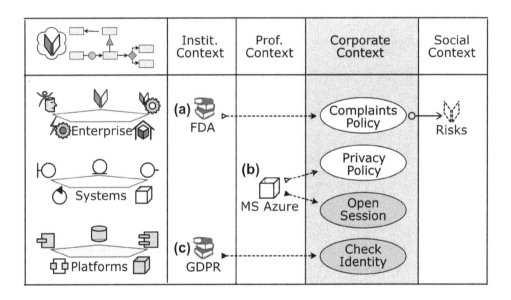

Figure 13-18. Monitoring Changes

All institutional changes don't have to be managed at the enterprise level; for example, compliance with the European Union's General Data Protection Regulation (GDPR) may be directly associated with a technical change at the platform level, which would be implemented through the ***Check Identity*** system case (figure 13-18c).

Changes in environments may also affect different EA levels, as is typically the case with strategic agreements negotiated in professional contexts. For example, a Microsoft (***MS***) ***Azure*** Cloud service contract would be associated with both organizational guidelines at the enterprise level (***Privacy Policy***) and a fully specified Use case (***Open Session***) (figure 13-18b).

Such dashboards concretize the role of Use cases (and their extension with business and system cases) at the nexus of EA decision-making, between objectives and realizations, organization and systems, and environments and enterprise. The next chapter will consider the engineering processes linking objectives and realizations.

CHAPTER 14.

Enterprise Architecture & Model-based Systems Engineering

Workshops combine Agile and Model-based systems engineering

Managing changes in complex organizations that operate in competitive environments is clearly a primary objective of enterprise architecture (EA). Previous chapters have laid the groundwork with regard to the perimeter of EA requirements (chapter 11), their refactoring (chapter 12), and the mapping of projects to changes in architectures (chapter 13). This chapter sets forth the pivotal role of models for the engineering of enterprise architecture.

Three principles have already been established regarding the scope of enterprise architecture:

- EA should only be concerned by changes affecting resources or mechanisms shared across the enterprise.

- EA should not be concerned by the internal workings of self-contained (or autonomous) development processes.

- EA engineering processes should be comprehensively defined and managed in terms of maps and territories.

On that account, the engineering responsibilities of enterprise architects can be set on two axes: defining and managing work units through models, and transforming and reusing models in various ways.

Model-based Systems Engineering

As noted in the last chapter, when Agile conditions about shared ownership and continuous delivery cannot be met, phased development processes are required, with models introduced to manage intermediate outcomes.

Whichever monikers are employed (based/driven, system/software, development/engineering), the primary objective of Model-based systems engineering (MBSE) should be to support a smooth integration of EA engineering processes independently of the type of development model, Agile or phased. That can be done by replacing procedural (or imperative) approaches with declarative ones, which set the conditions for engineering steps, instead of detailing how they should be carried out.

Engineering & Models

From an EA perspective, engineering processes begin with Use cases (cf. chapter 13); at that point, decisions are made whether Use cases remain facades or mark the inception of projects managed within the architectural remit. That's when case models are introduced:

- Business cases (green background) define objectives; they are not meant to be executed and can thus rely on the whole range of EA's symbolic representations.

- Use cases (orange background) describe what happens between enterprises and business environments. They are meant to be executed and thus engineered. Therefore, Use cases should only rely on systems' information models: descriptive, prescriptive, or technical.

- System cases (orange background, slashed ellipse) are the part of Use cases that directly address systems capabilities; as such, they should only rely on prescriptive and technical models.

Starting with these cases, models can serve different purposes, acting as:

- Customary documents: models can fulfill regulatory or contractual obligations set in business environments.

- End products: models can be used to generate code for digital environments.

- Exchange: models can support collaboration between organizational units (business or engineering) and/or communication over time.

- Repository: models can embody canned knowledge that is used and/or reused in different contexts.

- Napkins: models without organizational purpose can be reduced to fleeting sketches supporting direct collaboration between business analysts and software engineers; that's the case for self-contained (or autonomous) developments.

Given that customary documents and end products are set on the margins of engineering processes, enterprise architects should focus on models serving as means of exchange and repository.

When models are the means of exchange, the Object management group (OMG)'s Model driven architecture (MDA) can serve as a reference (cf. chapter 3), with its three levels of description neatly aligned with architecture layers (figure 14-1):

- Computation independent models (CIM) for organization and business processes; they correspond to descriptive models.

- Platform independent models (PIM) for the functions supported by systems independently of their implementation; they correspond to prescriptive models.

- Platform specific models (PSM) for applications and systems components that support systems functionalities given an implementation technology; they correspond to technical models.

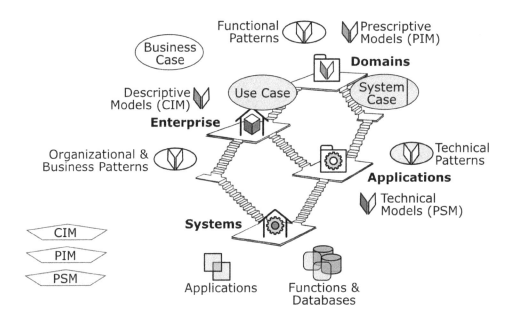

Figure 14-1. Engineering & Models

Data models, commonly known as conceptual, logical, and physical, are best understood as subsets of CIM, PIM, and PSM, respectively.

Finally, models can be used to capitalize on stable and reliable representations, or to embody business, organizational, or systems functional and technical patterns.

Using Models

Besides producing code, the raison d'être of engineering processes is to optimize the efficiency of work units, taking into account delivery and quality constraints. That rationale, often characterized as lean and just-in-time, is at the root of MBSE; since it also underlies Agile development models, it can serve to bring both approaches into a common engineering framework.

Applied to engineering processes, optimization implies a dynamic management of work units according to their status. With Agile, it can be done through direct collaboration between business analysts and development teams. But with phased processes, external dependencies prevent all-inclusive direct collaboration, and thus call for some mechanism to support the dynamic management of work units.

In addition to the direct editing of models by analysts, architects, or engineers, work units can handle models in two basic modes, mechanical or assisted (figure 14-2):

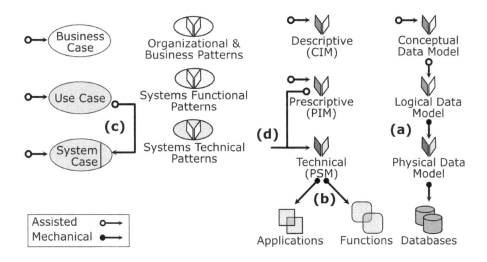

Figure 14-2. Using Models

Mechanical processing is deterministic: the outcome is defined by source models, targeted contexts, and parameters; for example:

- Generation of normalized databases' physical models (or schemas) (figure 14-2a)

- Generation of applications and functions (figure 14-2b)

By comparison, assisted processing combines decision-making with patterns or profiles (cf. chapter 8); for example:

- The design of system cases from Use cases, given systems technical patterns (figure 14-2c)

- The design (and then code generation) of applications, given prescriptive models that are expressed with a Domain-specific language (DSL), which takes into account systems functional and technical patterns (figure 14-2d)

By itself, sorting out full mechanical transformations from the ones calling for decision-making can greatly improve the traceability and transparency of engineering processes (cf. chapter 10). But even more substantial benefits come from the rationalization of the engineering processes.

Models & Work Units

If phased engineering processes are to reproduce Agile's dynamic definition and arrangement of work units, two conditions should be met:

- Artifacts must be set within a common engineering framework, defining the nature of their contents (e.g., document, model, code) and status (e.g., planned, complete, work-in-progress, delivered).

- Work units must be directly defined in relation to the processing of artifacts, without being folded into auxiliary activities (e.g., functional analysis, detailed design), and/or encumbered with ancillary documents.

Both requisites can benefit from digital formats, which enable a seamless integration of engineering flows independently of their nature (e.g., model, code, tests), as well as automated documentation processes. All engineering artifacts, from documents to code, can thus be expressed uniformly, thereby enabling work units to be defined directly in terms of model transformation, without introducing extraneous activities.

The departure from procedural solutions can be illustrated by taking a traditional V process and trimming the enclosing project-management activities (figure 14-3).

A simplified V development model (i.e., there is no consensus about the number or nature of phases) can be made of three basic tasks, doubled by corresponding validation (figure 14-3, left):

- The capture and analysis of requirements, dealing with business processes and descriptive (or CIM) models (a)

- Functional analysis and architectural design, dealing with Use cases and prescriptive (or PIM) models (b)

- Software design, development, and tests, implementing system cases and technical models, and delivering applications (c)

Applications would then be integrated with functions, deployed, and tested in operational environments (d).

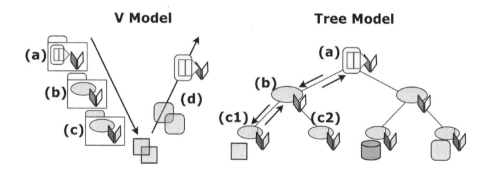

Figure 14-3. Processes & Work Units

Beyond the variety of alphabetic refinements (from Unified to Waterfall), procedural solutions suffer from a lack of flexibility. Instead of making room for decision-making in the course of developments, such processes are doubly constrained by predefined activities and requirements set upfront, not to mention the delays and overheads induced by the administration of encasing activities. Last but not least, such engineering processes make no provision for the specificity of enterprise- vs. systems-architecture projects.

By contrast, declarative engineering processes are built bottom-up from work units that are attached to targeted artifacts and driven by the state of development flows. Projects can thus be managed as trees that can be explored and developed dynamically according to the status of nodes and leaves (figure 14-3, right):

- Roots could be used to set contexts, business processes, and anchors in descriptive (or CIM) models (a, moving downward).

- Roots could also be associated with functions and anchors in prescriptive (or PIM) models.

- Use cases are first seen as black boxes (cf. chapter 13) anchored to descriptive (or PIM) models (b, moving downward).

- System cases are further detailed and anchored to technical (or PSM) models, and applications are developed and tested (c1, c2).

- Applications are integrated with functions, tested through use cases, and then used as white boxes; i.e., with their counterpart in systems (b, moving upward).

- Use cases are finally integrated, tested, and accepted in operational (processes') environments (a, moving upward).

It must be noted that the mapping between work units and models can be fine-grained and set dynamically depending on the operation (e.g., create, read, update, delete), scope (descriptive, prescriptive, technical), target (anchor, entity, aspect), and status (e.g., planned, current, suspended).

Transformation of Models

As already noted, the dynamic allocation of engineering work units is a key factor for the management of changes in enterprise architecture. That's not an issue for Agile projects, given their autonomy, direct collaboration, and collective responsibility. However, phased projects tasked with the development of architecture functions often answer to a plurality of stakeholders, preventing direct and continuous collaboration. Models provide an alternative communication mechanism.

A Taxonomy of Operations

Using models to support collaboration implies a common understanding of what can be done with them (figure 14-4):

- Development: new contents are added to models in line with their syntax, semantics, and purpose. Development is the default option at models' inception (e.g., requirements), but tends to be problematic downstream because new contents may affect the consistency of existing ones, thus inducing regression issues.

- Refactoring: the contents of models are reformulated or edited in accordance with the syntax and semantics of their modeling language. Refactoring operations should be explicit with purposes because they are not necessarily congruent; e.g., the respective outcomes of database optimization (with regard to digital processing) and normalization (with regard to business logic) are usually at odds.

- Translation: the contents of models are expressed using a different language. Translations are straightforward for syntax and semantics (e.g., between programming languages), but turn to interpretation when the pragmatics of business domains are involved (e.g., with DSL).

- Transformation: processes combine translation with development, mixing language and contents. Source and target models are associated with different engineering steps in order to change models' contents, either technical (e.g., reverse engineering and migration to new platforms) and/or business (e.g., code generation from DSL).

	Language	Contents	Examples
Development	=	>	Requirements, specifications
Refactoring	=	=	Optimization, normalization
Translation	>	=	Programs
Transformation	>	>	Reverse engineering, code generation

Figure 14-4. Processing of Models

In principle, refactoring and translation should be neutral (i.e., they should not involve decisions affecting the contents of models) in order to enable automated execution. In practice, such neutrality is conditioned by a clear divide between language constructs (syntax) and model contents (semantics): overlaps between modeling-language grammar and domain semantics would critically hinder the realization of the benefits of model transformations.

Prerequisites of Languages

If anything, model transformations must be nonregressive: automated refactoring or translations should not affect the validity of models' contents. To that end, there should be no blending between syntax and semantics; taking a simple example (figure 14-5):

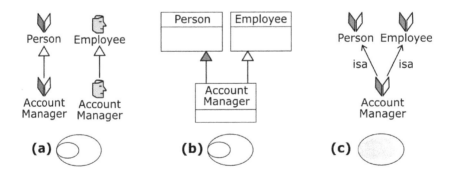

Figure 14-5. Transformations of Models (ellipses represent syntactic and semantic contents)

- A descriptive model could describe **Person** and **Account Manager** as business entities, and **Account Manager** and **Employee** as roles. The meanings would be unequivocal (ellipses neatly drawn): a subset of individuals with inheritance of features for business entities, and a subset of status with inheritance of abilities, responsibilities or authorizations for roles (a).

- The same clarity can be attained with nondescript classes and explicit connectors for structural (black triangle) and functional (white triangle) inheritance (b).

- By contrast, nondescript classes and connectors induce a blending between syntax and semantics (blurred ellipses): the *isa* connector takes different meanings when applied to **Person** (an agent) and **Employee** (a role). Such blending will critically affect the reliability of translations by introducing self-reproducing ambiguities in outcomes (c).

It bears reminding that the issue is not the validity of models' contents, whose determination should not be within the remit of enterprise architects, but the reliability of transformations. On that account, clear syntactic constructs interpreted by rules engines should be enough for the automated translation and refactoring of models. However, that's not the case for models' development and transformation, because in both cases, the semantics of the new contents will have to be taken into account.

Adding new contents to models means sorting out business and engineering semantics. While modelers, dealing with requirements or specifications, can be assisted by smart editors backed by patterns or profiles (cf. chapter 8), mechanical transformations can only rely on rules engines, which scale poorly with exponential complexity.

At the system level, complexity comes from the mix of modeling language and business semantics, first for the intrinsic contents of models, then for the rules in patterns. At the enterprise level, the difficulty is compounded by the semantic diversity and specificity of the different business domains.

Such complexity can be managed up to a point, providing that the scope of mechanical operations can be circumscribed, typically through DSL; but that's too limited an option at the enterprise level.

Meta-models' Limitations

Meta-models, being models of models (cf. chapter 8), may appear at first as a panacea for EA models. Taking our modeling paradigm as an example (cf. chapter 2), there would be two meta-models (figure 14-6):

- For descriptive models of environments (CIM): targeted categories (e.g., Account, Customer, Order) would be coalesced into meta-categories of objects or behaviors, actual or symbolic.

- For prescriptive models of systems (PIM): targeted classes would be coalesced into meta-classes of models, views, or controllers.

Rules in functional patterns, defined between meta-models, would be used to transform instances of meta-categories (descriptive models) into instances of meta-classes (prescriptive models).

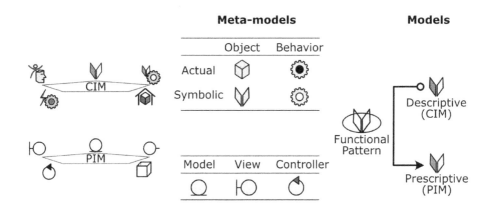

Figure 14-6. Meta-models & Transformation

Since meta-models' transformations still depend on rules engines, their effectiveness is determined by the modeling languages: transformations can be at their best when applied to clear and compact languages, or cumbersome and confusing when the translation of core syntax is polluted by semantic ambiguities.

That probably explains the patchy track record of meta-models with MBSE, from effective implementations of DSL to a motley of pointless profiles (around 230 and counting) from OMG.

OMG's Unified architecture framework (UAF) illustrates the dilemma of meta-models: in order to federate modeling languages, UAF meta-models have to climb the abstraction ladder well above the domains of concern (in that case, enterprise architecture). But up there, the meta-models become uprooted and detached from actual contexts or concerns. To compensate for the lack of concrete semantics, UAF introduces proxies under the guise of stereotypes (cf. chapter 8). Besides adding complexity, using stereotypes to rope meta-models to relevant meanings generates a double confusion:

- Between a core of syntax constructs and truth-preserving operations, supposedly shared by models and meta-models, and domain semantics, which are by nature specific

- Between the primary (or native) semantics of modeling languages, and the ones concocted by meta-languages to serve as proxies

As it happens, the confusion between the semantics of general-purpose and domain-specific languages mirrors the confusion between enterprise and systems architectures, both reflecting the limits of abstraction. For EA, the challenge is twofold: first, bringing together multiple and shifting business meanings; and second, bridging the conceptual gap between business and systems representations (cf. chapter 13).

The combination of MBSE with layered cases (business, Use, and system) provides an alternative to meta-models and abstraction.

MBSE & Enterprise Architecture

Model-based engineering processes are supposed to shore up some of the key issues of enterprise architecture, providing:

- Integration of engineering with EA

- Actionable maps, or the ability to manage changes directly from models without the trappings of administered activities whose only purpose is to mediate between objectives, projects, and realizations

- Comprehensive and principled liaison mechanisms between Agile and phased development models, supporting lean engineering and just-in-time delivery

- Mapping of long-term business objectives to EA transformation

These objectives can be achieved with engineering processes built from work units directly attached to enterprise architecture models.

Enterprise Architecture & Engineering Workshops

The rationalization of engineering processes is arguably a primary purpose of MBSE, and models' transformation, a key item in the toolbox. For enterprise architects, the transformation of models should therefore be crisscrossed with architecture layers; that is the aim of the four engineering workshops earmarked for enterprise, domains, applications, and systems issues (cf. chapter 3).

To be clear, workshops are not dry docks where architectures could be built or transformed, wholly or partially; neither are they supposed to be aligned with architecture layers. Instead, each workshop corresponds to an cross section of:

- Enterprise: descriptive models of organization and business processes anchors, business entities and aspects

- Domains: descriptive and prescriptive models of business domains

- Applications: development (technical) models

- Systems: deployment models and operations (code)

Engineering processes could then be organized across workshops, like production areas in job-shop manufacturing, depending on the nature of transformations (figure 14-7):

- At the software level, automated (or final) transformations generate code (or executable models) from technical models (figure 14-7d).

- At the system level, assisted transformations use patterns and profiles to generate parts of models or to support their editing (figure 14-7a, b, c).

- At the enterprise level, processes are integrated with operations and organization (e).

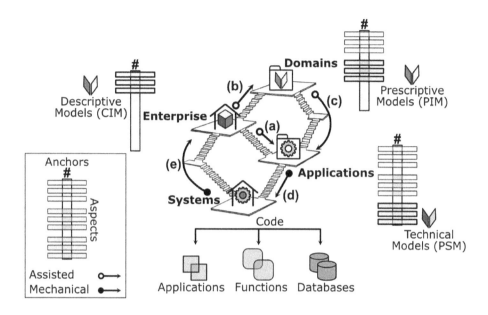

Figure 14-7. Engineering Workshops & Transformations of Models

Each workshop can thus serve as a starting point for projects, carried out through sequences of transformations that can be determined on the fly, according to the status of anchors (#) and aspects in models (cf. chapter 3).

Starting with requirements (cf. chapter 11) in the enterprise workshop, projects can be carried out directly through the applications workshop as self-contained developments (a), or can proceed to the domains workshop in order to deal with changes in shared domains or functions (b).

For direct developments through the applications workshop (figure 14-7a), the role of MBSE is to ensure the continuity and consistency of the new technical models with functional and technical architectures; that can be done with:

- Translation of the relevant anchors and facets from prescriptive to technical models (figure 14-7c)

- Integration of templates supporting the technical architecture

- Extension of prescriptive or technical models by developers using smart editors and DSL

For developments carried out through the domains workshop (figure 14-7b), the role of MBSE is to ensure the consistency of descriptive and prescriptive models (cf. chapter 7); that can be done through:

- Translation of the relevant anchors and aspects from descriptive to prescriptive models (figure 14-7b)

- Integration of profiles associated with business environments; e.g., regulatory contexts

- Integration of organizational patterns; e.g., for authorizations

- Integration of architecture functional patterns; e.g., the Model-View-Controller (MVC) pattern

Finally, code for applications, functions, or databases can be generated from technical models (figure 14-7d).

In any case, MBSE should ensure the strict complementarity (no overlaps) between direct developments and the ones carried out through prescriptive and technical models, with or without DSL editors.

Actionable Maps

The immersion of enterprises in digital environments represents a challenge as well as an opportunity: a challenge because enterprises are directly confronted by external moves; and an opportunity because the seamless continuity between systems and environments paves the way to a greater integration of architecture and decision-making processes (cf. chapter 10).

To that end, models must be turned into actionable maps, with MBSE providing the gears between Observation-Orientation-Decision-Action (OODA) loops and architectural changes (figure 14-8).

At the digital level, the objective is to combine the observation of changes in environments and systems, with the feedback of actions carried out through the systems engineering workshop (a). That can be typically obtained with Deep-learning technologies applied to data- and process mining.

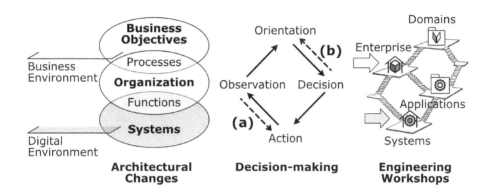

Figure 14-8. *Decision-making & Feedback (dashed arrows)*

At the business level, the objective is to hinge orientation and decision; i.e., to crisscross and compare ex-ante assessments of changes in business environments and processes with ex-post feedback from decisions carried out through the enterprise engineering workshop (b).

Actionable maps turn MBSE into a hub between business and systems changes. More generally, the approach positions the organization as the nexus of transformations, such that business processes match business models with enterprise capabilities, and systems functions match enterprise and systems capabilities.

Agile & MBSE

Scaling up MBSE from the system to the enterprise level calls for an equivalent move for representations and liaison mechanisms.

With regard to representations, ontologies should be decisive in bridging the conceptual gap between information models, managed at the system level, and the assortment of thesauruses, data vaults, statistical models, and Knowledge graphs employed to describe actual or virtual business environments and objectives (cf. chapter 9). Given an ontological basis, business, Use, and system cases (cf.

chapter 13) provide the modeling interfaces between business models and objectives, on the one hand, and organizational changes and engineering processes, on the other hand (figure 14-9).

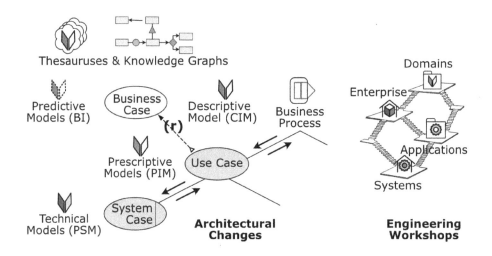

Figure 14-9. MBSE & Enterprise Architecture

At the enterprise level, objectives would be formulated as business cases, supported by predictive models, business intelligence (BI), and Knowledge graphs, and mapped to actual or planned (or virtual) descriptive models.

At the system level, projects would be organized as dynamic trees (cf. figure 14-3) rooted in business processes or functions, with Use cases as subtrees, and system cases as leaves. The traceability between objectives and architectural changes is achieved through realization connectors (r) between business- and Use cases (cf. chapter 13).

With regard to liaisons among engineering processes, the objective is to apply a common control and collaboration mechanism to both Agile and phased projects, and more specifically, to replace imperative sequences of predefined activities with dynamic arrangements of work units. Such a mechanism, an extension of the Agile backlog, should rely on:

- Agreed-upon descriptions of objectives, models, artifacts, and work units; that is to be done through ontologies (cf. chapter 9)

- Agreed-upon descriptions of standard operations on models and artifacts; namely, development, translation, refactoring, and transformation

- Standard tree-management operators

That mechanism can be seen as a knowledge-driven backlog; for example (figure 14-10):

Assume two Use cases (*UC1, UC2*) that share a common system case associated with a business function (*SC5*) are developed by separate teams (*T1, T2*). A backlog is initiated as a double Last-in, first-out (LIFO) structure, knitting dynamically the relative sequencing of the teams' work units.

For example *UC1>* (inception) must be carried out before *UC1<* (completion):

- *T1*: *UC1>, SC6, SC5, UC1<*

- *T2*: *UC2>, SC9, UC2<*

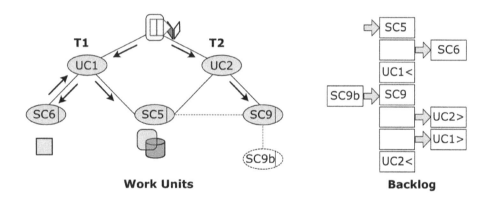

Work Units   **Backlog**

Figure 14-10. Management of Work Units

The backlog is then managed dynamically to reflect the status of work units:

- Removed when completed: *UC1>, UC2>, SC6*

- Activated when conditions are met: *SC5*

- Introduced when needed: *SC9* is redefined as *SC9b* when *SC5* is factored out

The use of a backlog mechanism to manage EA engineering processes is pivotal in securing the dynamic integration between business-driven and architecture-based projects, and more specifically, between Agile and phased development models. Moreover, the benefits can be extended to EA and knowledge-driven engineering.

Knowledge-driven Enterprise Transformation

Maintaining a comprehensive and consistent representation of environments, business objectives, organization, and systems, as well as of predicted, planned, or engineered changes, should be at the top of the EA agenda; that can be achieved with extended backlogs.

To begin with, backlogs can be represented as graphs, with work units as nodes and sequencing constraints as connectors. The constraints can then be refined using generic ontology connectors (cf. chapter 9), for example (figure 14-11):

- Time association: **SC6** and **SC5** to **UC1<**

- Functional association: **UC1>** to **SC6** and **SC5**

- Structural association: **SC9** to **SC9b**

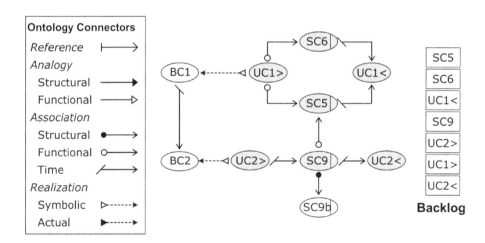

Figure 14-11. Augmented Backlog

Once translated into graphs, backlogs can be upgraded to encompass broader enterprise objectives defined by business cases (e.g., **BC1** and **BC2**), with realization connectors (actual or symbolic) mapping the dynamics of change between environments, objectives, organization, and systems.

Like geographic maps combining economic and demographic data, graphs can be combined to build knowledge-based dashboards that weave business objectives and engineering projects with the relevant items of environments and systems architecture (figure 14-12).

Such a mapping of objectives, assets, and realizations across systems, organization, and business will help to integrate systems transformations and enterprise modernization.

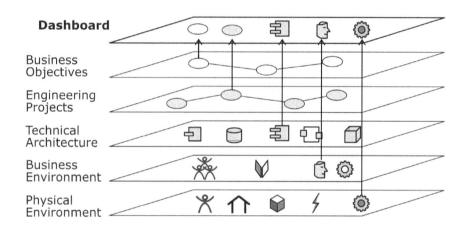

Figure 14-12. From MBSE to EA Dashboards

Reuse & Modernization

Models' transformation, typically with DSL, constitutes the current mainstay of MBSE; yet, transformation also has a counterpart, which is reuse. Often neglected at the system level, the reuse of models comes to the fore with enterprise architecture, especially with regard to legacy and modernization.

The Matter of Reuse

Scaling up MBSE to enterprise architecture entails a separation of concerns (represented by business, Use, and system cases; cf. chapter 13) and a selective management of modeling assets (represented by descriptive, prescriptive, and technical models). In between, objectives, options, and undertakings can be detailed in terms of reuse (figure 14-13):

- Anchors and business entities, identified in descriptive models (a), are meant to be reused all along engineering processes.

- Aspects (attributes and operations) are first introduced by descriptive models (d), and then refactored to set apart business aspects from systems functional ones; specifically, the messages exchanged at the architecture level, defined by Use cases (e) and prescriptive models (f), are set apart from the features (or interfaces) at the component level, defined by system cases and technical models (g).

- Business logic is defined by descriptive models (b) and possibly refined by Use cases (c).

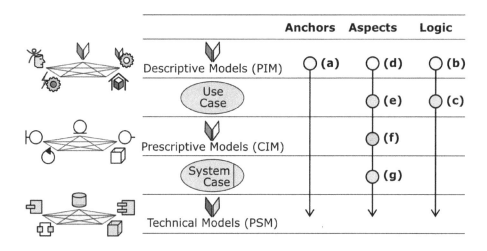

Figure 14-13. The Matter of Reuse

The reuse of anchors and business entities (a) is necessary because it determines the continuity and consistency of the whole of enterprise architecture. It is also straightforward because anchors can be unambiguously defined and managed by business stakeholders. Likewise for business logic: assuming it can be factored out, its reuse in business domains (b) or Use cases (c) can be unequivocally decided by business analysts (cf. chapter 12).

By contrast, the reuse of aspects is front and center for disputed architecture issues:

- For aspects defined in descriptive models, the purpose of reuse is to set apart the intrinsic semantics of enterprise anchors (e.g., accounting) from their understanding by business domains (d).

- For aspects defined in Use cases, the purpose is to share user interfaces across business applications (e).

- For aspects defined in prescriptive models, the purpose is to share access to business functions; e.g., invoicing or establishing a credit rating (f).

- For aspects defined in system cases, the purpose is to share access to supporting functions or services; e.g., authentication or authorization (g).

The reuse of models thus appears as the logical counterpart of their transformation; but reuse should also be considered in the broader context of enterprise architecture.

The Economics of Reuse

Reusing artifacts (including symbolic ones like models) means using them in contexts or for purposes different from the original ones. That may be set ex ante, when designers take into account broader objectives, or ex post, when existing artifacts are used in ways that were not identified upfront. In both cases, enterprise architects have to consider three related issues:

- Returns on investment: if the additional costs of developing reusable artifacts can be readily traced, the expected benefits are by nature more difficult to assess.

- Visibility and usability: business and systems modelers must be made aware of available, relevant, and reliable modeling assets without having to stray from their regular modus operandi.

- Overheads: ensuring the transparency, traceability, and consistency of reusable models cannot be achieved without a supporting organizational and technical environment.

As long as reuse remains an engineering issue for systems architects, contexts and purposes can be circumscribed and MBSE platforms should provide the supporting environments.

But for enterprise architects, the assessment of models' reuse and transformation revisits the choice between business (domain-specific applications) and architectural (shared business functions) perspectives (cf. chapter 4). That issue can be solved by resetting MBSE within ontologies (figure 14-14):

- Core engineering should encompass Use and system cases, and descriptive, prescriptive, and technical models. Development dependencies between work units are represented by ontological connectors for association and realization.

- Thesauruses, systems functional and technical patterns, and analogy connectors are added to support the transparency and traceability of reuse within and beyond systems architecture representations.

- Business cases, business and organizational patterns and profiles, and Knowledge graphs are introduced to integrate the engineering of systems with the transformation of enterprise architectures.

Bringing together the technical (system cases), functional (Use cases), engineering (MBSE), and economic (business cases) dimensions of EA undertakings enables focused, consistent, and reliable roadmaps that encompass systems legacy, EA transformations, and enterprise modernization.

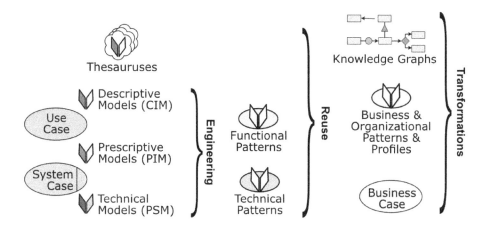

Figure 14-14. Conceptual Extensions to MBSE (see figure 14-11 for connectors)

Refactoring & Modernization

The term modernization can be misleading because it suggests a single and definite transformation of architectures. But for enterprises immersed in digital environments, changes are by nature plural and continuous:

- Plural: legacy issues must be tackled differently depending on their mark on architecture capabilities.

- Continuous: modernization should play with the direction of time: backward by restoring past requirements from opaque legacy code, and forward by developing new capabilities.

For systems architectures, modernization can combine three basic schemes (figure 14-15):

- Reuse: wrapping of legacy components into encasings adapted to the new environment, thus enabling the legacy components to be run unmodified (a)

- Refactoring: developing new components that reproduce the legacy functions in the targeted environment (b)

• Transformation: updating applications with extended functionalities and improved Quality of service (c)

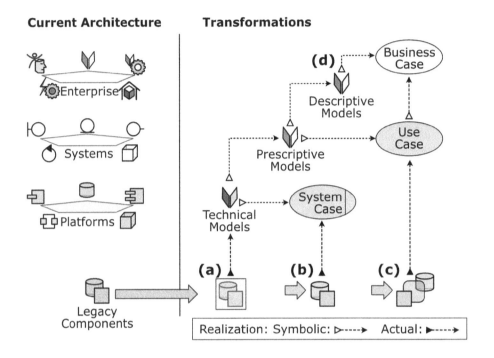

Figure 14-15. *Modernization as a Work in Progress*

These options can be integrated into broader EA-modernization roadmaps, linking architectures, projects, and business objectives in terms of actual (models to components) and symbolic (between models) realizations:

• Wrapping legacy components without affecting cases or models (a)

• Refactoring system cases through a change in technical models (b)

• Refactoring Use and system cases through a change in technical and prescriptive models (c)

• Setting future developments, with business cases pointing to changes in descriptive models and leading to cascading consequences for prescriptive and technical models, as well as Use and system cases (d)

Modernization projects could then be organized as workflows that are managed dynamically, depending on the status of model-driven engineering processes, which are themselves built on work units; for example (figure 14-16):

• Collect and organize legacy code (a)

• Translate into system cases (SC) (b)

• Refactor technical (or Platform specific) models according to architecture technical patterns (c)

• Redesign Use cases (UC) (d)

• Refactor prescriptive (or Platform independent) models according to changes in Use cases and architecture functional patterns (e)

• Edit or create descriptive (or Computation independent) models in line with business cases (BC) (f)

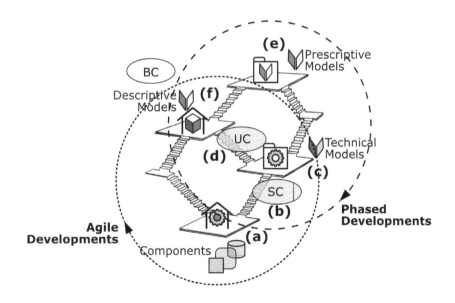

Figure 14-16. Modernization Workflow

Augmented backlog mechanisms (as described above) could then be used to control the execution of all work units, whether set with Agile or phased development processes; the former would be focused on Use and system cases, and the latter, backed by descriptive and prescriptive models.

For enterprise architects, the integration of engineering backlogs with ontologies means that profiles and Knowledge graphs could be used to support the whole scope of the decision-making process (cf. chapter 10).

The next chapter will consider the benefits of upgrading MBSE to EA for enterprises' capacity and maturity.

PART V.

Enterprises as Viable Organizations

Part I presented enterprise architecture (EA) as symbolic representations of environments, organizations, and systems, and suggested two defining differences between EA and brick-and-mortar architectures:

- Evolution: sustainability in competitive environments means continuous and consistent changes.

- Self-consciousness: since the core of enterprise architecture is itself made of symbolic matter, its immersion in digital environments opens the door to osmosis and homeostasis.

Part II described the objectives of EA as a discipline and the role of frameworks, and introduced the Pagoda blueprint.

Part III dealt with the mix of architecture layers and symbolic representations: content (data, information, knowledge), forms (models, thesauruses, graphs, ontologies), and roles (architecture and decision-making).

Part IV focused on the engineering of changes: how to manage EA transformations using Model-based systems engineering (MBSE) as a glue between iterative and business-driven developments, on the one hand, and phased and architecture-based engineering processes, on the other hand.

Taking our cue from the pioneering work of Stafford Beer (cf. bibliography), this part of the book considers enterprises as viable organizations and examines what happens to evolution when enterprises immersed in digital environments are confronted with systemic disruptions. Chapter 15 considers architecures' intrinsic capabilities in terms of agility and entropy; chapter 16 puts the focus on the significance of organizational behavior and collective intelligence for intangible assets; and chapter 17 takes the broader perspective of externalities.

CHAPTER 15

Agile Organizations

*Versatility is the ability to change usage without changing structure;
plasticity is the ability to change structure without affecting usage*

As social entities, enterprises are understood according to three symbolic dimensions: statutory, organizational, and economic. As a result of the digital transformation, enterprises, systems, and operations are also brought into the same symbolic fold. Therefore, promoting MBSE to the enterprise level provides a common harness for changes in environments, organizations, and systems.

When seen through cybernetics' glasses, enterprises are viable systems whose sustainability and capabilities hang on their ability to track changes in their environment and exploit opportunities before their competitors. For enterprises, success thus depends on their capacity to support fast, accurate, and purpose-driven readings of environments, as well as to harness the transformation of their organization and systems.

But the flattening of traditional physical (i.e., nondigital) barriers brings external disorder and confusion to enterprises' doorsteps. Unless a robust and flexible organization can serve as a buffer between changes in environments and systems, variety will progressively clog systems with sequences of piecemeal information that are introduced to support specific adjustments.

To prevent such debasement (or entropy) of their information systems, enterprises need to leverage the benefits of digital osmosis and homeostasis across their architectures.

Capacity to Change

Change is a matter of time for enterprises confronted with a shifting balance between assessments (which improve with time until becoming redundant) and commitments (which bear the costs of missed opportunities if kept waiting too long).

For enterprises immersed in competitive digital environments, their capacity to change depends on their ability to:

- Perceive changes in environments in terms of facts (data), meaning (information), and consequences (knowledge)

- Perform effectively and efficiently at both levels of environment (operations) and enterprise (systems and organization)

- Improve performance and learn from experience

Applied to viable systems, these abilities can be described in terms of osmosis, homeostasis, and self-improvement.

Perceptions: Digital Osmosis

Enterprises' digital immersion leads to an overhaul of their perception of business environments:

- Markets: the lines between products (materialized by physical flows) and services (materialized by digital flows) are fading fast; first, because more and more products are marketed as or packaged with services and, second, because even the engineering processes of physical products are turning digital.

- Resources and assets: with software, smart or otherwise, tightly woven into the fabric of products and services, and a plurality of business processes driven by knowledge, intangible assets like data and information are taking the lead from tangible ones like IT infrastructures.

- Time frames: the ironing out of established distinctions across markets, as well as assets, also erases the corresponding milestones used to plan business prospects over managed horizons (e.g., operational, tactical, strategic).

To maintain their grip on business moves, enterprises must take advantage of the digital osmosis that can be fostered between their systems and environments. First, systems must integrate the processing of data and information into a knowledge chain (cf. chapter 9):

1. Mining data: to reflect factual changes in environments

2. Mapping data into meaningful categories (or models): predictive (business intelligence), descriptive (managed business objects and processes), or prescriptive (supporting systems)

3. Morphing information into knowledge through decision-making processes

Then, digital osmosis should be used to integrate knowledge chains with decision-making loops (cf. chapter 10) (figure 15-1):

- Orientation (information) is achieved by applying knowledge to observations (data) (figure 15-1a); in this case, digital osmosis means that orientation can be adjusted by improving the quality of the data that supports observations (figure 15-1b).

- Observation apparatuses are built to serve specific purposes, taking into account current information models and knowledge (figure 15-1c); here, digital osmosis means that observation can also take into account the way decisions are implemented as well as their impact, thus providing feedback on the information models and knowledge behind these decisions (figure 15-1d).

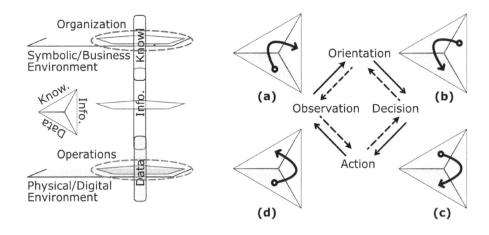

Figure 15-1. Digital Osmosis Adds Feedback (dashed arrows) inDecision-making

Such generalized osmosis can only be achieved with ontologies that secure the integration of systems architecture layers (technical and functional) and organization, on the one hand, with the corresponding symbolic representations (data, information, knowledge), on the other hand (figure 15-1, left).

Performance: Homeostasis

In differentiated environments (physical operations, digital observations), actual interventions may lag behind digital perceptions. By contrast, in digital environments, acting on the understanding of changes without delay may be necessary if enterprises are to keep their momentum in line with shifting environments. For viable systems (a term borrowed from Beer), the ability to maintain a sustainable equilibrium (or homeostasis in cybernetics' parlance) depends on the sensory-motor apparatus. For enterprises, maintaining the equilibrium requires a tight integration of symbolic representations (cf. chapter 9) with processes of decision-making (cf. chapter 10) and engineering (cf. chapter 14).

On that basis, the effectiveness of homeostasis will be conditioned by the mapping of perceptions, representations, and decisions:

First, the mapping of perceptions must cope with size and complexity. Since viable organizations combine a large plurality of dedicated structures and functions, the indiscriminate processing of continuous and massive flows of observations (or Big Data) would generate an exponential number of options. That outcome can be prevented by the alignment of platforms, systems, and organizational capabilities, on the one hand, with the processing of data, information, and knowledge, on the other hand. This alignment would enable a selective processing of inputs, depending on their nature; e.g., personal data from social media vs. customers' information.

Second, ontologies provide a built-in transparency and traceability between changes in territories (environments and systems) and the corresponding maps (models, thesauruses, graphs) at the levels of data, information, and knowledge.

Third, MBSE is the engine that makes maps actionable; i.e., such that work units defined from maps can be carried out directly without the need for additional organizational constructs (cf. chapter 14).

The granularity of changes can thus be aligned in environments and systems, on the one hand, and engineering workshops, on the other hand; this alignment allows for (figure 15-2):

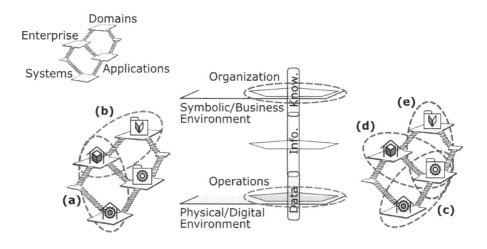

Figure 15-2. Engineering Workshops & the Granularity of Changes

- Adjustment of operational configurations (systems workshop) to changes in physical environments (enterprise workshop); e.g., locations or volumes (figure 15-2a)

- Adjustment of models (domains workshop) to changes in organization or business processes (enterprise workshop) (figure 15-2b)

- Deployment of applications on systems platforms (figure 15-2c)

- Development of business-specific applications (figure 15-2d)

- Development of functions shared across architectures (figure 15-2e)

That alignment of work units and architecture capabilities with decision-making loops and knowledge chains will enable returns on experience and improvements across systems and organization (cf. chapter 10).

Self-improvement

Self-improvement is clearly a key success factor for enterprises competing in digital environments, but it is also very elusive. Yet, the roots of self-improvement appear more clearly when defined in terms of decision-making and Machine-learning (ML) technologies (figure 15-3):

- Observation: betterments in the relevance and quality of data can be obtained through data mining and Deep-learning (DL) technologies.

- Orientation: Knowledge graphs and ML can be used to assess the reliability of supporting models and profiles, and to proceed with adjustments.

- Decisions: models and profiles (business, organizational, functional, technical) that support decision-making can be assessed and amended, taking into account observed outcomes.

- Actions: process mining (for operations) can be combined with data mining (for environments) in order to improve the way decisions are carried out.

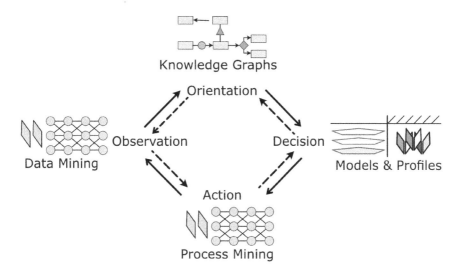

Figure 15-3. Learning from Experience

The significance of the multifold integration of systems, representations, and decision-making loops should not be understated: it constitutes the nexus of enterprises' self-improvement capacity. This integration enables the leveraging of Machine-learning technologies across the whole of enterprise architecture.

Such capacity is a key factor preventing the increase of entropy in enterprises' systems.

Architecture & Entropy

The imprint of cybernetics on the understanding of enterprise systems has been frustrated by a supposed correspondence between energy in physics and information in economics. This has occurred despite cybernetics' focus on regulatory systems and Claude Shannon's pivotal adjunct for information theory.

That supposed equivalence between energy and information should become redundant with the digital mutation of business environments.

Entropy: From Physics to Economics

As understood in thermodynamics, the entropy within a system is the quantum of energy that cannot be converted into mechanical work. Formalized by Shannon in terms of leakage along communication channels, entropy has become a pillar of information theory.

Translated to economics, entropy could be understood as unexplained data or, to mirror energy in thermodynamics, as the part of data that cannot be translated into useful information. Yet, that transposition faces two hurdles.

To begin with, the second law of thermodynamics states that entropy as a whole is uniform and constant: the gains in one system are balanced by the losses in another. Economics laws, if there are such a thing, beg to differ: as far as business environments are concerned, data is not a given and uniform resource, free to be picked up. Quite the contrary, it is an ephemeral resource with very specific relevance.

Moreover, in contrast to the binary dimension of digits in communication channels, business information combines an open-ended number of interdependent dimensions: physical (e.g., demographics, climate), socio-economic (e.g., income, education), and symbolic (e.g., religion, politics, culture).

It ensues that for enterprises in competitive environments, Shannon's understanding of entropy occurring during communication is irrelevant: the issue is what happens before and after communication; namely, how the exchanged information affects the internal states of enterprises. On that point, as noted above, conditions are drastically modified by digital osmosis and homeostasis, and by their leveraging effect on entropy across the whole of architectures.

In principle, the leveraging effect of digital osmosis and homeostasis can play in both directions: rounding out the rough edges of external disorder or speeding up improvements across architectures. In practice, the level of entropy will be determined by the self-improvement capability of decision-making processes (cf. chapter 10) and their ability to cope with complexity.

Entropy & Complexity

Entropy in systems can be understood in terms of disorder and randomness; for enterprise systems, it means the misalignment of observed data with the expected values, given the categories managed by the enterprise (e.g., are VIP customers meeting sales managers' expectations?). That understanding of entropy can be neatly aligned with the symbolic architecture of the Pagoda blueprint (cf. chapter 9): data for disorder (environment), information for categories (systems), and knowledge for their managed alignment (enterprise).

It is thus possible to more precisely assess enterprise architecture capacity in terms of entropy as the quantum of data that can be accounted for by enterprises' symbolic representations (figure 15-4):

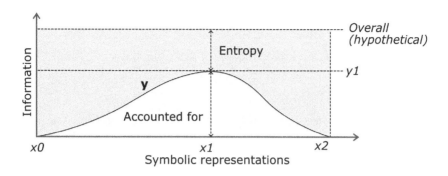

Figure 15-4. Information Systems & Entropy

The vertical axis represents the quantum of information supposedly contained in a given set of targeted items (e.g., demographic data from a population sample). The horizontal one represents the size and complexity of the categories supporting the representations (e.g., descriptive models), from an all-inclusive classification made up of single category (x0) to a bijective mapping of each observation (or fact) to a specific category (x2). Given an overall quantum of hypothetical information (gray color), the function y represents the part (blue color) of that quantum that can be accounted for, depending on the complexity of the categories used by the representations. This complexity ranges between the equally pointless options of full abstraction (everything in one concept) and full detail (a concept for everything).

Entropy is thus implicitly defined as the difference between the part accounted for and the overall quantum of information, such that entropy is at the hypothetical minimum when the part accounted for is at its maximum $(x_1 \cdot y_1)$.

In principle, the part accounted for by a given representation is defined by the ratio between the size and complexity of targeted items (or microstates in thermodynamics parlance), and the size and complexity of the categories used to represent them (or macrostates in thermodynamics parlance).

In practice:

• The estimation of the size and complexity of targeted items is a technical issue routinely handled with statistical methods like regression analysis.

• The size and complexity of representations can be assessed with metrics like function points, and applied to descriptive models at the enterprise level and prescriptive ones at the system level (cf. chapter 11).

Even if computed from crude estimations, descriptive and prescriptive complexity ratios should still provide empirical indicators of entropy and, consequently, of the effect of changes on the complexity of systems' symbolic representations.

Versatility & Plasticity

For enterprises, homeostasis means the adaptation of organizations and systems to changes in environments. Policies aiming to prevent entropy should thus focus on improving the part of data accounted for by its mapping to information, which can be achieved through the betterment of data analytics (for the reliability of microstates) and/or more relevant information models (for the representation of macrostates) (figure 15-5).

Digital osmosis should significantly help with the perception of changes in microstates (environments), as demonstrated by the use of data mining to fine-tune the sampling of targeted items (e.g., customers' behavior). Other things being equal, digital osmosis should thus increase the effectiveness of representations; i.e., the quantum of information accounted for by a given set of categories (**x1**), moving the function (**f**) upward (figure 15-5, *f1 - f2*), and so reducing the minimum entropy that corresponds to the optimal point (**x1**) (figure 15-5, *y1 - y2*).

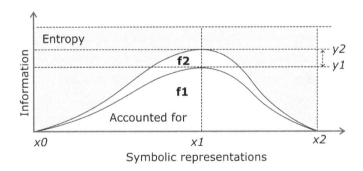

Figure 15-5. Digital Osmosis & Reduced Entropy

Regarding the leveraging effect of homeostasis, a distinction can be made between systems' versatility and plasticity.

Versatility (figure 15-6, left) is the ability of systems to adjust processes to shifting environments without inducing significant changes to architectures. With regard to EA, it means improving the relevance of descriptive models (*fd*) without increasing the complexity of prescriptive ones (*fp*). That would induce a better set of categories representing business environments and objectives (**x1** – **x2**) and, consequently, a decrease of the corresponding entropy (**d1** – **d2**), without a negative impact on systems' complexity (*po*).

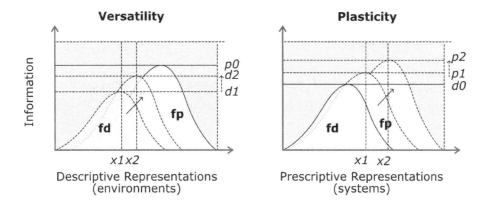

Figure 15-6. Agility vs. Entropy

Plasticity (or flexibility) (figure 15-6, right) is the ability of systems to improve architectures without impairing the effectiveness of supported processes. With regard to EA, it means reducing the complexity of prescriptive models (fp) without introducing discrepancies with descriptive ones (fd). That would induce a better design of the system (x1 – x2) and thus a decrease of the corresponding entropy (d1 – d2), without a negative impact on the validity of business representations (po).

If, as noted above, rough but consistent and unbiased estimates can be obtained for versatility and plasticity ratios, they could be used to assess the agility of enterprises' architecture.

Quality vs. Entropy

Quality, understood as the probability that nothing will go amiss during the life-cycle of a product or service, can be seen as the opposite of entropy.

Here again, systems- and enterprise architectures take different views: the former considers quality at the delivery point, whereas the latter should also take into account a part (to be determined) of products' life-cycles. That's the reason why EA quality management should distinguish between issues that can be managed before delivery, and issues that could arise later from changes in environments.

EA Quality Management

Quality issues may stem from unsound requirements, flawed engineering, or unexpected changes in environments. Considering the ubiquity of software components in business processes and their immersion in digital environments, sorting out these issues may be challenging.

While the specifics of quality management are not under their remit, enterprise architects should ensure the transparency, traceability, and accountability of the policies carried out by engineering and business units. To that effect:

1. Requirements must be documented according to their scope: applications, systems architecture, or enterprise architecture (cf. chapter 12).

2. Projects' objectives and responsibilities must be defined in terms of business, Use, and system cases (cf. chapter 13).

3. EA engineering processes must be built from work units defined in terms of models' transformation (cf. chapter 14).

4. Decision-making processes must be structured by EA stakes and ensure detailed traceability (observations, reasoning, and judgement) and accountability (cf. chapter 10).

Assuming these conditions are met, EA quality management should be combined with quality assurance with regard to internal issues, and risk management with regard to external ones.

Quality Assurance

The primary objective of EA quality assurance (QA) is to ensure a seamless integration of all the relevant undertakings that contribute to the overall quality of outcomes (figure 15-7):

• Consistency of descriptive models (or CIM) with regard to business objectives, as represented by business cases (BC)

• Validity of prescriptive models (or PIM) with regard to descriptive models (or CIM) and Use cases (UC)

- Validity of technical models (or PSM) with regard to prescriptive models (or PIM) and system cases (SC)

- Integration and acceptance tests carried out in reference to models and non-functional requirements.

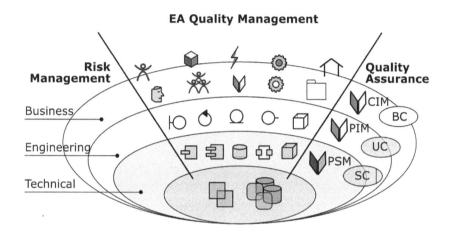

Figure 15-7. EA Quality Circles

Not surprisingly, models constitute the backbone of EA quality assurance, at least for issues that can be fully managed at the enterprise level. Yet, as a remedy to entropy, quality management must also take charge of external ones.

Risk Management

As noted above, quality is a probability that reflects risks. In theory, risks are either external (business or technical environments) or internal (engineering processes). In practice, for enterprises competing in digital environments, the continuity of fine-grained deliveries means that quality is affected by a mix of external and internal issues. As a corollary, QA policies can help with external issues; e.g., quality checks on models (internal) may give some clues to latent hazards in business or technical environments (external). More generally, the versatility and plasticity of architectures improve their ability to cope with unexpected changes.

Nonetheless, in competitive digital environments, external hazards become the new normal for quality assurance. These hazards can be grouped into three figurative categories:

- Ducks: run-of-the-mill external contingencies that can be fully or partially handled through quality assurance; e.g., platform redundancy would limit the consequences of external disruptions, and model reuse and code generation would iron out sudden changes in technical environments.

- Grey swans: a watered-down version of Nassim Nicholas Taleb's Black Swan (cf. bibliography), for improbable yet well-identified contingencies whose handling cannot be integrated into the architecture; e.g., an unexpected regulatory change or a delay in a drug-approval process. For that kind of contingency, QA must provide fallback solutions.

- Black ducks: disruptive contingencies whose handling can be priced and weighted by likelihood. In that case, QA should monitor the risks and itemize the costs; e.g., the costs induced by a delay in a drug-approval process should be identified in addition to the costs of alternatives.

For enterprise architects, the objective is thus to make sure that risks can be continuously mapped to relevant data, information, and knowledge (cf. chapter 9) and decision-making processes (cf. chapter 10).

EA quality can also be managed from a process perspective. Taking into account the constraints of digital immersion in competitive environments, enterprise architectures could be assessed in terms of their ability to change with shifting environments.

Agile Architectures

Most EA practitioners would readily confirm that capacity to change is the litmus test of enterprise architecture. However, assessing actual realizations is of limited use for planning, when a more principled basis is needed.

The Capability maturity model integration (CMMI) is an attempt in that direction, at least for processes, and can thus provide a starting point to assess the capacity of enterprise architectures to transform themselves.

Capability Maturity Model

The objective of CMMI, initially developed at the Software Engineering Institute at Carnegie Mellon University, is to create "reliable environments where products, services and departments are proactive, efficient and productive." These few words sum up the intent of addressing simultaneously the assessment of processes and of supporting environments, typically architectures.

That original confusion between processes and architectures goes some way to explain the disputed record of CMMI; the need to conciliate asymmetric, if not conflicting, perspectives has induced cumbersome procedures, as well as steep and open-ended learning curves. For enterprise architects, the objective is therefore to set apart the two issues.

Regarding the assessment of processes, CMMI's five levels of maturity are straightforward and can be readily applied to systems engineering processes:

1. Initial: no process, each engineering project is managed on an ad hoc basis

2. Managed: processes are specific to projects

3. Defined: processes are defined as profiles (cf. chapter 8) of engineering objectives and contexts, and applied to projects accordingly

4. Measured: benchmarks are used to assess the effectiveness of processes

5. Optimized: the effectiveness of processes is analyzed and processes are improved accordingly

Process areas (e.g., measurement, integration, performance management, training, monitoring, planning, quality) are meant to support the ranking of supporting environments. But their number (more than 20), specificity, and cross dependencies turn assessment into a full-fledged methodology, overloaded with procedures and fogged by interpretations. CMMI V2.0 introduces guidelines to smooth and customize implementations, but the focus remains on the assessment of the different processes' areas, and consequently on the miscellany of associated methodologies; architectural issues are just an afterthought.

In addition to the necessary (if overlooked) distinction between processes and architectures, CMMI brings to the fore two critical points.

On the positive side, CMMI emphasizes the significance of a seamless and fine-grained integration of processes' assessment and improvement.

On the negative side, CMMI illustrates the need for assessment schemes to meet two provisos:

- They must be unbiased; i.e., assessment schemes should not prioritize specific metrics or methodologies.

- Their adoption should not induce additional activities or organizational structures other than those directly associated with assessment.

That sets the agenda for a revised understanding of the CMMI.

EA Maturity & Capacity to Change

Notwithstanding their approximative measurements, versatility and plasticity ratios meet both provisos and can thus provide rough indicators for the capacity to change and maturity of architectures. And the shortcomings of measurement can be managed:

- The lack of accuracy of the ratios is a practical issue open to continuous improvements.

- The associated methods and tools, typically regression analysis and requirements metrics, have a proven track record in a number of enterprise activities.

Using the complexity of models as a yardstick for processes' assessment, policies combining versatility and flexibility can further architectures' agility (figure 15-8):

- Versatility policies pivot on Use cases. Changes in descriptive models are rooted in business processes in order to meet new requirements through aspects and business logic without affecting architecture anchors (cf. chapter 14). Data analytics can be used to provide metrics of the complexity of targeted environments, metrics that could then be used to assess the effectiveness of changes in descriptive and prescriptive models (cf. chapter 11).

• Plasticity (or flexibility) policies pivot on system cases. Changes in prescriptive models are rooted in functions supported across the architecture in order to change architecture anchors without affecting the aspects used by business processes. The impact on plasticity can be assessed by comparing the respective changes in descriptive and prescriptive models.

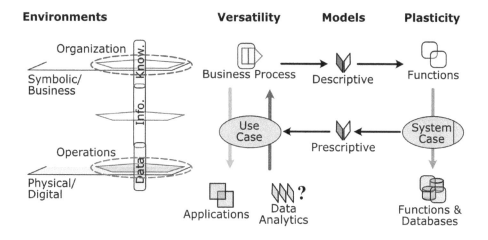

Figure 15-8. Agile Architecture

The final step is to reset processes' maturity levels in terms of enterprise architecture.

Enterprise Architecture Maturity Levels

The objective here is to bypass CMMI process areas and to assess the maturity of engineering processes directly from the way they operate on enterprise architecture:

1. *Initial*: The first maturity level deals with managed projects, which requires a set of common characteristics; typically, size and architectural footprint (cf. chapters 11 & 12).

2. *Managed*: Processes can be assessed in relation to purposes. This implies that work units are defined by engineering objectives, without the need for extraneous organizational constructs to link tasks with outcomes. That can be achieved with processes built as dynamic trees from work units that are associated with models and Use cases (cf. chapter 14).

3. *Defined*: If processes are to be assessed and improved, work units must be defined with regard to some reference model so that their effectiveness could be compared and work units recombined as necessary. MBSE appears to be the best option, with work units defined with regard to business, Use, and system cases, on the one hand, and the transformation of descriptive, prescriptive, and technical models, on the other hand (figure 15-9).

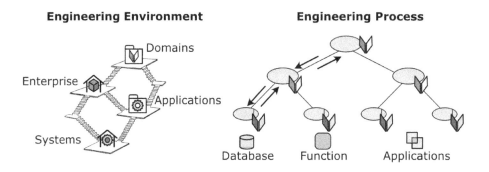

Figure 15-9. Engineering Process & Work Units (cf. chapter 14)

4. *Measured*: Processes are not only assessed as a whole but also through their work units; it ensues that the choice of areas (e.g., quality, resources), tools, and methods is not predetermined but can be left to enterprises to decide according to their context and experience (figure 15-10).

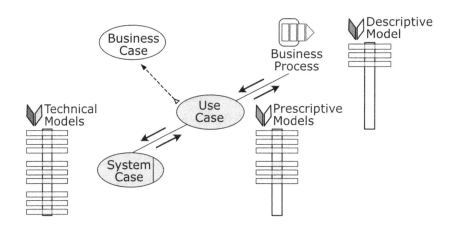

Figure 15-10. Work Units & Model-based Systems Engineering

5. *Optimized*: For all intents and purposes, processes' improvement implies that work units can be switched or recast. The corollary is that assessing work units on their own (as done at maturity level 4) is not enough: they should also be assessed in relation to their impact on the whole process.

The optimization of processes as a whole puts processes' assessment in their architectural context; for example (figure 15-11):

- Business cases (BC) set anchors in descriptive models; their realization may involve system and Use cases over an undetermined period of time (cf. chapter 14) (a).

- Architecture-oriented processes are rooted in system cases (SC); they use descriptive anchors as inputs, add aspects, and deliver prescriptive models to system cases that target databases and functions. System cases dealing with databases can rely on automated tools to generate physical schemas — but that is not so for system cases dealing with functions. Yet, automated models' transformation means that system cases for databases and functions don't have to be carried out sequentially (b).

- Some business-oriented engineering processes can be reduced to single Use cases, which are developed iteratively across descriptive, prescriptive, and technical models (c). Otherwise, Use cases are needed to develop descriptive models that are meant to be shared between Use cases; some are developed directly (d), whereas others require new system cases (e).

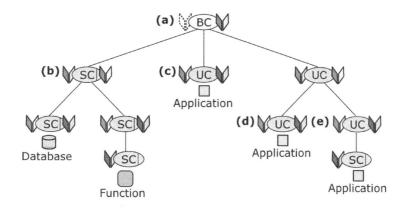

Figure 15-11. Optimizing EA Engineering Processes

With work units associated with changes in models, engineering processes could be assessed on their own with regard to the relevant process areas, or with regard to their impact on the architecture's complexity. That explicit separation of concerns sets the groundwork for a balancing act between business processes' agility and EA sustainability.

Business Processes & Architecture Capabilities

Topping the job description, enterprise architects are meant to serve as brokers between business and systems stakeholders; to that end, they must be aware of the intrinsic difference between their respective agendas. Agility is a case in point.

For business stakeholders, Agile means customer-centric, lean, and just-in-time engineering processes — something that could be considered as a yardstick for the fourth maturity level.

For systems stakeholders, Agile refers to the versatility and plasticity of architectures — something that could be achieved at processes' fifth maturity level.

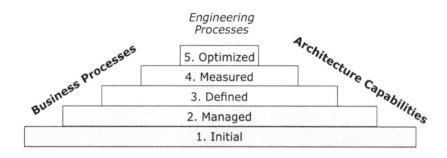

Figure 15-12. A Double-sided Ladder for Business Processes & Architecture Capabilities

Maturity levels could thus provide a double-sided ladder for business and systems perspectives, with processes and capabilities being improved independently along the first four levels, and brought together at the fifth. All along, alignments would be carried out in a piecemeal fashion, according to the level of maturity achieved (figure 15-12) by engineering processes:

At the second (managed) level, the lining up of business and systems perspectives is shallow and limited to the feasibility of objectives concerning capabilities, without being specific about problems and solutions; that mapping of objectives and capabilities can be done through Use cases (cf. chapter 13).

At the third (defined) level, alignments can go deeper and chart engineering paths between processes and supporting capabilities, taking advantage of MBSE and model transformations (cf. chapter 14).

At the fourth (measured) level, with both perspectives consistently defined and assessed, the aim is to balance the pros and cons of specific vs. architectural changes; that can be achieved by assessing versatility and plasticity ratios from a process perspective.

Finally, at the fifth (optimized) level, the balancing of versatility and plasticity can be assessed in the broader context of enterprise architecture.

That double-sided maturity scale may help to clarify some confusion surrounding the so-called business architecture. While the term may make some sense when business processes and architecture capabilities are meant to converge at the fifth (optimized) maturity level, using it indiscriminately simply sidesteps the main issue of enterprise architecture, which is to dynamically manage the bevel gears linking architecture assets and mechanisms to business moves.

Business Acumen vs. Systems Entropy

When it comes to business, agility is all about observation, judgment, and decision-making. On that account, the immersion of enterprises in digital environments is giving new relevance to the works of two trailblazers of the 1960s. Both combined cutting-edge ideas and in-depth, hands-on experience: Stafford Beer applied cybernetics to enterprise governance, and John Boyd applied fighter pilots' decision-making to business competition.

Beer (cf. bibliography) is best known for bringing cybernetics to management, both theoretically, by developing his Viable system model (VSM), and concretely, by trying to implement it with computers and applying it to the case of Chile's economic planning under Salvador Allende. Despite the foresight of the projects, Beer and his team could not overcome the technological impediments of the time, not to mention Chile's military backlash. But Stafford Beer's theory left its mark, which appears clearer in today's digital world: the behavior of organizations mixing people and computers can be governed through a symbolic representation of their interactions with environments.

John Boyd (cf. bibliography) was also a trailblazer: he started as a fighter pilot during the Korean War, then theorized his experience of dogfights for the Pentagon, and went on to adapt his decision-making loop to business competition. Combined with the leveraging impact of Machine-learning technologies on decision-making environments (cf. chapter 10), Boyd's Observation-Orientation-Decision-Action

(OODA) loop has direct relevance for the development of Systems of Systems (SoS), which is meant to mix a miscellany of human and manufactured brains, driven by varying friendly or hostile intents. In that context, autonomous decision-making, all-inclusive assessment, and instant feedback are critical.

Beer's VSM and Boyd's OODA point to a cybernetic understanding of business agility.

From the VSM perspective, business agility requires a seamless integration of architectures and representations, and more specifically, of neuro-motor and cognitive capabilities. These capabilities can then support self-improving decision-making loops:

- Observation: separate the wheat (information) from the chaff (data)

- Orientation: identify risks and opportunities

- Decisions: weight risks

- Action: carry out decisions and learn from experience

Assuming that homeostasis operates in full duplex between perceptions, orientation, and actions, enterprises' competitive edge not only depends on preventing imported entropy, but equally on successfully exporting entropy; i.e., inducing confusion and disorder in the human minds and artificial brains of their competitors.

The next chapter will take a prospective view on the impact of new technologies on EA evolution, and the last one will consider how it could help with EA resilience to systemic upsets.

CHAPTER 16.

Brainy Organizations

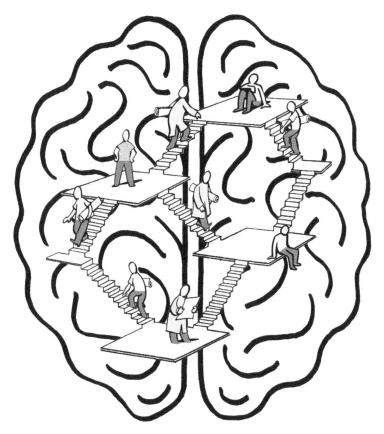

The digital weaving of intangible assets, organization, and systems, puts collective intelligence on enterprises' driving seat

Artificial-intelligence (AI) and Machine-learning (ML) technologies have become part and parcel of software engineering, affecting almost every field supported by computer systems — in other words, every human activity: personal, social, or professional. At the same time, the digital revolution is shaking the foundations of enterprises' organization:

- The digital revolution is eliminating many of the signposts used to mark the boundaries between physical environments and computer systems, not to mention the ones between the contributions of human and artificial brains.

- Combined with the merging of business and engineering processes, the fusing of material and digital flows subverts the traditional division of labor in enterprises' organization.

- The immersion of their systems in digital environments opens enterprises' innards to new regulatory constraints and exposes their brand and image to abrupt and massive shifts in consumers' whims through social media.

While the changes in technologies, organizations, and business environments are driven by specific momentums, it's safe to assume reciprocal influences and synergies. These should define EA's sustainable strategies.

Intelligence as Capability

For enterprises competing in digital environments, sustainability depends on continuous improvement, which means learning. Just to maintain their position, enterprises must continuously weave data and information into the fabric of new knowledge. That's what AI and ML technologies do best.

A Brief Technology Reminder

In some ways, artificial brains have taken longer to mature than their human counterparts, lingering in infancy for almost half a century before their abrupt and sweeping development. With hindsight, it's easy to understand why computers have been late bloomers: they could be taught but they couldn't learn. Hindsight also provides the twofold explanation of the growth spurt: a direct and wide-ranging exposure to environments combined with enough neurons to cope with massive amounts of rough data.

Two technologies are behind the AI breakthrough: Knowledge graphs (KG) and Deep learning (DL).

Behind the variety of names for Knowledge graphs (e.g., conceptual graphs, semantic networks) and employs for them is an all-purpose, graph-based representation built from nodes, properties, and connectors (cf. chapter 8). Yet, the expansion of KG is less the result of technological advances than a combination of:

- Graphs' proven track record for the actionable representation of complex issues

- KG's natural implementation as neural networks

- KG's universality in representing almost any kind of knowledge

By contrast, the upsurge in Deep-learning applications is mainly due to technological leaps, which can be summarily described in three steps:

1. Traditional Machine learning (ML): symbolic representations and rules reproduce human expertise

2. Supervised Deep learning (DL): neural networks reproduce cognitive processes and are trained with profiled data samples

3. Reinforcement learning (RL): extensive raw inputs and statistical inference replace profiled samples for the training of neural networks

Successes are compounded by the synergies engendered by interoperability — both KG and DL technologies are driven by neural networks — and complementarity — the former handling explicit knowledge, and the latter, implicit.

In-depth synergies between KG and DL technologies can be demonstrated by their use in natural-language interfaces (figure 16-1).

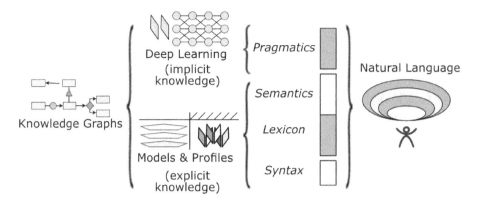

Figure 16-1. Language & Knowledge

On the one side, natural languages use pragmatics to weave together syntax, lexicon, and semantics (cf. chapter 9). On the other side, Knowledge graphs produce knowledge from models and profiles, and from Deep learning. In between, pragmatics materialize the overlapping of language and knowledge, and the flux between implicit and explicit contents.

These advances in symbolic computing capabilities must be put in parallel with technological advances in their physical counterpart: one already well established (Cloud computing), and the other still probing business opportunities (Blockchains).

Intelligence as a Learning Capability

For systems, intelligence implies the ability to learn; i.e., to acquire new knowledge (cf. chapter 9):

1. From observations of enterprises' environments (data) or through the running of their applications (information): observation itself is an activity and its outcome can be affected by attitudes and smart applications.

2. Through reasoning, by applying models (information) and logic to observations (data): reasoning by itself is supposed to be reliable and transparent, yet outcomes are contingent on the adjustment of symbolic representations to contexts and concerns.

3. Through judgment, by combining observations and reasoning: in contrast to observation and reasoning, which can be defined (if not performed) independently of agents, judgment — no matter the name (intuition, common sense, expertise) — takes a different meaning if it is individually or collectively made.

Taking advantage of ontologies and integrated representations (Use cases, models, thesauruses, Knowledge graphs), enterprises can combine observation, reasoning, and judgment into a seamless learning loop (figure 16-2).

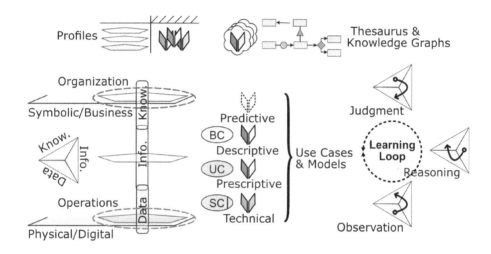

Figure 16-2. Enterprise Learning Loop

That learning loop can be used to leverage the benefits of AI and ML technologies across enterprise architecture:

Observation is the main locus of DL technologies, with advances obtained through a shift from Supervised to RL. Beyond its economic benefits (from downsizing the armies of tutors who redundantly put names on pictures), the significance of RL comes from detaching learning from human common sense. But cutting off common sense from Machine learning relies on the implicit assumption that meanings can be extracted from raw data like gold nuggets from river beds, independently of what humans may think. That (literally) open-minded approach may be a boon for the discovery of emerging consumers' fancies, but not so for the development of well-thought-out strategies. More generally, the difference is between pattern matching, open to discovery, and policy making, focused on purpose: when policies are considered, Deep learning must be combined with the reasoning capabilities of Knowledge graphs.

Reasoning is the realm of KG technologies, whose ubiquity can be explained by one technical rationale and two functional ones (figure 16-3):

- The implementation of KG with neural networks enables a seamless integration with DL applications.

- Serving as semantic networks, KG provide modular and versatile interfaces with natural languages.

- Serving as property graphs, KG provide robust interfaces with systems modeling languages (in particular, relational models). They can then combine with DL to mine data from applications and databases.

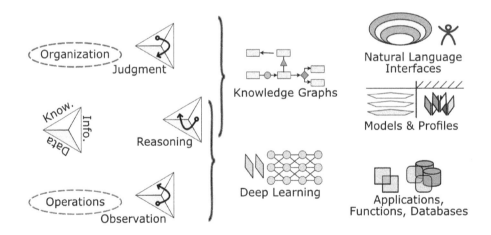

Figure 16-3. Enterprise Learning Apparatus

For EA, the main benefit of KG is their seamless integration with ontologies and, consequently, their ability to leverage learning across the full range of systems, organization, and business representations.

Judgment represents the ultimate yardstick of learning; at the enterprise level, that yardstick is both collective and individual:

- Collective, because judgments should be backed by transparent and traceable knowledge and reasoning, independently of individual beliefs or opinions

- Individual, because when judgments translate into decisions, even ones taken collectively, their traceability also implies personal accountability

That pivot from learning (individual and collective knowledge) to decision-making (individual accountability) is arguably a critical issue for organizations. It can be analyzed with regard to the problem at hand, or from the broader perspective of organizational behavior.

Intelligence as a Problem-solving Capability

Intelligence doesn't come naturally to organizations, and it can only be observed through its benefits in terms of problem-solving. The influence of AI and ML on enterprise governance should thus be probed in relation to the kind of problems under consideration (cf. chapter 9):

- *One-sided* problems don't involve identified parties, and thus don't call for decision-making and accountability at the enterprise level; they can be handled by algorithms (e.g., pattern-matching, optimization) and/or delegated to business or systems units.

- *Zero-sum* problems involve identified parties with conflicting agendas set in well-defined contexts (e.g., calculation of annual bonuses). Outcomes can therefore be fully defined so that the sum of all gains is balanced by corresponding losses. In addition to algorithms, the handling of such problems also requires fully traceable decision-making.

- *Nonzero-sum* problems involve identified parties with conflicting agendas set in open-ended contexts. Outcomes cannot be fully defined, which allows for win-win solutions and, consequently, for mutually beneficial collaborations. Such issues call for both traceability and accountability.

At the enterprise level, the significance of AI and ML technologies starts with zero-sum problems, as illustrated by the achievements of Google's AlphaGo. Beyond its algorithmic wizardry, AlphaGo's breakthrough stems from its combination of both symbolic and nonsymbolic knowledge — a critical issue for fully fledged Reinforcement learning and the harnessing of intuition with reasoning.

Intelligent devices built on that kind of blueprint can thus operate back and forth between the capture of emerging patterns (to analyze problems) and the fine-tuning of representations (to design solutions).

The benefits of a seamless integration between observed phenomena (Deep learning) and explicit causal chains (Knowledge graphs) may seem boundless for businesses competing in digital environments. Yet, there is a proviso: that kind of achievement relies on a shift from Supervised to Reinforcement learning; i.e., on the assumption that facts on the ground can be captured directly, without the filter of prior knowledge. That assumption can work for zero-sum problems because the context and possible outcomes can be mapped out, or at least circumscribed, thus leaving little room for emerging new concepts or erratic reasoning. But that's not the case for nonzero-sum issues.

Judgments related to nonzero-sum issues rely on observing ill-defined contexts, and reasoning about open-ended outcomes. In such circumstances, fully fledged RL can introduce self-reinforcing biases — biases that need to be redressed through supervision or Knowledge graphs.

When DL technologies are used to support decision-making processes, a clear distinction should thus be maintained between:

- Self-contained issues: for which judgments must be upheld by the traceability of supporting data (observation) and causal chains (reasoning)

- Open-ended issues: for which accountability is required, not only for judgments but also for the selection of causal chains and the provision of supporting data

Crossing learning steps (observation, reasoning, judgment) with the nature of problems (self-contained or open-ended) marks the benefits and limits of DL and KG technologies:

- Regarding the traceability of causal chains, KG can provide reasoned guidance to the freewheeling potency of DL, that is forceful but unconstrained by purpose or causality.

- Regarding the accountability of decisions, the benefits are conditioned by the integration of individual judgments with collective behaviors.

At the enterprise level, the real challenge is therefore to morph individual learning into collective knowledge and decision-making.

Organizational Behavior

No matter the disciplinary perspective, from developmental psychology to linguistics, thinking is rooted in communication. For enterprises, thinking means collective intelligence and collaboration.

Creativity & Collaboration

For enterprise organizations, two aspects of intelligence as a social capability are especially significant:

- With regard to behavior, emotional intelligence (usually defined in terms of motivation, empathy, and social skills) can significantly enhance people's ability to learn and handle issues. The ways emotional intelligence translate into collective accomplishments may be perplexing, but the results are not in doubt: enterprise successes are always backed by strong corporate identity and culture.

- With regard to outcome, creativity and innovation give enterprises their competitive edge. If anything, they give name to the puzzling alchemy that turns individual initiatives into collective momentum.

Both aspects are contingent on collaboration that is alive and kicking, and fed with renewed ideas and assumptions; this active collaboration prompts opposite viewpoints and opens new perspectives. As expounded by cognitive psychologists like Robin Dunbar (cf. bibliography), and confirmed by empirical studies, human brains differentiate between two levels of collaboration: one set for around 10 trusted personal contacts, and the other set for around 150 untested social ones (cf. chapter 10). Since that distinction broadly matches the imprint of digital networks on people's personal and professional connections, it should serve as a template for enterprise collaboration mechanisms.

On that basis, AI and ML technologies can be turned into gatekeepers securing spaces for trusted personal collaborations (no bots allowed), such that the impact of such collaboration on creativity and innovation would be enhanced. The specificity of personal interactions can be characterized by:

- Pragmatics: the meanings exchanged in conversations are determined by the context and the flow of what is said, with syntax and semantics serving as the supporting structure.

- Empathy: people in personal interactions believe (rightly or not) that they can understand what their counterparts have in mind.

- Guarded trust: people in personal interactions expect qualified truth from their interlocutors; they assume that people sharing the same environment on a regular basis will try to preserve their credibility and will consequently speak truthfully as often as possible.

As a corollary, if organizations are to further individual motivation and creativity, digital collaboration should make sure that people are in no doubt about whom they are talking to: a bro or a bot. Conversely, using DL or KG to mimic human behaviors would be counterproductive:

- As illustrated by real-time subtitling, talking pragmatics is like walking a tightrope: a single misstep can throw away the whole thread of understanding, with no chance to retrieve or reprieve.

- Any misgivings in people's minds about the nature of their interlocutor will switch off empathy and the emotional intelligence behind creativity and innovation.

- The mix of contributing brains (human and artificial) is bound to impair accountability.

Organizations should thus use AI and ML technologies to secure collaboration swimlanes with unambiguous behavioral expectations and commitments.

Collaboration & Cognition

As noted above, the weaving of individual creativity into the fabric of collective innovation must be supported by collaboration mechanisms that preserve the intuitive (by nature, individual) part of thinking. The matter of reasoning is different: compared to intuition, reasoning is set in two dimensions, individual and collective; an organization should thus strive to achieve more as a whole than the sum of its individual parts.

As a matter of fact, that sum can turn into a dramatic net loss as demonstrated by the hoped-for wisdom of the crowd, found stillborn in the cradle of social media. When artificial brains are embedded in social networks, evidence suggests an equivalent of Gresham's law for money: "bad judgment drives out good." In order to prevent such a dereliction of collective intelligence, enterprises need to secure a pivot between individual and collective thinking.

That juncture can be illuminated by the work of Amos Tversky and Daniel Kahneman (who received the 2002 Nobel Prize in Economics). Their analysis of decision-making distinguishes two levels:

1. Decision-making that "operates automatically and quickly, with little or no effort and no sense of voluntary control." Contributions are intuitive and prompted by immediate circumstances.

2. Decision-making that "allocates attention to the effortful mental activities that demand it, including complex computations." Contributions stem from an assessment of circumstances and are justified by reasoning and past experience.

Not surprisingly, these levels neatly align with intuition and reasoning; they can also pair up with the cognitive levels of collaboration mentioned above. That triple perspective of cognition (intuition vs. reasoning), decision-making (instant vs. planned), and collaboration (individual vs. collective) is at the core of organizational behavior and determines the osmosis between individual contributions and collective innovation. On that account, enterprise architects could use AI and ML technologies to improve the integration of cognition and collaboration mechanisms.

With regard to *collaboration*, the objective is to emphasize the specificity of human contributions, while ensuring a seamless and traceable integration of all contributed contents. That can be achieved with interfaces fed from a unified representation of contents and reasoning capabilities, but structured according to organization, agents, and roles (cf. chapter 10). Such interfaces should ensure:

- Traceability: nature of resources (data, information, knowledge), language (syntax, semantics, epistemics, and pragmatics), and reasoning capabilities

- Accountability: roles (systems or people), kind of collaboration (direct or mediated), and decision-making process (observation, orientation, decision, action)

With regard to *cognition*, DL and KG technologies can support forward and reverse gears between personal intuition and reasoning, on the one hand, and collective knowledge and innovation, on the other hand:

- Forward: personal moves (intuitive or reasoned), engendered by circumstances, issues at hand, or exchanges, can be captured and assessed — either directly (DL) or after being translated into symbolic representations (KG).

- Reverse: direct feedback from changes in collective knowledge provide incentives for individual learning and further initiatives.

These changes in organizational behaviors intermingle with the transformation of an enterprise's organization and architectures.

Emerging Organizations

For all intents and purposes, organization is the shape taken by enterprises' activities, and changes in organization have always been brought about by changes in the division of labor. The question is, what happens to organizations when knowledge-driven activities are immersed in digital environments? Some indications can be found by probing changes in EA capabilities:

- Roles: division of labor and innovation

- Outcomes: knowledge hybrids

- Activities: hybrid value chains

- Location: edges of the Cloud

- Processes: homeostasis

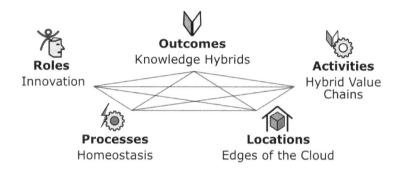

Figure 16-4. EA Capabilities & the Knowledge Economy

Innovation

As epitomized by Henry Ford, industrial-era organization was defined by a clear-cut division of labor:

- At the execution level, manual tasks were fragmented and specialized.

- At the management level, analysis and decision-making were centralized and abstract.

That organizational paradigm put a double restraint on innovation:

- On the execution side, the fragmentation of manual tasks prevented workers from assessing and improving their performances.

- On the management side, knowledge was kept in conceptual boxes and was bereft of feedback from actual application.

Such railings between supposedly smart brains and dumb hands may have received just enough results for mass manufacturing processes, limited to material flows and subject to circumscribed and predictable technological changes.

But hierarchies had to grow with processes' complexity, generating overheads and rigidities in need of repeated prunings. Then, to deal with the rise of services and the crisscrossing of informational and material flows, enterprises had to introduce matrix organization, which has blurred the lines between management and execution, yet has maintained hierarchies. The digital mutation and the knowledge economy can be seen as the last stage of that trend: the dematerialization of industrial and business flows means that the distinction between execution and management is pointless at best and cripples innovation at worst. Interestingly, that point has been made by robots.

Whereas smart tools may be able to perform a wide range of physical tasks without human supervision, innovation is driven by what happens on the front lines — where humans and machines collaborate in the processing and delivering of mixes of products and services, and learn from their mutual experience. That's where DL technologies are at their best: tackling one-sided or zero-sum problems, in well-defined contexts, in collaboration with human supervisors.

Compared to symbolic flows, the processing of material flows can be directly and effectively assessed and improved, as demonstrated by the ubiquity of Deep-learning technologies. Moreover, the possibility of actual and direct feedback removes the traceability issues that hamstring Reinforcement learning in symbolic processing. It ensues that the distinction between manual and cognitive skills is erased from both sides:

• Manual workers can learn from reasoning robots.

• Robots can adjust their behavior to humans and learn from their intuitive skills.

That pairing of human and mechanical brains brings together implicit (intuition) and explicit (reasoning) learning, and puts judgment in the hands of the former who can combine action with knowledge.

Knowledge Hybrids

A ten-second overview of the ten biggest market capitalizations tells the whole story: there is no business like the business of knowledge. No matter which product or service, what counts is knowledge — sold directly (e.g., higher education), or as software embedded in products (e.g., cars), services (e.g., maintenance), or licensed designs (e.g., silicon chips).

As illustrated by the history of intellectual property, there is nothing new in knowledge as an economic factor; what is new is the impetus it has received from the digital transformation and the upsurge in AI and ML technologies. Knowledge can no longer be seen only as an asset, but must also be accounted for as an input to be bought (cf. chapter 15), transformed, and marketed. More importantly, the spreading of knowledge in value chains (cf. chapter 4) is not limited to a subset of knowledge-driven activities but potentially affects a wide range of industries. That possibility is materialized by patent trolls, shell companies whose only purpose is to bag as many apparently pointless patents as possible in the hope that one of them will turn into a lucrative industrial stranglehold.

Summarily, patents can be defined by two basic characteristics:

1. As formal descriptions, patents belong to the realm of symbolic representations.

2. Patents do not secure the rights to use what is described, only the rights to exclude others from using the patented descriptions.

The first characteristic puts patents at the heart of the knowledge economy; the second one makes them a barrier to entry and, consequently, positions them against knowledge as a business. That paradox was mostly irrelevant as long as knowledge wasn't bought and sold by and for itself; but knowledge is now a key resource that should be traded as freely as any other one.

The purpose of patents has never been to promote competitive markets, only to protect new designs of artifacts and modus operandi. For two centuries, the targets of patents have been mainly physical (until the addition of software) — yet as a special kind of device, not as a symbolic artifact. Nonetheless, the patenting of software has paved the way to patent any kind of symbolic construct; most notably, representations of biological structures (e.g., stretches of DNA), financial products, and business processes.

Besides the implementation hurdles, exemplified by the swelling delays, costs, and litigations generated by the filing of patents, extending the scope of patents to symbolic representations themselves has introduced an intrinsic flaw in the way intellectual property is regulated: if patent P refers to artifact Ap, the issue is about the possibility of using P (a symbolic description) to achieve Ax (an artifact); but if Ap is itself a symbolic description, the issue turns into a debate about the semantics of two symbolic descriptions — not far from patenting the number of angels standing on the point of a pin.

By doing away with the differentiated natures of patented items (artifacts or modus operandi) and the patent itself (symbolic representation of the patented item), a new species of patented items has emerged:

- The first generation are crossbreeds, combining physical and symbolic items held together by patents.

- The second generation are digital hybrids of the first generation.

- The third generation are intelligent (or knowledgeable) hybrids.

For enterprises, the spreading of patented intelligent hybrids in value chains implies their reassessment in terms of open-source information (free to use), market prices (e.g., from data factories), proprietary information (traded), and internal prices (cf. chapter 10).

In addition to these advances on the symbolic side, digital hybrids open new perspectives on the physical one when combined with the Internet of things (IoT) and Cloud computing. The benefits for the traceability and authenticity of supply chains can be illustrated by crypto-anchors, microchips embedded in material flows which embody the concept of anchor employed in this book.

Significantly, advances on the symbolic and physical sides of digital hybrids can be combined through Blockchains and pave the way to an overhaul of patent regulations.

Blockchains are encrypted digital ledgers that can be used to track and authenticate the provenance of physical or symbolic artifacts without disclosing their innards; that technological specificity could be suitably applied to the untangling of patents and patented contents.

Hybrid Value Chains

The organizational consequences of knowledge-driven activities should be examined in light of the evolution of manufacturing- and software-engineering methods, and the merging of business and engineering processes.

Established manufacturing and engineering methods, epitomized by Lean Six Sigma, put the focus on minimizing the different categories of waste:

• Outcomes: overproduction, inventories, defects (as defined by capabilities)

• Human resources: unemployment or underemployment of skills

• Activities: unnecessary steps or moves

• Time: processes waiting for equipment or equipment waiting for processes

The merging of business and engineering processes suggests that the objective of minimizing waste should be simultaneously applied to the physical and symbolic dimensions of processes. But that would be waiving the convenience of software flows in order to handle them with the impediments of physical ones. Alternatively, morphing the whole of processes into digital hybrids may offer a way out of the dilemma.

Digital hybrids rely on three basic ideas:

• Products, equipment, or systems are a combination of physical and software artifacts.

• Being digital, such artifacts can be uniformly described through models.

• Analysis, design, and engineering can be carried out through iterative building, simulating, testing, and adjusting of various combinations of hardware and software.

Popularized by digital twins, digital hybrids have been primarily employed to reproduce physical devices and mimic their behavior; as such they can be seen as dynamic extensions of 3D computer-aided designs (CADs), or as a reverse of digital-to-physical 3D printing.

But digital hybrids have a broader significance as ultimate surrogates:

• Digital hybrids fuse software components and business processes.

• They integrate actionable maps (models) and territories (systems and artifacts).

• They materialize the integration of data, information, and knowledge.

Taking into account the potential of Blockchains, that puts the processing of digital hybrids on the front line of EA transformation.

Edges of the Cloud

At the system level, Cloud computing is without a doubt the most visible realization of the digital transformation. And the term is an understatement: the Cloud is much more than computing and can accommodate most of systems architectures' capabilities, as many enterprises of various sizes have experienced.

Enterprises' rapid and comprehensive move to the Cloud has been facilitated by the Cloud's organizational neutrality and the modularity of implementations:

- Deployments to the Cloud can be done at the application or system level, or for functions or databases.

- If and when required, a migration to the Cloud can be carried out with limited impact on systems' functionalities or enterprises' organization.

As a result, there has been a marked contrast between the dated organization of enterprises and the transformation of Cloud-based technical architectures. But the COVID-19 pandemic and the technical and organizational mutations mentioned above have combined with Cloud neutrality to upturn EA geography.

Within a few weeks in early 2020, the pandemic's health hazards for office work and mass public transport emptied offices all around the world. As if curtains were drawn on a stage, deserted cubicles and open-plan offices have given a concrete image of the overlooked obsolescence of organizations structured around offices.

All at once, the stars aligned for a shake-up of enterprises' topology: an outdated structure (the office), a dire necessity (health), a proven facility (the Cloud), and a toolbox of advanced technologies (AI and ML). As they happen, shake-ups often also redefine perspectives and possibilities; with regard to enterprises' topology, the new frontier is commonly known as Edge computing.

As already mentioned (e.g., in chapter 12), EA edges are doubly significant: first, they mark the divide between enterprise and systems architectures, and second, they are the locus of the digital revolution and the merging of physical and digital realms. From a functional perspective, Edge computing is meant to deal with issues like security, privacy, and authenticity; from a technical perspective, Edge computing involves IoT, digital hybrids, Blockchains, and naturally, AI and ML technologies. Given the diversity of issues and the rapid advances of technologies, redefining EA topology in physical and symbolic environments should be top of the enterprise architects' agendas.

Homeostasis

The ubiquity of smart software components in business processes and the immersion of systems in digital environments leads to the fusing of external (business) and internal (engineering) time frames.

On the business side, time is relative and episodic: as suggested by Lewis Carroll's Red Queen, the survival of enterprises in a Darwinian-like contest of natural selection doesn't depend on absolute speed, but on their relative rate of change compared to the moves of their competitors.

On the engineering side, time can be both continuous and periodic: continuous for the deliveries of Agile developments, and periodic for the deployment of phased ones (cf. chapter 14).

Planners must therefore take into account both the pulse of business environments and the time frames of architecture-based developments. That two-pronged focus corresponds to a typical shuttle configuration, with boarding decisions determined by the optimization of business values under the constraint of the Lean principles mentioned above. That kind of problem (what to put in shuttles and when) can be directly integrated into the dynamic backlog presented in chapter 14.

Dynamic planning by itself is a well-known optimization problem that can be handled by traceable algorithms. But the continuous delivery and deployment of applications in digital environments induces a wide range of ill-defined uncertainties. Enter process mining.

Process mining is process management on steroids, materialized by two key functional extensions:

- Process mining enables the continuous monitoring and improvement of actual processes in digital environments.

- It can apply Machine-learning technologies to operational data and information models.

Taking advantage of the dynamic integration of DL technologies into business operations, process mining becomes the key to homeostasis between enterprises and their digital environment (cf. chapter 15).

With business and organizational issues accounted for by decision-making processes (cf. chapter 10), DL technologies can probe data logs from both sides of operations:

- Environment: to identify shifts in markets; e.g., customer expectations or competitors' moves

- Enterprise: to identify failings in operations; e.g., supply chains or systems' performances

These observations can be continuously fed into the dynamic planning of software updates, used to improve operations, or conveyed into business intelligence.

Deep-learning technologies can be especially effective for process mining, because the focus put on operational concerns (instead of open-ended organizational and business concepts) means that options can be clearly defined and/or circumscribed, laying the groundwork for Reinforcement learning.

As the embodiment of homeostasis, process mining thus stands at the forefront of enterprises' sustainability in digital business environments. For the same reason (i.e., homeostasis), process mining is also where new forms can emerge from digital primordial DNA and morph into new architectures.

Octopuses & Swarms

Emerging forms and behaviors of enterprise architectures suggest two complementary metaphors.

At the enterprise level the aim is to bring together top-down and bottom-up learning and decision-making processes. On that account, distributed agents sharing experience, intuition, and reasoning appear to parallel the nervous system of octopuses, with each arm outfitted with its own local brain, yet with neuronal connections coordinating all learning and decision-making.

From the perspective of the environment, the top-down rationales of enterprises' governance are masked. What remains is the conflicting logic of operational interactions between devices and systems with cognitive capabilities, shifting agendas, and differentiated access to a multi-layered pool of data. That mix of competition and collaboration points to swarms of agents whose highly developed capabilities and autonomy can only exist as part of a collective. That collective will be considered in the final chapter.

CHAPTER 17.

Evolution, Resilience & Externalities

Systemic disruptions call for adaptive changes supported by shifts in representation paradigms

As established upfront, enterprises can be seen as living organisms whose sustainability depends on their continuous adaptation to changes in environments and, consequently, on their ability to learn from observation, reasoning, and experience. But for enterprises set in competitive environments, learning is just a prerequisite; the deciding factors for success are their capacity to evolve and their resilience when confronted with abrupt and massive upheavals.

Evolution & Resilience

Evolution in Four Dimensions

As summarized by Eva Jablonka and Marion J. Lamb (cf. bibliography), the extended evolutionary synthesis defines the evolution of live organisms in four dimensions:

1. Genetics: changes in phenotypes (the actual forms and capabilities of organisms) are carried out through the combination of genotypes (the coded parts of DNA).

2. Epigenetics: changes in genotypes between generations (genetics) can also take place in transmission, induced by the noncoded (or perhaps still undeciphered) parts of the DNA (or epigenetics).

3. Behavioral: changes occur through socially mediated nonsymbolic learning (e.g., imitation).

4. Symbolic: changes occur through socially mediated symbolic learning (e.g., political systems).

For enterprises, the equivalent dimensions of evolution would be:

1. Corporate identity: changes in status, assets, and ownership

2. Business model: changes in targeted markets, resources, and organization

3. Business processes: changes in channels and operations

4. Architecture: changes in symbolic representations

In line with the epigenetics metaphor, the evolution of enterprises would be governed by the double thread of information between data and knowledge, supporting both behavioral (emerging) and symbolic (planned) evolutions (figure 17-1).

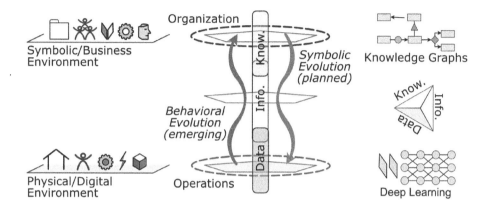

Figure 17-1. *Enterprise Evolution*

The question is: how can adaptive changes learned through observations and experience can be accumulated into perennial (or inherited) strengths that are embodied in systems, organization, and corporate culture? As far as enterprises are concerned, the yardstick should be their capacity to change; in particular, the versatility and plasticity of their architecture (cf. chapter 15).

With regard to versatility, behavioral evolution stems from innovation and collaboration on the human side, and process mining on the systems side. A better use of representations can then translate into an improvement of the representations themselves.

With regard to plasticity, symbolic evolution stems from the analysis of descriptive and prescriptive models, and is meant to reduce the complexity of architectures and processes.

Yet the COVID-19 pandemic has been a brutal reminder that changes can be disruptive and throw entire industries into the ditch. With the looming hazards of climate change in mind, enterprises' architectures should add resilience to sustainability.

Risks & Resilience

Like evolutions in nature, the evolution of organizations is not linear but rather the combined result of random and targeted changes, possibly but not necessarily related. As long as the curve of transformations remains steady, there is time for enterprises' stakeholders and architects to set the path of evolution between changes with adaptive value and extraneous variations. That long game didn't play out with the sudden onset of the COVID-19 pandemic, and neither will it happen with the much wider range of potential climate-related upsets.

Compared to the COVID-19 pandemic — an inflated and speeded up replica of an otherwise known hazard — the upshots of climate change, beside being abrupt and massive, are bound to come from unexpected directions. Systemic and in-depth disruptions will be set across:

- Physical environments (e.g., extreme rainfalls, heat waves)

- Operations (e.g., infrastructures, distribution channels, supply chains)

- Markets (e.g., shifts in consumption, products' obsolescence)

- Regulations (e.g., environment, health, privacy)

It ensues that piecemeal and focused adjustments through enterprise architecture capabilities, effective for plain-sailing sustainability, will not cope with systemic risks such as these. To prepare for the wide range of foreshadowed fallouts, enterprises should focus on their capacity to change and anticipate.

Regarding their capacity to change (cf. chapter 15), enterprises should replace closing perspectives, focused on business-specific domains, with all-inclusive ones embracing all possible dimensions. To that effect, EA should rely on:

- Homeostasis and Deep-learning for behavioral evolutions

- Brainy architectures and Knowledge graphs for symbolic ones

- Agile architectures for enabling swift and pointed adaptations, as well as for securing long-term mutations

Regarding anticipation, climate-related hazards can serve as a benchmark for the impact of systemic changes on enterprises' architecture. Such an impact can be summarily mapped by crossing the dimensions of EA evolution with the taxonomy of contexts introduced in chapter 8 (figure 17-2):

Dimension	Institutional	Professional	Corporate	Social
Corporate Identity	Regulations	Alliances	Ownership Assets	Brand
Business Model	Taxes	Partnerships	Carbon Footprint	Demographics
Business Processes	Regulations	Supply Chains	Operations	Channels
Symbolic Representations	Simulations	Game Theory	Strategic Planning	Marketing

Figure 17-2. The EA Imprint of Climate-related Changes

Corporate Exposure

Preparing for climate-related upshots epitomizes the purpose of strategies; namely, to compensate for unreliable facts and doubtful causal chains (cf. chapter 10).

Given the open-ended time frame, extensive scope, and countless cross-effects of the changes concerned, a reliable cost/benefit assessment of options is nearly impossible. Nevertheless, the four dimensions listed above can help to identify enterprises' potential exposure.

Regarding corporate identity, brisk and extensive shifts in business environments may introduce discrepancies between the agenda of corporate stakeholders (e.g., Big Oil) and enterprises' prospective business models (e.g., thermal insulation). Accordingly, enterprise architects need to appraise the sway of corporate ownership on strategic decision-making.

The exposure of business models can be assessed through potential shifts in the value of corporate assets and, more specifically, enterprises' carbon footprint. While ML and KG technologies can help to assess the future of assets' prices, they cannot offset the unreliability of available facts and causal chains. By contrast, carbon foot-prints can provide an indirect yet more reliable indicator of enterprises' resilience to climate change, and thus lay the groundwork for the assessment of the carbon contents of value chains.

Regarding physical exposure, the potential impacts of climate change can be best apprehended through business operations, combining scientific research (e.g., about rainfalls or heat waves), simulations (e.g., to inform infrastructures' cost/benefit analysis), and critically, process mining.

Finally, symbolic representations, set at the juncture between planned and emerging transformations, are key to align policies with exposure; specifically:

- Mapping climate-related issues with enterprise architectures' capabilities

- Integrating the assessment of strategic alternatives with decision-making processes (cf. chapter 10)

- Providing actionable maps in support of Agile architectures (cf. chapter 15)

Corporate exposure to climate-related changes can then be associated with the corresponding factors in contexts.

Institutional Context

As far as climate change is concerned, taxes and regulations should play a key role in institutional contexts.

Dealing with taxes, on carbon or otherwise, is a well-established corporate discipline with no special application to climate change; by contrast, coping with climate-related regulations may call for a radical overhaul of customary schemes.

To begin with, such regulations are set across a wide range of domains (e.g., physical environments, health, processes, safety), with multiple overlapping effects. Moreover, these regulations are issued by a plurality of authorities with different and often overlapping agendas. Finally, these regulations are in constant flux, which make them moving targets for enterprise architects.

As it happens, these issues are a good match for KG and DL technologies:

- Regulations are by nature symbolic, comprehensive, and formal; they can thus be represented by KG and, consequently, be subject to different kinds of reasoning and judgment.

- Data- and process mining can be used to flesh out symbolic reasoning with data analytics and simulations, with DL in-between to uncover and try out hypothetical causal chains and outcomes.

That should give enterprise architects a better understanding of how climate-related regulations can affect processes and operations.

Professional Context

Compared to institutional contexts which, lobbying notwithstanding, are not meant to be affected by corporate policies, professional contexts are swayed by enterprises' competition and/or cooperation initiatives.

On the planned axis of evolution, enterprises should consider the implications of climate change for structural alliances (corporate identity) and business partnerships (business model).

On the emerging axis, the objective should be to identify potential cracks to be fixed (e.g., weaknesses in supply chains) — or to be exploited, to get ahead of competitors.

The priority should be supply chains, which are bound to be directly affected by climate change through physical disruptions, taxes, or regulations. Once again, the combination of DL and KG technologies can be decisive in bringing together actual observations and simulations, confirmed and hypothetical causal chains, and decision-making (e.g., with Game theory).

Social Context

Like professional contexts, social ones can be affected by enterprises' policies; but the difference is that agents in social contexts are anonymous and are supposed to remain so.

Regarding corporate identity, the impact of climate-related disruptions can be felt through company brands in a variety of ways depending on circumstances and the perception of corporate policies; e.g., a supply chain could be associated with deforestation, or a sudden focus could be put on the environmental impact of palm oil used as ingredient. Business models could thus be affected by demographic, geographic, and socio-economic consequences of climate changes.

The objectives here are essentially tactical and defensive (e.g., the monitoring of social media), with limited relevance for enterprise architecture.

Personal Context

Albeit temporarily, most innovations start with individuals. Depending on innovations' turnover, new ideas may remain dormant for some time before either withering or achieving some business and/or social status. Given the range of still-to-be-solved climate issues, a miscellany of initiatives and experiments are continuously scrutinized and renewed. Enterprises can keep track of the ones deemed relevant (e.g., typical climate-related litigations) with Document management systems (DMS). But DMS cannot cope with the myriad of individual facts and ideas that form the primordial soup of innovation. For that purpose, enterprises need the ontological distinction between facts and representations.

The raison d'être of ontologies is to set apart epistemic levels of knowledge: concepts, categories, and facts (cf. chapter 8). That's especially useful for organizations that have to cope with rapid and extensive changes without a reliable and comprehensive understanding of contexts and phenomena. With ontologies, knowledge managers can keep track of relevant individual facts and interpretations, and continuously build, assess, improve, or reject representations.

Externalities & Social Responsibility

Enterprises are confronted with a wide array of changes — some gradual, others seismic — and the primary objective of enterprise architecture is to make the best of these changes (cf. chapter 15). But what if the changes don't make sense or defy a clear rationale for a foreseeable future?

Enterprises & Digital Edges

Enterprises stand on both edges of the digital sphere: the physical one, materialized by IoT, and the symbolic one, actualized by social networks.

On the *physical edge*, enterprises must prevent security breaches of their own data, while protecting the personal data of individuals in environments.

IoT is typical of the physical edge's exposure to security breaches. From its inception, it has been a paradoxical endeavor: trying to integrate physical devices into the symbolic web. Not surprisingly, hackers have caught sight of that new wealth of chinks in the internet's armour, combining brute force (e.g., denial-of-service attacks) and cunning ploys (e.g., Trojan horses) to wreak havoc in enterprises' systems. While DL and KG technologies can provide a first line of defense, artificial brains are at an inherent disadvantage against real ones: effective defenses require hackers' supervision.

Yet, over the long term, the protection of enterprises' internal data could benefit from the protection of external personal data, as dictated by regulatory constraints like the General Data Protection Regulation (GDPR). Accordingly, EA strategies should rely on digital walls to separate data from information (cf. chapter 8). And these walls could double as defenses against security breaches, taking advantage of Edge-computing technologies like crypto-anchors (to combine physical and digital spheres) and Blockchains (to combine validity and anonymity).

That kind of synergy could herald a convergence between the enterprise's own concerns and social responsibility.

On the *symbolic edge*, social networks' lack of accountability is creating a semantic Wild West. The same kind of massive (e.g., swarms of bots) and deceptive (e.g., fake identities) instruments are at play on the physical and symbolic edges. But the targets differ in nature: actual items in enterprises' repositories on the physical edge, and symbolic items (or memes) in social representations on the symbolic one.

Not directly concerned by the tumult of social networks, enterprises may simply try to set apart the wheat of reliable facts from the chaff of deceptive ones — or they could get into the fray and build their own narratives in support of their goals and strategies. But storytelling in social networks is not without risk for business entities, because they are, for all intents and purposes, the only ones held accountable.

That specific exposure of enterprises to social accountability suggests, as noted earlier, a potential convergence between their business interests and social responsibility.

Digital Identities & Managers' Responsibility

As contended at the outset of this book (cf. chapter 2), enterprises' architecture is set on three dimensions: physical and business environments, on the one hand, and systems' symbolic representations, on the other hand. The digital fusing of these dimensions into a single nexus has radical and directly observable consequences for people and money, arguably two key aspects of business.

Whereas digital money is already on a fast track, driven by the endeavors of financial institutions as well as nonfinancial big retailers, digital identities are still entrusted to a physical counterpart, with practical issues at the physical as well as symbolic levels:

- At the physical level: what is at stake is compliance with privacy regulations.

- At the symbolic level: it is to have managers personally accountable for corporate decision-making.

As noted before, crypto-anchors could be used to build digital identities, with Blockchains securing both the anonymity and authenticity of physical identities. But Edge-computing technologies are of little help at the symbolic level, where what is at stake is managers' authority, responsibility, and accountability:

- Authority is an enterprises' internal matter to be decided with regard to their organization and decision-making processes.

- Responsibility, once fully defined by organization, must now take into consideration the part played by knowledge-based supporting systems (cf. chapter 10).

- Accountability, once essentially an internal matter, has taken a new dimension since the 2008 financial crisis, as illustrated by regulations like the United States' Yates Memorandum or the United Kingdom's Senior Managers and Certification Regime.

But compliance with regulations surrounding managers' responsibility may introduce debilitating consequences for decision-making if digital identities are not used to differentiate between physical and symbolic ones, and to manage the latter according to their organizational or functional context.

That sets up another point of enterprises' exposure to social responsibility — an exposure best shielded with the knowledge component of enterprise architecture.

Enterprises as Social Matrices

As viable organisms, enterprises constitute a basic unit in social ecosystems; their structures and behaviors reflect their adaptive evolution, which in turn, reshape their ecosystems.

From the perspective of economic liberalism, the feedback of enterprises' transformation on business environments is meant to be governed by the invisible hand of the markets; the corollary is to circumscribe enterprises' responsibility to their shareholders and stakeholders.

But enterprises' stakes and options are bound to be redefined by systemic disruptions; for example:

- Extensive and unpredictable shifts in business environments undermine the reliability of short-term shareholders' policies.

- Ethical considerations cannot be ignored in the face of societal hardship.

- Health issues often entail difficult trade-offs between individual choices and collective gains.

- Social media are the greenhouses of corporate brands, but can also turn into minefields in cases of public relations' missteps. Success in such hothouses induces a delicate balance between business benefits and social responsibility.

Put together, these factors mean that, nolens volens, enterprises need to extend the scope of their responsibilities beyond shareholders and stakeholders to encompass not only their actual socio-economic and ecological footprint, but also the associated representations and, more generally, their public image.

That progressive integration of enterprises into their social ecosystem, while driven by clear business motivations, also reflects a better understanding of the cross-dependencies between enterprises and social issues. That shift in enterprise governance is paralleled by a return of active public policies driven by the expansion of regulatory domains and the need for economic stimulation in the wake of COVID-19.

These trends put enterprises' architecture at the nexus of technical (digital sphere), functional (knowledge economy), and social (ecosystems) transformations, and consequently, at the core of enterprises' strategies.

Notations

Environments, Architecture Layers & Models

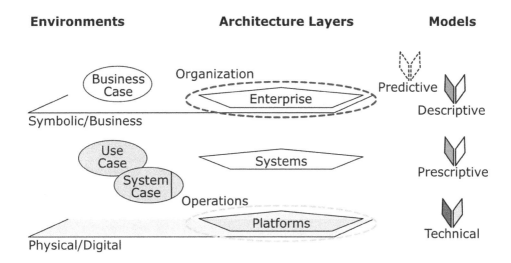

Figure A-1. *Environments, Architecture Layers & Models*

Symbolic Representations

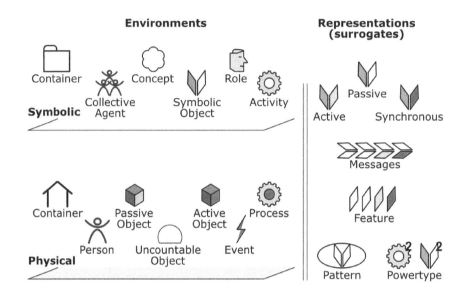

Figure A-2. Symbolic Representations

Connectors

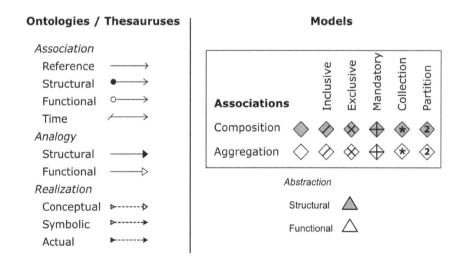

Figure A-3. Connectors

Enterprise Architecture's Capabilities

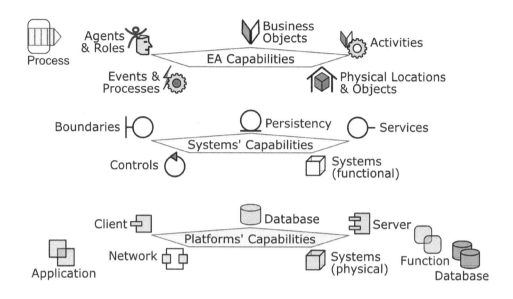

Figure A-4. EA Capabilities

Workshops

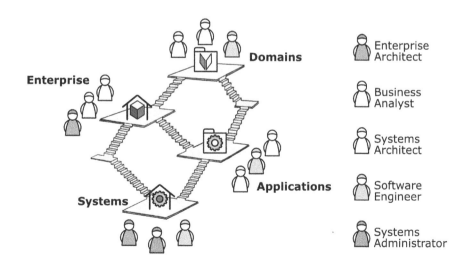

Figure A-5. Workshops

Conceptual Kernel & Enterprise Architecture Thesaurus

Preamble

Objective

When considering thesauruses, it may help to remember that "define" literally means setting limits. The aim here is thus not to embark upon a futile quest for truths (or to play definition games), but to borrow Occam's razor and cut meanings to the bone of necessary, sufficient, and consistent definitions:

- Necessary: a definition must serve a purpose.

- Sufficient: meanings are by nature unbounded, so looking for all-inclusive definitions is self-defeating.

- Consistent: definitions must be unequivocal and free of circular references.

As an illustration, quality is defined as *the probability that nothing will go amiss during the life cycle of a product or service.*

The objective of this thesaurus is therefore to build a conceptual kernel from which such definitions could be formally derived, discussed, probed, corrected, or amended. It must be noted that this objective comes as a necessary complement to the open-modeling approach (cf. chapter 9). From a broader perspective, it's easy to argue that closed and rigid definitions would go against Agile objectives.

Ontologies developed with that kernel are set on three tiers:

- A backbone is built of ontological hierarchies, set according to the epistemic nature of entries: aspects, categories, concepts, documents, and individuals. These hierarchies are purely semantic and devoid of architectural meaning.

- Seven axioms provide the roots of acyclic semantic networks; they serve as semantic firebreaks, preventing circular definitions.

- Knowledge graphs connect EA concepts, categories, aspects, and instances.

The kernel presented here, implemented using the OWL Web Ontology Language on the Stanford/Protégé portal, is meant to support open and actionable descriptions of enterprise architectures:

- Open: kernel definitions (suffix "_") only cover minimally incontrovertible assertions, which are meant to be extended according to the specifics of industries and contexts, whether organizational or technical.

- Actionable: the distinction between kernel elements and specific contents enables formal quality checks and the reliable transformation of models.

Axioms

To be ecumenical and avoid endless controversies, kernel entries must be built on a limited set of unambiguous and effective assertions:

- Limited: since axioms serve as roots to acyclic semantic graphs, there should be as few axioms as possible.

- Unambiguous: axioms are meant to be either accepted or rejected, which implies that their meaning should be clear and leave no wiggle room for misunderstanding.

- Effective: the axioms singled out are not meant to be the pillars of some absolute truth, but rather to serve as logical hubs for sound and effective EA categories. They should therefore only be judged on their effectiveness in supporting clear and concise EA definitions.

On that account, and assuming standard logic, seven axioms have been selected as a necessary and sufficient basis for an enterprise architecture (EA) thesaurus:

Instances

Physical or symbolic occurrences of objects or phenomena (both accepted as postulates): The distinction between physical and symbolic instances is not exclusive (consider hybrids); additionally, fictional instances are instances (physical or symbolic) that are not meant to be realized. Instances are represented by individuals in OWL.

Collection

Set of instances managed uniformly, independently of their nature.

Identity

Unique value associated with an instance: External identities are defined independently of the organization or system under consideration. External identities can be biological, social, or designed; they are not exclusive (e.g., social security number and fingerprints). Internal identities are used to manage components independently of environments.

Symbolic Representations

1. A symbol is a sign pointing to something else (referent).

2. A symbolic representation is a symbol pointing to a set of instances.

3. A symbolic object is an object representing a referent; this means that symbolic objects can be physical, as they usually are.

Behavior

The ability of an instance to change the state of instances, including itself: Objects are either active (with behavior) or passive (without behavior), and the propriety is exclusive.

State

Named sets of values that characterize instances of objects (actual or symbolic), processes, or representations, between events. Stateful objects and activities come with a finite number of discrete states; stateless ones don't have this limited array, and may indeed have an infinite number of discrete states.

Event

Change in the state of objects and phenomena: External events are changes triggered from outside the organization or system under consideration.

Example

Axioms serve as roots and firebreaks in acyclic semantic networks of EA definitions. These definitions are not meant to be "true," comprehensive, or exclusive; but rather, effective (to make a difference), as simple as possible (Occam's razor), and open to refutation.

The semantics of entries in the thesaurus are thus defined by hierarchies and semantic connectors. For example (figure B-1):

- *System* is defined as *Container* and *Agent* (hierarchies).

- The semantics of *Container* make references to *Collection* and objects' *Identity*.

- The semantics of *Agent* make references to *Behavior* and *Identity*.

Hierarchies and semantic connectors constitute the kernel of the thesaurus, which can then be fleshed out to build EA Knowledge graphs.

Given the layered organization (axioms and acyclic networks for semantics, and graphs for EA knowledge), consistency checks can be formal with regard to the kernel (e.g., no circular definitions), but pragmatic and customized with regard to EA definitions.

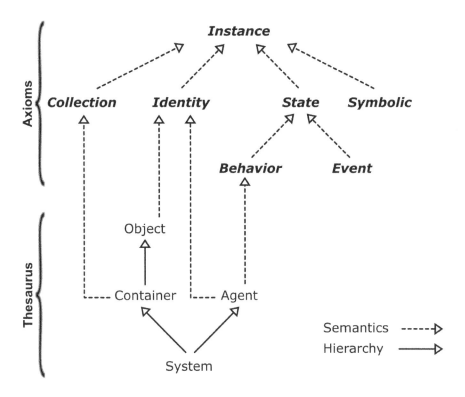

Figure B-1. *Axioms* (**italics**) *& Thesaurus*

Online

A beta version of the ontology using OWL 2 is available for comments on the Stanford/Protégé portal (details of access at https://caminao.blog/knowledge-architecture/ontologies-models/ea-in-bowls/).

Thesaurus

OWL Entry Level

The conceptual kernel is built around four kinds of *things* (in OWL 2 parlance), plus one for individuals, corresponding to the epistemic nature of targeted elements:

Aspects

Descriptions without external instances of their own: Aspects cannot be directly instantiated (or identified) in environments; they can only be observed as attached to external objects or phenomena, and instantiated as digital components (or internal objects) within systems.

Categories

Symbolic descriptions of sets of objects or phenomena: Categories can be associated with actual (descriptive, extensional) or intended (prescriptive, intensional) sets of instances.

Concepts (or ideas)

Pure semantic constructs defined independently of instances or categories.

Documents

Entries for documents represent their symbolic contents.

Individuals (or instances)

Physical or symbolic occurrences of ontological things.

EA Thesaurus (selected entries)

Abstraction

Cognitive process meant to focus on features deemed relevant, and to ignore the others.

Accountability

Ability to trace the organizational origins of decisions.

Activity

Symbolic description of a set of operations meant to be carried out by agents: Activities should not be confused with their execution, which may or may not change the state of objects, processes, or expectations.

Actor

Defined by UML as the roles played by agents interacting with systems. On that account, and to avoid confusion, actors, as defined by UML, can be seen as a subset of roles, generally defined at the enterprise level, independently of systems.

Agent

Identified instances with symbolic representations and behavior.

Aggregation

Collection of instances that are functionally bound together by a root instance, while keeping their own separate identities: The aggregate root guarantees the consistency of changes but doesn't prevent external objects from holding direct references.

Agile

Iterative development method characterized by shared ownership, collective responsibility, and continuous delivery.

Analysis

Classification of given sets of instances into (descriptive) categories; by comparison, design, used to define (prescriptive) features that could be implemented by an unlimited number of instances.

Analytics (data)

A variant of analysis focused on data; by comparison, the purpose of analysis is to go further and morph data into information models.

Anchor

Entity whose external (environment) instances are meant to be continuously and consistently represented by internal (systems) surrogates.

Application

Active digital object that can be executed by a computer system.

Architecture

Both an activity and its outcome: As an outcome, it's a structured collection of shared assets and mechanisms, which is intended to support a set of activities.

Asset

Resource used but not directly transformed by processes: The natures of assets determine how they are affected when they are used.

Association
Connection between instances of objects or behaviors identified on their own.

Attribute
See Property.

Blockchain
Encrypted digital ledger that can be used to track and authenticate the state and provenance of physical or symbolic artifacts, while disclosing only the information that is deemed necessary.

Boundary (or interface)
Symbolic or physical object marking the limit of a container.

Business
Whatever is deemed relevant in the environment of the organization considered.

Capability
Set of states that can be achieved by an object or process.

Category
Symbolic description of a set of instances with shared aspects (or features).

Class
Symbolic representation of digital objects identified in computer systems.

Coding
Building of executable models.

Communication
Exchange of objects between agents.

Composition
Collection of instances that are structurally bound (identified) together by a root instance, preventing external objects from directly referring to them and, as a result, ensuring the internal integrity of the composition.

Context

Container with semantics.

Data

Digital object with undetermined context and, therefore, undetermined semantics: Data can only be identified as a whole (no properties). Compared to information, data can only be taken at face value; i.e., without the mediation of interpretation.

Design (software)

Specification of resources and mechanisms directly and immediately available within a single address space and actionable within a single time frame (under a single clock). By comparison, architecture deals with resources and mechanisms distributed across multiple address spaces, which are subject to different time frames.

Domain

Context with models.

Entity (business)

Symbolic representation of actual or symbolic objects with a perennial identity (biological, social, or manufactured) defined in the environment.

Entropy

As understood in thermodynamics, entropy is the quantum of energy in a system that cannot be converted into mechanical work. For EA, entropy is the part of data that cannot be translated into useful information.

Environment

All instances outside a container; by default, all instances outside an organization.

Epistemic Level

Determination of the nature of what is known: concepts, categories, and facts.

Epoch

Event used as the origin of a time frame.

Expectation

Symbolic representation by agents of the future state of a context.

Explicit (knowledge)

Knowledge with symbolic representation.

Extend (connector)

Introduces an option to an object, activity, or Use case; the tail of the *extend* connector adds (aggregation) features to the connector's head.

Extensional (category)

Characterizes categories representing instances of objects or phenomena; as opposed to intensional.

Fact

Information (data + structure + context) that represents the state of objects or phenomena in a specific context: Facts can be observed directly or obtained through communication with agents.

Feature

Property or operation that characterizes a set of objects.

Framework

Symbolic container whose aim is to manage consistent descriptions of typical artifacts and associated modus operandi, and to support their realization.

Functional (partition)

Partitions with subsets characterized by the states of the same features, and can change during the life cycle of instances.

Generalization

Symbolic operation that extends the scope of a definition or a description.

Graph

Symbolic structure made of nodes, properties, and connectors.

Homeostasis (EA)

Process by which information is exchanged between a system and its environment in a way that ensures the system's sustainability.

Hybrid

Digital object that holds digital and physical identities simultaneously.

Implicit (knowledge)

Knowledge without symbolic representation.

Include (connector)

Introduces a necessary component of an object, activity, or Use case; the head of the *include* connector is part (composition) of the connector's tail.

Information

Structured sets of data set in a context.

Inheritance

Relationship between modeling constructs set at different levels of abstraction: The semantics of the inheritance are defined by modeling languages.

Intensional (category)

Characterizes categories representing specifications; as opposed to extensional.

Knowledge

Information associated with an intended purpose.

Layer (architecture)

Structured subsets of descriptions of interrelated categories and concepts; the terms tier and level are also employed as substitutes.

Legacy

Part of a system whose functional or technical evolution cannot be guaranteed.

Message

Object identified within a communication between agents; equivalent of a value object.

Model

Symbolic representation of instances pertaining to a domain of concern; by extension, meta-models are symbolic representations of models.

Models can be formally defined as extensional (or **descriptive**) or intensional (or **prescriptive**). The former deal with (or denote, in semiotic parlance) actual populations; the latter deal with categories, types, or features of artifacts.

Models can also be categorized as conceptual, for organization and business objects and activities defined independently of supporting systems; logical, for symbolic representations managed by systems independently of technical implementations; or physical, for the actual implementation of symbolic representations as binary objects.

Executable models are ones that can be run on a computer and reproduce the behavior of what they represent.

Nonzero-sum (Game theory)

Characterizes games set with open-ended outcomes, making room for win-win solutions.

Object

Catch-all category for instances (physical or symbolic) with perennial identities.

Objective

Expectation with intent.

Observation

Activity whose objective is to get information from the environment without affecting the state of the environment.

Ontology

Systematic account (what makes sense) of the nature of existence for whatever is considered (i.e., named).

Operation (or action)

Targeted behavior: Symbolic operations affect the state of representations; physical operations affect states in environments.

Opinion

Agent's state of mind with regard to a specific issue.

Organization

1. an active and collective social entity
2. the associated representations of objects, roles, and activities

Osmosis (digital)

Process by which data is exchanged as digital flows between a system and its environment.

Partition

Classification of instances (objects or phenomena) into subsets based on the value of shared properties: Partitions can be structural, functional, phased, or analytical.

Pattern

Symbolic description of recurring forms or functions deemed relevant: A pattern can also refer to the mapping of typical problems and solutions.

Perennial

Capacity of instances to keep their identity independently of external events.

Phased (partition)

Combines functional partition with triggering events and sequencing constraints.

Phenomenon

Physical change in the environment.

Physical

Things that can be perceived.

Plasticity

Ability of a system to improve its architecture without impairing supported processes.

Polymorphism

Object-oriented mechanism that lets the same messages be interpreted differently according to the receiver.

Powertype

Symbolic representation of the subsets defined by a partition: Introduced when all instances of subsets share the realization of some aspects; not to be confused with subtypes, which are introduced when subsets have specific aspects.

Process

Actual execution of a set of ordered activities.

Project

Ordered set of activities with a purpose and time frame.

Quality

Probability that nothing will go amiss during the life cycle of a product or service.

Property

Range of values characterizing the state of objects or phenomena: litterals, references, coded values, and binary values.

Realization (connector)

Connects representations across epistemic or abstraction levels.

Refactoring

Change in the technical implementation of a component without a concurrent change in its functionalities.

Relationship

Connector between entities.

Requirements

What is expected from an artifact.

Role

A set of activities for agents to perform as defined by the organization. Contrary to agents, roles cannot be identified outside the organization considered.

Semantics

Meaning of terms defined by a language.

Specialization

Symbolic operation that reduces the scope of a definition or a description.

Stanford Paradigm

"Computer systems, robots, and people are all examples of symbolic systems, agents that use meaningful symbols to represent the world around them so as to communicate and generally act in the world" (Stanford University's Symbolic Systems Program).

Stereotype

Fixed set of features used to characterize instances: Stereotypes cannot be generalized or specialized, and they are not supposed to be aligned with the definition of categories.

Structural (partition)

Partitions with subsets characterized by different features, and are thus set for the whole life cycle of instances.

Surrogate

Digital substitute meant to reflect the state of objects or phenomena identified in the environment.

Sustainability

Ability of a system to carry on with its activities without degrading its environment.

Symbol

Sign pointing to something else (a referent, in semiotic parlance); not to be confused with a symbolic object, which is an object representing a referent.

Symbolic System

See Stanford Paradigm.

Syntax

Rules governing the organization of lexical categories independently of their semantics.

System

Structured set of objects and activities meant to serve a purpose.

Taxonomy

Reasoned set of categories.

Testing

Running executable models or applications in supervised conditions.

Thesaurus

Structured set of definitions.

Time

Intervals between events: Given a primary (or initial) event, intervals can be completed with the occurrence of a secondary event, or measured by repeated events, which are generated by some active instance that is triggered by the initial event.

Time frame

Temporal scale defined at the outset by a root event (or epoch), and at the end, by either a closing event or periodic ones.

Traceability

Capacity to retrieve the structural, logical, or functional origin and context of artifacts.

Transparency

Facility to understand the purpose, structure, and behavior of artifacts.

Type

Symbolic description of a set of objects or activities: Types can be understood as categories with features. Compared to classes, which are focused on the description of system surrogates (in prescriptive or technical models), types are more ecumenical and can be employed for any kind of description.

Use Case

Symbolic representation of interactions between a system and its environment: Business (Use) cases apply to enterprise organization, and technical (Use) cases to computer systems.

User Story

Narrative describing the actions performed by an agent in order to achieve an objective.

Value Chain

Charts the activities associated with the delivery of products or services to customers, in order to map business values to the resources and assets involved.

Value Stream

Steps that an organization follows to implement value chains: Operational value streams put the focus on the business perspective; development value streams, on the engineering one.

Versatility

Ability of systems to adjust processes to shifting environments without inducing significant changes in their architectures.

Virtual

Unrealized instances.

Zero-sum (Game theory)

Characterizes games set with fully defined outcomes, with gains balancing losses.

Bibliography

Arlow, J., and Neustadt, I. (2004) *Enterprise Patterns and MDA: Building Better Software with Archetype Patterns and UML.* London: Addison-Wesley.

Beer, S. (1995) *Brain of the Firm,* 2nd edition. Hoboken: Wiley.

Beer, S. (1985) *Diagnosing the System for Organizations.* Hoboken: Wiley.

Boldrin, M., and Levine, D.K. (2008) *Against Intellectual Monopoly.* Cambridge: Cambridge University Press.

Booch, G., Jacobson, I., and Rumbaugh, J. (2005) *Unified Modeling Language User Guide,* 2nd edition. London: Addison-Wesley.

Cockburn, A. (2000) *Writing Effective Use Cases.* London: Addison-Wesley.

Davis, R., Shrobe, H., and Szolovits, P. (1993) What is a knowledge representation? *AI Magazine* 14 (1): 17.

Deacon, T.W. (1998) *The Symbolic Species: The Co-evolution of Language and the Brain.* New York: Norton.

Devlin, B. (2013) *Business unIntelligence: Insight and Innovation beyond Analytics and Big Data.* Basking Ridge: Technics Publications.

D'Souza, D.F., and Wills, A.C. (1998) *Objects, Components, and Frameworks with UML: The Catalysis (SM) Approach.* London: Addison-Wesley.

Duffy, D.J. (2004) *Domain Architectures: Models and Architectures for UML Applications.* Hoboken: Wiley.

Dunbar, R. (2014) *Thinking Big: How the Evolution of Social Life Shaped the Human Mind*. London: Thames and Hudson.

Evans, E. (2004) *Domain-driven Design: Tackling Complexity in the Heart of Software*. London: Addison-Wesley.

Ferber, J. (1999) *Multi-agent Systems: An Introduction to Distributed Artificial Intelligence*. London: Addison-Wesley.

Frankel, D.S. (2003) *Model Driven Architecture: Applying MDA to Enterprise Computing*. Hoboken: Wiley.

Gamma, E., Helm, R., Johnson, R. et al. (1994) *Design Patterns: Elements of Reusable Object-oriented Software*. London: Addison-Wesley.

Génova, G., Valiente, M.C., and Marrero, M. (2009) On the difference between analysis and design, and why it is relevant for the interpretation of models in Model Driven Engineering. *Journal of Object Technology* 8 (1): 107–127.

Gleick, J. (2011) *The Information: A History, a Theory, a Flood*. New York: Pantheon.

Godfrey-Smith, P. (2016) *Other Minds: The Octopus, the Sea, and the Deep Origins of Consciousness*. New York: Farrar, Straus and Giroux.

Gomaa, H. (2011) *Software Modeling and Design: UML, Use Cases, Patterns, and Software Architectures*. Cambridge: Cambridge University Press.

Halpin, T. (2008) *Information Modeling and Relational Databases*, 2nd edition. Burlington: Morgan Kaufmann.

Harel, D. (1998) *Modeling Reactive Systems with Statecharts: The Statemate Approach*. New York: McGraw-Hill.

Havey, M. (2005) *Essential Business Process Modeling*. Sebastopol: O'Reilly.

Herzum, P., and Sims, O. (2000) *Business Component Factory: A Comprehensive Overview of Component-based Development for the Enterprise*. Hoboken: Wiley.

Hofstadter, D.R. (1979) *Gödel, Escher, Bach: An Eternal Golden Braid*. Basic Books.

Jablonka, E., and Lamb, M. (2020) *Inheritance Systems and the Extended Synthesis*. Cambridge: Cambridge University Press.

Jacobson, I. (2001) *The Object Advantage*, 2nd edition. London: Addison-Wesley.

Jacobson, I., and Cook, S. (2010) The road ahead for UML. *Dr Dobb's* (May 12).

Jacobson, I., Griss, M., and Jonsson, P. (1997) *Software Reuse: Architectures, Processes, and Organization for Business Success*. London: Addison-Wesley.

Jacobson, I., and Pan-Wei, N. (2005) *Aspect-oriented Software Development with Use Cases*. London: Addison-Wesley.

Kahneman, D. (2011) *Thinking, Fast and Slow*. New York: Farrar, Straus and Giroux.

Kruchten, P. (1995) The 4+1 View Model of architecture. *IEEE Software* 12 (6): 42–50.

Kulkarni, P., and Joshi, P. (2015) *Artificial Intelligence, Building Intelligent Systems*. Delhi: PHI.

Lakoff, G. (1997) *Women, Fire, and Dangerous Things*. Chicago: University of Chicago Press.

Lavi, J.Z., and Kudish, J. (2004) *Systems Modeling and Requirements Specification Using ECSAM: An Analysis Method for Embedded and Computer-based Systems*. New York: Dorset House.

Leffingwell, D. (2011) *Agile Software Requirements: Lean Requirements Practices for Teams, Programs, and the Enterprise*. London: Addison-Wesley.

Martin, R.C. (2002) *Agile Software Development, Principles, Patterns, and Practices*. New Upper Saddle River: Prentice Hall.

Mayr, H.C., Guizzardi, G., Ma, H., and Pastor, O. (2017) Conceptual Modeling. Conceptual Modeling: 36th International Conference, ER 2017, Valencia, Spain. Berlin: Springer.

Object Management Group. (2014) *MDA Guide*, revision 2.0 (June).

Odell, J.J. (1998) *Advanced Object-oriented Analysis & Design Using UML*. Cambridge: Cambridge University Press.

Pearl, J., and Mackenzie, D. (2018) *The Book of Why: The New Science of Cause and Effect*. New York: Basic Books.

Peirce, C.S. (1992) *Reasoning and the Logic of Things.* Cambridge: Harvard University Press.

Porter, M. (2008) *Competitive Advantage: Creating and Sustaining Superior Performance.* New York: Simon and Schuster.

Provost, F., and Fawcett, T. (2013) *Data Science for Business.* Sebastopol: O'Reilly.

Rotem-Gal-Oz, A. (2012) *SOA Patterns.* Shelter Island: Manning.

Russell, N., van der Aalst, W., and ter Hofstede, A. (2016) *Workflow Patterns: The Definitive Guide.* Cambridge: MIT Press.

Sowa, J.F. (2019) *Natural Logic Is Diagrammatic Reasoning about Mental Models.* Amsterdam: Elsevier Procedia.

Sowa, J.F. (1999) *Knowledge Representation: Logical, Philosophical, and Computational Foundations.* Pacific Grove: Brooks/Cole.

Sowa, J.F., and Zachman, J.A. (1992) Extending and formalizing the framework for information systems architecture. *IBM Systems Journal* 31 (3): 590.

Taleb, N.N. (2007) *The Black Swan.* New York City: Random House.

Van der Aalst, W., and Stahl, C. (2011) *Modeling Business Processes: A Petri Net-oriented Approach.* Cambridge: MIT Press.

Van Lamsweerde, A. (2009) *Requirements Engineering: From System Goals to UML Models to Software Specifications.* Hoboken: Wiley.

Weilkiens, T., Lamm, J.G., Roth, S., and Walker, M. (2015) *Model-Based System Architecture.* Hoboken: Wiley.

Wiegers, K.E. (2013) *Software Requirements*, 3rd edition. Redmond: Microsoft Press.

Winograd, T., and Flores, F. (1987) *Understanding Computers and Cognition: A New Foundation for Design.* London: Addison-Wesley.

Wright, R. (2001) *Nonzero: The Logic of Human Destiny.* New York: Vintage.

Index

CPSIA information can be obtained
at www.ICGtesting.com
Printed in the USA
BVHW010004170521
607527BV00008B/108